A Student's Guide to *We the People*

SECOND EDITION

Marilyn S. Mertens

MIDWESTERN STATE UNIVERSITY

W • W • NORTON & COMPANY • NEW YORK • LONDON

Printed in the United States of America

Composition/Layout by Roberta Flechner Graphics

ISBN 0-393-97321-2 (pbk.)

W. W. Norton & Company, Inc., 500 Fifth Avenue, New York, NY 10110
http://www.wwnorton.com

W. W. Norton & Company Ltd., 10 Coptic Street, London WC1A 1PU

1 2 3 4 5 6 7 8 9 0

CONTENTS

To the Student

Many students entering college believe that reading the book is sufficient for understanding, but reading is only the beginning. One must invest time and involve oneself deeply in the material to gain understanding and build the vocabulary necessary for learning. One of the problems of political science is that much of the vocabulary we use is common language which students think they understand. In the discipline of political science, however, the language acquires specific definitions which must be learned. Because it is easier to read an American government book than, say, a chemistry book, students are lulled into thinking the material is simple. If you want to learn, you must develop an active learning strategy.

Begin by accepting the fact that this will take time. That is, the more time you spend on a subject, the more you learn. To help you study, let's structure the learning tasks. For *We the People,* you will need to:

- keep a weekly calendar
- *never* miss a class
- read the textbook
- use the Study Guide
- check the Internet site
- do outside work, such as reading articles, watching movies, or completing projects as assigned by your professor
- review for major examinations.

Keep a weekly calendar

Establishing good study habits early in your college career will pay dividends later. Treat going to school like a job. The traditional study rule for college is, for every hour you spend in the classroom, you should spend two hours in out-of-class study. If you are taking a twelve-hour class load, you should be spending an *additional* twenty-four hours studying. We know that learning is related to time-on-task. Keep a weekly calendar in which you schedule study time just as you would record your work schedule for an outside job. You will be a happier and more successful student if you put your studies first.

Never miss a class

Recently, I was advising a student who was put on academic probation at the end of his first semester of college. "You didn't go to class, did you?" I asked. "I went most of the time," he replied, "but they always seemed to test stuff they taught when I was absent."

Not true. Learning is cumulative: what you learn today is built upon what you learned yesterday. Missing class causes big gaps in your learning. *Attendance is critical.* My own studies show that students' grades go down about five percent for each day they are absent. You can't learn if you don't go to class.

Read the textbook

Before you begin to read the first chapter, find a study partner. One of the curiosities of American education is its emphasis on learning alone, when in fact all the learning research indicates that learning together is more beneficial. The most effective learning takes place with a partner; the next most effective learning occurs with a small group; and the least effective learning occurs alone. So find a partner, or ask your instructor to help interested students set up study partnerships. Small study groups work well if the group stays focused, but all too often they become gab fests, so use the following method to avoid wasting everyone's time.

With your study partner or small group, find a comfortable place to sit and write. Then turn to the box at the beginning of each chapter that outlines the key topics and questions. Take a minute to go over these so that you are mentally prepared for what you are reading. Then turn to the study outline at the end of each chapter and have one person read aloud the key points of the first section, so that the seeds of the topic are planted in your memory.

The next step is to have one person read the first paragraph of the text, while the second person listens, without reading the book. When the reading is finished, the second person tells the first what he or she read, while the first person corrects and clarifies. Then trade places: the second person reads a paragraph while the first person listens. Together, discuss any figures or tables that appear on the page. Return to the study outline at the end of the chapter before proceeding to each new section. Going back and forth like this takes time, but it is a proven and effective way to learn.

The process of verbalizing what you know helps you learn in two ways. First, if you can't verbalize it, you don't really know it. Go back over that section again until you can clearly express its content. The second reason for verbalizing is that it incorporates another sense—hearing—into the learning process. Hearing, as well as seeing, help memory retention.

Even if you don't have a study partner, try to use this system anyway. Read a paragraph, cover the book, and repeat aloud what you just read. If you can't verbalize it, read it again.

Take frequent breaks, but make them short. Get up and move around, grab a snack, do some stretching exercises. Then get right back to work. Save your social conversations for the end of the study period.

Some students find that outlining the chapter also helps their retention. Again, outlining involves another sense—touch—and forces you to think through what you are writing. Don't just copy the words in the text; always paraphrase so that your mind is actively involved. You can write the outline by hand or type it on a computer if that is faster. Also, computer copies are easier to read and provide great test reviews.

Use the Study Guide

The Study Guide provides you with a ready-made learning strategy for use with *We the People.* For each chapter the Study Guide offers a brief summary; key terms; a fill-in-the-blank quiz to reinforce newly acquired vocabulary; a multiple choice quiz; questions for discussion and further thought; projects intended to help you understand the importance of government in your daily life; outside readings; and a list of popular movies that enhance the themes of political science. Properly used, this resource should enhance your understanding and introduce questions that require serious reflection about the fundamental values of liberty, equality, and democracy.

Check the Internet site

Spend some time going through the Internet site. Here you will find the study guide quizzes online, with instant feedback, and additional resources, including stories from National Public Radio and the *Washington Post,* forums for discussion, in-depth policy analyses, and links to other sites.

Review for major examinations

By this time, you've done all of the hard work, and reviewing for tests should be easy. Tests are difficult when you procrastinate; you can't possibly read and remember everything you need to know when you cram. But a little bit of study every day makes preparing for exams almost effortless.

The formula for success in college is very simple: The more you study, the better grades you will get. The better your grades, the happier you will be. Have a good semester.

Marilyn S. Mertens
Midwestern State University

Acknowledgments

This study guide is really a collaborative effort. Joel O. Reid wrote the chapter summaries and Robert England wrote the multiple-choice questions for the first edition of the study guide. Much of their material has been incorporated into this edition. My special thanks to them both. W. W. Norton & Company has supplied me with an outstanding editor, April Lange, whose careful work through two editions has been most helpful. I also want to thank Jane Carter, Kate Barry, and Scott McCord of Norton for their assistance. I hope that this guide will be a helpful companion to *We the People,* Second Edition, and that, as you use it, you will become aware of the importance of being an active, informed, participating citizen.

Marilyn S. Mertens
Midwestern State University

CHAPTER 1 American Political Culture

THE CHAPTER IN BRIEF

Are you one of those people who think that the American democratic system will be here forever? Or do you think about the future of our system and wonder if it will survive the constant stresses that it undergoes? Let's start with the scary part: the American democratic system is the oldest one in history at nearly 225 years, and there are only about two dozen democratic nations in the world today. Americans have one of the lowest voter turnouts of all of these countries, and many Americans cannot even name the three branches of government (see Table 1.1 of your text). Now, let's ask that again: should you worry about the future of democracy?

Here's the good part. You're in this class to understand how important it is that everyone be informed and participate in our government to ensure that it continues to exist. We hope that by the time you have finished this course you will have a deeper understanding of the important themes of this text: liberty, equality, and democracy. The great British politician Edmund Burke once said, "The only thing that is necessary for evil to triumph is for good men [and women] to do nothing." For democracy to triumph, it will take the personal involvement of everyone, not just a few.

The American democratic system evolved out of the Founders' fear of "tyranny," or the subjugation and oppression that they believed the British government had exerted over the colonies. Hence, Americans have always had a healthy distrust of power. Still, we have also learned that sometimes government must provide services for us that are necessary for our survival and for our growth. Since the 1960s, though, trust in government has steadily declined.

There are many theories about why this has happened. Certainly as government has grown in size, it has intruded into our lives in many ways, with regulations, higher taxes, and benefits. We like the benefits and don't want to give them up, but we are often unhappy with the performance of government. Many Americans believe that government is wasteful and inefficient.

In reality, government has been very effective in some areas, such as lessening poverty among the elderly and reducing air and water pollution. Also, Americans' attitudes toward government are heavily skewed by how well the economy is doing; prosperity makes us less critical, and recession makes us more dissatisfied. Younger Americans' attitudes reflect those of their elders; the majority are critical of government. Consequently, it becomes more difficult for government to recruit competent employees, government's ability to respond to problems is damaged, and Americans' sense of political efficacy is weakened, leading to even more cynicism about government.

What makes a good citizen? The ancient Greeks defined citizenship as more than just voting; it involved public discussion and rational thought. We have enshrined this responsibility in the First Amendment, which guarantees freedom of speech. The authors of the text define citizenship as "enlightened political engagement." A good citizen should have a knowledge of government, politics, and democratic principles. Let's examine each of these in turn.

Government is the formal structure that rules a people. Governments are classified according to two questions: who governs? How much government control is permitted? In an autocracy, only one person rules. If several people rule together, an oligarchy exists. Government by the people is democracy. Government control is, in theory at least, determined by a constitution which limits the powers of government. In many nondemocratic societies, institutions other than the constitution are used to control the people. Authoritarian societies may use the military or other societal groups to enforce their power. Totalitarian societies destroy all social institutions, such as the church, labor unions, and political parties, in order to exert total control.

The evolution of our democracy began in Europe in the seventeenth century. The key force behind the imposition of limits on government power was a new social class, the "bourgeoisie," which comes from a French word meaning "freeman of the city." These people were "middle class" and were associated with being in commerce or industry. They sought to change existing conditions, especially parliaments, into instruments of real political participation. Although motivated by the need to protect their own interests, they advanced many of the principles of individual liberty that our government is based on, such as freedom of speech, freedom of assembly, freedom of conscience, and freedom from arbitrary search and seizure. They also were advocates of electoral and representative institutions, although they favored property requirements to limit participation. The writings of John Locke, Adam Smith, and John Stuart Mill were important influences on their thinking.

The expansion of participation took two paths. In some nations, the crown or aristocracy saw common people as potential political allies against the bourgeoisie and thus expanded popular participation hoping to build political support among the lower orders. In other nations, competing segments of the bourgeoisie sought to gain political advantage by reaching out and mobilizing the support of working- and lower-class groups who craved the opportunity to take part in politics.

The term "politics" refers to conflicts over the character, membership, and policies of any organization to which people belong. "Politics is the struggle over 'who gets what, when, how.'" Its goal is to have a share or a say in the composition of the government's leadership, how the government is organized, or what its policies are going to be. Having a share is called "power" or "influence." In this country, every adult citizen has the right to participate, or have influence. A system of government that gives citizens the opportunity to elect the top government officials is called a representative democracy, or a republic. A regime that permits citizens to vote directly on laws and policies is called a direct democracy. At the national level, America is a representative democracy because citizens do not vote on legislation. But some states do have provisions for direct legislation through popular referendum and initiative petitions.

Politics can also occur through the interaction of groups, a process we call pluralism. Direct action can occur through either violent politics or civil disobedience, both of which attempt to shock rulers into behaving more responsibly, or it can be revolutionary politics, which rejects the system entirely and attempts to replace it with a new ruling group and a new set of rules.

Americans share three basic values that are the core of our political culture. We generally agree on these principles but sometimes disagree over their application. The first of these values is liberty. We have documents that guarantee our liberty. The first is the Declaration of Independence, which says we have certain unalienable rights. Then there is the Preamble of the Constitution. Most important is the Bill of Rights, which guarantees us the freedom of speech and writing, the right to assemble freely, and the right to practice religious beliefs without governmental interference. We also have the interpreted rights of free enterprise, the right to enjoy the fruits of our own labor, and the right to free competition.

The second core value is political equality. A clear distinction is made in the public mind between political equality and social or economic equality. The former is strongly supported, the latter much less so. Because we support the right of individuals to live their own lives, we are also willing to tolerate greater inequality of results.

The third value is democracy, the right of the people to choose their rulers and to influence what those rulers do. Political power ultimately comes from the people, and voting is a key element. Ideally, democracy involves an engaged citizenry prepared to exercise its power over rulers.

The ideals of our system can easily conflict with one another in practice. What is liberty and freedom for one could possibly infringe on the freedoms of others. The issue of slavery was a key conflict in the early years of this country. Many regulations today are seen as protecting the liberties of certain segments of society, while other segments see the same rules as restricting their freedom in some way.

There have been several debates over equality. As far as equality of access to public institutions is concerned, the case of *Plessy v. Ferguson* (1896) decided that separate but equal accommodations constituted equality for the races. But then, in *Brown v. Board of Education* (1954), the *Plessy* decision was overturned, and the Supreme Court decided that separate is *not* equal. The second debate was over the public role in ensuring equality of opportunity in private life. Supporters of affirmative action claim it is necessary to compensate for past discrimination, and that equality should not acknowledge gender or racial differences.

A third debate is over differences in wealth and the quality of income. The traditional view is that economic success is possible for anyone and is a product of individual effort. Where concern over economic inequalities emerges is usually over the issue of taxation and fairness. The growing division between rich and poor may lead to politics by class.

Until very recently, our ideal of democracy was not a reality in the United States. The United States was not a full democracy until the 1960s, when African Americans were guaranteed voting rights. Early in our history, restrictions were much greater. Property restrictions on the vote were eliminated by 1828. The Fifteenth Amendment to the Constitution in 1870 granted African Americans the vote, although later exclusionary practices invalidated that right. In 1965, the Voting Rights Act finally secured the right of African Americans to vote. In 1920, the Nineteenth Amendment gave women the vote.

Another concern about democracy is the relationship between economic power and political power. Money often determines who runs for office, it can exert a heavy influence on who wins, and it can affect what elected politicians do once they are in office. A final consideration about democracy concerns the engagement of the citizenry. There is a low turnout for elections in American politics today and many people seem filled with apathy and cynicism. Many people do not participate because they feel that their single vote doesn't matter. This undermines the vitality of democracy and reduces the accountability of those in office to the public.

As we attempt to resolve conflicts among our core beliefs, America's political principles change and evolve. Even core values should be understood as works in progress rather than immutable facts. In principle, liberty and democracy can be reconciled, but in practice, over time democracy poses a fundamental threat to liberty. And with social policy such as affirmative action, what one person thinks is a guarantee of liberty, another thinks is an infringement of liberty. However, in the United States, it has been the institutions of democratic government that have been critical in guaranteeing both liberty and equality.

REVIEW QUESTIONS

1. What percentage of Americans lost trust in their government in the period from the early 1960s to today?

2. What reasons are given to explain this decline in trust?
3. Do the attitudes of younger Americans differ from those of older Americans? In what ways?
4. What problems are created by popular mistrust of government?
5. What is political efficacy? Why is its loss "bad news for American democracy"?
6. How did the ancient Greeks define citizenship? How do we define it today? What obligations are imposed by citizenship?
7. What are the three important things that Americans need to know in order to be participating citizens?
8. Define government according to the number of people who rule.
9. Who were the bourgeoisie and why are they important to the history of democracy?
10. What important concepts from the writing of John Locke were borrowed by Thomas Jefferson in writing the Declaration of Independence?
11. Why is Adam Smith, an economic theorist, also an important political theorist?
12. Explain the importance of John Stuart Mill's writings for the Bill of Rights.
13. Explain Harold Lasswell's definition of politics as "who gets what, when, how."
14. Compare a republic with a democracy.
15. What are the three core values developed throughout this textbook?
16. List three historical documents where "liberty" is declared as an important value in American government.
17. Do we have *laissez-faire* capitalism today? Explain.
18. Explain the difference between equality of opportunity and equality of results.
19. Define popular sovereignty.
20. How is the power of the majority checked in the Constitution?
21. What was the greatest issue America ever faced in regard to liberty?
22. What is the relationship between economic power and political power?

KEY TERMS

authoritarian government
autocracy
citizenship
constitutional government
democracy
direct-action politics
direct democracy
efficacy
equality of opportunity
government
laissez-faire capitalism
liberty
limited government
majority rule/minority rights
oligarchy
pluralism
political culture
political equality
politics
popular sovereignty
power
representative democracy (or republic)
totalitarian government

FILL-IN-THE BLANK QUIZ

Use the key terms to complete the following sentences.

1. Rule by one person is a(n) _________________; rule by several people is a(n) __________.
2. An institution that rules a society is known as a(n) _________________, while the struggle for power within that institution is called ____________.
3. A government that relies on force and control of other social institutions in order to make its will known may be either a(n)_________________ government or a(n)_________________ government.
4. A political system that elects people to serve in a law-making body is a _____________
5. An economic system that allows near-total freedom in the economic sphere is termed _________.
6. The political __________ of the American political system values equality, ____________, and ________.
7. Americans generally favor __________ equality and believe all people should have equality of ___________.
8. A political system in which groups dominate the distribution of public goods is called a(n) _______ system.
9. Constitutions are important because they create ______________.
10. The will of the people is often called _____________________.

11. If people believe that they have influence or _______ over their government, they have political ________.

12. When all of the people together make the laws for their government, their government is known as ________________.

13. There is an inherent conflict between majority rule and __________________.

14. ______________ can be defined as "enlightened political engagement."

15. When the people take matters into their own hands and use methods outside of the formal channels of government, they are using __________________.

16. A government that lives by formal rules is a(n) ______________ government.

MULTIPLE-CHOICE QUIZ

1. Political involvement among 18 to 24-year-old Americans is:
   a. higher than people over 65.
   b. higher than people 35 to 55, but not as high as people over 65.
   c. lower than people over 65, but higher than people 25 to 35.
   d. lowest of all age groups.

2. The trend line of Americans' trust in their government:
   a. has declined steadily since the early 1960s.
   b. declined during Watergate, but rose again during the 1980s.
   c. has risen since 1990.
   d. rose during the 1970s and 1980s, but has declined since 1992.

3. Public opinion about how well government is doing is strongly influenced by:
   a. how much taxes rise or fall.
   b. which party controls Congress.
   c. how well the economy is doing.
   d. which party controls the presidency.

4. The belief that citizens can affect government is called:
   a. political culture.
   b. political socialization.
   c. political efficacy.
   d. political satisfaction.

5. In ancient Greece, citizenship was defined as the right to:
   a. vote.
   b. discuss and argue about politics.
   c. have a trial in Athens.
   d. run for public office.

6. According to the authors of the text, good citizenship requires:
   a. political knowledge.
   b. political engagement.
   c. a good education.
   d. both a and b.

7. Approximately what percent of Americans can name the length of a U.S. Senator's term?
   a. about 50 percent
   b. about 25 percent
   c. about 75 percent
   d. about 90 percent

8. Government run by a few people is called:
   a. autocracy.
   b. totalitarianism.
   c. pluralism.
   d. oligarchy.

9. The concept of government resting on the "consent of the governed" comes from:
   a. John Locke.
   b. Thomas Hobbes.
   c. Adam Smith.
   d. John Stuart Mill.

10. "Who gets what, when, and how" is a definition of:
    a. government.
    b. politics.
    c. pluralism.
    d. political culture.

11. Democracy in ancient Greece was:
    a. a republic.
    b. an autocracy.
    c. authoritarian.
    d. direct democracy.

12. Which of the following was a totalitarian regime?
    a. the Soviet Union under Stalin.
    b. Spain under Franco.
    c. Portugal under Salazar.
    d. Hungary after World War II until 1989.

13. The *bourgeoisie* of western Europe wanted to:
    a. open up political participation to all social classes.
    b. restore the divine right of kings.
    c. restrict political participation to the middle classes.
    d. overthrow parliaments.

14. Adam Smith is considered to be a liberal philosopher because he advocated:
    a. revolution.
    b. life, liberty, and the pursuit of happiness.
    c. the social compact theory.
    d. freedom to allow for individual economic advancement.

15. In nineteenth-century Prussia, Otto von Bismarck introduced social reforms to aid the lower class because he:
    a. wanted to introduce modern democratic ideas.
    b. was trying to offset the growing power of the middle class.
    c. had a religious conversion that told him to aid the poor.
    d. needed support from the middle class which was advocating greater representation of the poor.

16. A student council is an example of:
    a. direct democracy.
    b. representative democracy.
    c. limited democracy.
    d. an oligarchy.

17. Which of the following is NOT part of the American political culture?
    a. belief in equality of results.
    b. belief in equality of opportunity.

c. belief in individual liberty.
d. belief in free competition.

18. *Laissez-faire* capitalism has been limited by:
a. public opinion, which opposes capitalism.
b. voluntary actions by big businesses.
c. government regulation.
d. papal encyclicals.

19. Many of the conflicts in American politics today revolve around:
a. the proper scope of government.
b. whether government should exist at all.
c. allowing minorities to participate in government.
d. consolidating the three branches of the military into one.

20. The principle of equality in America means:
a. equal results.
b. equal opportunity.
c. equality before the law.
d. all of the above.
e. both b and c.

21. In a democracy, sovereignty is vested in:
a. the president.
b. the federal government.
c. the people.
d. Congress.

22. The authors of the text state that the American definition of liberty has been formed primarily through its experiences with:
a. revolt against British control;
b. communist threats in the twentieth century;
c. Hitler and fascism;
d. slavery.

23. Regarding income inequality, Americans:
a. have the widest gap between rich and poor of any developed nation.
b. believe that government should undertake major programs to reduce inequality.
c. believe that taxes should be raised on the rich and middle class to aid the poor.
d. have the smallest gap between rich and poor of any developed nation.

24. Realistically, the United States did not become a full practicing democracy until:
a. 1789.
b. the Civil War.
c. the New Deal.
d. the 1960s.

25. America's core political values are fixed and unchanging.
a. True
b. False

26. Which of the following is NOT a principle of our democracy?
a. majority rule
b. complete freedom
c. minority rights
d. equality of opportunity

27. The two important questions to ask about government are:
a. Why are we here? Who should become a citizen?
b. How can we create a perfect society? Who should determine what constitutes a perfect society?
c. Who governs? How much government control is permitted?
d. Who governs? How can we create equality?

QUESTIONS FOR DISCUSSION AND THOUGHT

1. James Baldwin wrote, "Words like 'freedom,' 'justice,' 'democracy' are not common concepts; on the contrary, they are rare. People are not born knowing what these are. It takes enormous and, above all, individual effort to arrive at the respect for other people that these words imply." Do you think you know what these words (freedom, justice, democracy) actually mean? How did you derive your own meaning for these words?

2. The textbook discusses **liberty** as a key component of American democracy. What sort of liberty did the Founders have in mind in the Bill of Rights? What kind of liberty was Adam Smith promoting? Are there limits to how much liberty we can allow and still maintain a stable society? What sort of limits on personal freedom do you think are acceptable? What sort of actions are not acceptable?

3. The term **equality** has several dimensions: political, social, economic. What sort of political equality exists in the United States? Where do we fail to provide political equality? How much social equality do we have? How much do you want? How much economic equality would you want?

4. The development of a public educational system is based on the idea that democracy requires an educated population trained in rational discussion and decision making. Yet countries like Mali and India, with low literacy rates, are creating democracies that include free elections and protections of basic freedoms. What are the practical requirements for democracy to exist? Can any country where so few are educated really be a democracy? If you were the democratic leader of such a country, how would you go about trying to create democracy?

5. Is it possible for people in a democracy to choose poor leaders? What, in your opinion, would constitute a poor leader? Which is more important: choosing good leaders, or letting the people decide, even if they choose poorly?

6. The draft was abolished in the United States in 1973. Some people believe that everyone ought to perform at least one year of mandatory public service, either in the military or in community service. Do you agree? What benefits do you see to mandatory public service? What problems? If there were mandatory service, should it be required of both men and women? Which would you choose: military service or community service?

7. What do we mean by "tyranny of the majority"? Can the majority in a democracy be as tyrannical as a dictator? If democracy is based on majority rule, can we still allow the minority to get around the will of the majority? If so, why? How?

THE CITIZEN'S ROLE

You cannot really understand government in action until you *see* government in action. Attend a meeting of some local or state government agency, such as a city council, school board, or government advisory committee meeting. Spend at least one hour at the meeting and take careful notes.

1. Describe the meeting you attended. What were the main items on the agenda?
2. Who were the officials running the meeting? Did the officials seem to have the public interest at heart or did it seem that they were following their own political agendas?
3. How did the officials treat the general public? Were they respectful, patient, rude, indifferent? How did the general public treat the officials?
4. Were the major issues discussed openly? Were all sides of the issue considered? Did you think the officials were open to hearing other sides? Were any formal actions taken?
5. What is your opinion of public officials? Would you ever want to run for public office? Would you be willing to speak before this group if you felt strongly about an issue? If this is democracy in action, what is your opinion about it?

GOVERNMENT IN YOUR LIFE

To understand why it is important to study American government, you need to see how government affects your everyday life. On page 5 of the text, Figure 1.1 shows some of the ways in which government is involved in the life of a recent college graduate. But government doesn't wait until you graduate from college to intervene in your life. Below, make a list of at least ten items that show how your life has intersected with government (state, local, and national today). For example, this morning you may have used a municipal water supply or taken a medication controlled by the Food and Drug Administration. After making your list, answer the questions below.

What you did	Government action involved
1.	
2.	
3.	
4.	
5.	
6.	
7.	
8.	
9.	
10.	

1. Were you surprised at the number of government actions surrounding your life today? Explain.
2. What was the purpose of these government actions? Do you think that the private sector could perform some of these actions more efficiently? Explain.
3. Are there some government actions that you think are unnecessary? Which ones? Why should government get out of those areas?
4. What would happen to American society if government were small and weak? Would a smaller government provide student loans and grants? Support medical research? Assemble a manned mission to Mars? Should government be doing those things? Explain.
5. Do you think most Americans understand the importance of government in their lives? Explain.

ANSWER KEY

Fill-in-the Blank Quiz

1. autocracy, oligarchy
2. government, politics
3. authoritarian, totalitarian
4. representative democracy (or a republic)
5. laissez-faire capitalism
6. culture, liberty, democracy
7. political, opportunity
8. pluralist
9. limited government
10. popular sovereignty
11. power, efficacy
12. direct democracy
13. minority rights
14. Citizenship
15. direct-action politics
16. constitutional

Multiple-Choice Quiz

1. d
2. a
3. c
4. c
5. b
6. d
7. b
8. d
9. a
10. b
11. d
12. a
13. c
14. d
15. b
16. b
17. a
18. c
19. a
20. e
21. c
22. d
23. a
24. d
25. b
26. b
27. c

CHAPTER 2 The American Political Community

THE CHAPTER IN BRIEF

The history of America has been the history of the expansion of democracy. As we noted in the last chapter, America did not really become a democracy until the 1960s, when African Americans were finally allowed to practice their constitutional rights of voting and participation. This chapter examines that history and explores the complex relationships between race, class, gender, religion, and political participation.

From our beginnings as a collection of colonies until the late nineteenth century, most immigrants to America came from Europe; we refer to these people as "white ethnics." Whites still comprise almost three-quarters of the U.S. population. The immigrants to urban areas were integrated into the political and social systems through political machines, which controlled the election process by parceling out favors, jobs, and other benefits to needy newcomers.

But not all Americans were welcomed and given the rights of citizenship. African Americans, in particular, fought to be able to exercise their right to vote. First, as slaves, they were denied citizenship; then, in the late nineteenth century, many southern states passed laws that made it nearly impossible for them to vote, even though this had been secured in the Fifteenth Amendment. In the interim period from 1865 to 1877, African Americans generally joined the Republican Party, and some even held state and federal offices. But in the Compromise of 1877, federal troops were withdrawn and the southern states immediately began a process of disenfranchising black Americans. The Republican Party, meanwhile, dropped its support of civil liberties for all.

Full participation rights were demanded by organizations such as the NAACP, which organized protests, filed lawsuits, and applied political pressure at both the state and federal levels. Eventually the rights of citizenship were granted through the 1964 Civil Rights Act and the 1965 Voting Rights Act.

Today, black Americans tend to vote as a bloc and support the Democratic party. Segregation still exists *de facto* (in fact), even though it has been officially outlawed. Many blacks believe that the Democratic party takes the black vote for granted and so feels little pressure to advance civil rights issues; the Republicans, on the other hand, show little interest in black voters, even though many blacks (especially in the middle class) are more ideologically comfortable with the Republicans.

Latinos in America come from diverse backgrounds. Mexicans, the largest single group, include those whose families were here prior to the American Revolution as well as the more recent newcomers. Most live in the states of the Southwest and have throughout history also experienced segregation, discrimination, and denial of voting rights. In the absence of political machines in these more rural areas, the white elites ran the society and controlled political office.

After World War II, two political organizations formed that were based on Mexican American membership: the League of United Latin American Citizens (LULAC) and the GI Forum. After seeing the success of black Americans in the civil rights movements, these organizations developed their own strategies. The first was to organize voters, the second to file lawsuits demanding equal rights.

Puerto Ricans, the second largest group, were made American citizens in 1917, which allows them to migrate easily to the United States. Most of these immigrants have settled on the east coast, particularly in New York. The political participation rates of Puerto Ricans are very low.

Cubans, on the other hand, came primarily as refugees in the 1960s and were from the conservative middle class. While Mexican Americans and Puerto Ricans are concerned about issues such as bilingualism and discrimination, Cubans are noted for their fervent anticommunism, which leads them to support the Republican Party.

Other Latino groups include immigrants from the Caribbean, and Central and South America. The Hispanic vote is often called a "sleeping giant" because of the low voter participation among all groups. One reason for this is because so few of the Mexican immigrants become American citizens.

Another ethnic group that is marked by diversity is the Asian American population. Asians were used as cheap labor in nineteenth century America, but they were not given rights of citizenship until 1898, when in *United States v. Wong Kim Ark*, the Supreme Court declared that anyone born in the United States was a citizen. Several times in our history Congress has passed laws excluding or severely limiting Asian immigration. The anti-Asian hostility reached a peak during World War II, when over 110,000 Japanese Americans were forcibly removed from their homes and sent to live in "relocation camps" until the war's end.

The Japanese fought back by attacking the laws that restricted their rights. In 1952, Congress passed the McCarran-Walter Act, which rescinded a law passed in 1790 that allowed only whites to become citizens. Later, in 1988, Congress authorized reparation payments to those displaced during the war.

The 1965 Immigration Act abolished discriminatory quotas on immigration, which allowed an influx of immigrants from Asia to enter the United States. Many Vietnamese and Cambodians came after the Vietnam war. Other immigrants came from the Philippines, Korea, China, and Taiwan. Because of the diversity of languages and cultures, Asians have not yet been a powerful political force, except in California.

Native Americans were not granted citizenship until 1924, which delayed their political organization. In the 1960s, in the aftereffects of the civil rights movement of black Americans, Native Americans organized their own action group, the American Indian Movement (AIM). The Supreme Court ruled in 1987 that Indian tribes were exempt from state gambling regulations, which has led to many tribes opening casinos on their reservations. While this has brought considerable wealth to some tribes, Native Americans as a whole are still the poorest group in America.

The immigration issue today raises a number of troubling questions. We are, after all, "a nation of immigrants" but we also recognize that the nation cannot absorb everyone who wants to come to America. How many people can we accommodate each year? What people should be allowed to enter? What rights do we extend to those who are legal residents but not citizens? What about illegal immigrants, especially their children—what rights, if any, should they have? What sort of nation will we be in the future if the new immigrants are increasingly unlike the white ethnics who settled this land? There have been several anti-immigrant movements in the past, such as the Ku Klux Klan and the American (Know-Nothing) Party. Will we see a rise in resentment-based political groups in the future?

Social class is another dividing factor in American political life today. While most Americans call themselves middle class, in reality the United States has the widest gap between rich and poor of any developed nation. Surprisingly, this has not led to class-based political movements which are common elsewhere. The Democratic Party is in a difficult position: it must appeal to low-income voters by stressing greater income equality without alienating its middle-class support.

Gender politics in America focus on the rights of women. Although women had long been active in political movements, such as abolition, temperance, and ending political corruption, they were denied the vote until the suffragette movement demanded the vote. The first state to grant women full voting rights was Wyoming, followed by several other western states. Finally, in 1920, women were able to vote in all states after the passage of the Nineteenth Amendment. When demanding the right to vote, women argued that they would clean up politics, but in fact women's voting rates have never been high, and the women's equality movement almost disappeared, until it was revived in the late 1960s.

The galvanizing issue for women at that time was equal pay. Women were entering the workforce in large numbers and were dismayed to discover that it was not illegal to pay men more than women doing the same job. Several women's organizations organized to promote a constitutional amendment (the Equal Rights Amendment), which was never ratified. The women's movement did, however, secure an Equal Pay Act and the right to an abortion. Today, the women's vote is more liberal than men's on most social issues. Because fewer women vote, however, the impact of their attitudes is weakened at the polls. Still, today there are many more women in public office because of the feminist movement, and women's issues are increasingly on the public's agenda.

Another political issue that divides us is our religious beliefs, particularly as exercised in the political arena. The Christian religion has long been imbedded in our public life. Churches and religious people have always been active in politics. *Roe v. Wade* mobilized many evangelical Christians into political action, primarily through the Christian Coalition, which is aligned closely with the Republican Party. Pat Robertson, the founder of the Christian Coalition, has even run for president. The Christian Right believes that traditional Protestant values are under attack today and it will take their active political participation to restore religion to what they perceive to be its rightful role in America.

Certainly Americans are divided by many factors when it comes to their political beliefs and participation. The history of America has been marked by expansion of the electorate: to immigrants, Native Americans, women. But in spite of the long battles for the right to vote, the sad fact is that American political participation rates are very low. Fewer than half of the eligible voters turned out for the last presidential election, few engage in political dialogue or activities, and it appears that only the wealthy can influence our system.

While it is true that more people of higher socioeconomic status participate in politics, education, race, and age can also affect participation rates. A recent study showed that political participation is heavily influenced by resources such as time and money, civic engagement (political interest and efficacy), and being asked by someone you know to participate. As more Americans go to college, we would expect higher participation rates, but in fact, the opposite is occurring. Why is this happening? Theories include high crime rates, television, lack of galvanizing political issues, voter registration laws, and reduced efforts by political parties to recruit new activists. There are serious consequences to our decline in civic participation. "Checkbook democracy" leads to government by elites or powerful groups. The elites themselves are withdrawing further into a world of separate schools, neighborhoods, and social institutions. Maintaining liberty, equality, and democracy will not be possible if ordinary people withdraw from civic life. Our system can disappear under the weight of apathy, cynicism, and alienation.

REVIEW QUESTIONS

1. What is "white ethnic"? Describe the waves of immigration of white ethnics.
2. What is a political machine? Why were they important in the immigration process?

3. How long did it take for African Americans to achieve their full political rights?
4. Explain the Thirteenth, Fourteenth, and Fifteenth Amendments.
5. What was the Compromise of 1877? Why was this important in the history of black voting?
6. Describe the strategy used by the NAACP for achieving political rights for blacks.
7. What were the three strategies used by black Americans to achieve full citizenship rights?
8. Why have black voters been a powerful voting bloc when other groups such as Latinos and Asians have not?
9. What sort of diversity is captured in the term "Latino"?
10. Name two organizations that pursue citizenship rights for Latinos.
11. What are the two political strategies used by Latinos?
12. Contrast the immigration experiences of Mexicans, Puerto Ricans, and Cubans.
13. Why is the Latino vote called the "sleeping giant"?
14. What was the significance of *United States v. Wong Kim Ark*?
15. Contrast the Chinese Exclusion Act with the McCarran-Walter Act.
16. What was a "relocation camp"? What are reparations?
17. What was the constitutional status of Native American tribes? How was that changed in 1924?
18. What is the major Native American political organization? What strategy does it emphasize today?
19. What was the purpose of Proposition 187 in California?
20. What problems might America face if we deny basic services to illegal immigrants?
21. What is the "English Only" movement? Why is it important?
22. What strategy did the American Federation of Labor choose to advance its causes?
23. Why does America not have class-based politics?
24. What was the suffragette movement? What strategies were used by women to influence politics before the Nineteenth Amendment was passed?

25. What political strategies were used by the feminist movement to influence politics?
26. What was the Equal Rights Amendment?
27. Name three ways in which women affect politics today.
28. What political issues have helped to mobilize religious groups in the last forty years?
29. What is the Christian Coalition? Why is it important today?
30. Why is political participation necessary to the survival of liberty, equality and democracy?
31. How does socioeconomic status affect political participation?
32. What three things are necessary for successful political participation?
33. After spending two hundred years fighting for full political participation, many of the groups discussed in this chapter have very low voter participation rates. Why?
34. Does the American political system actually reflect the fundamental values of liberty, equality, and democracy?
35. What are the dangers of "checkbook politics"?

KEY TERMS

American political community
civic engagement
coalition
efficacy
gender gap
mobilization
political institution
political machine
political participation
poll tax
socioeconomic status
white ethnics
white primary

FILL-IN-THE-BLANK QUIZ

Use the key terms to complete the following sentences.

1. Two ways in which the South kept blacks from voting prior to the civil rights movement of the 1960s were the ____________ and the __________ .
2. Immigrants to America's cities were often assimilated with the help of a ____________ .

3. ___________ describes the different political values and voting patterns of men and women.

4. Two important strategies for groups attempting to influence the political system are to form a ___________ with other groups and to run voter ___________ drives.

5. One's social class or ___________ heavily influences one's political ___________ .

6. This chapter summarizes the struggle that minority groups have undergone in order to be able to participate fully in the ___________ .

7. Citizenship is defined as "enlightened ___________ .

8. A formal structure of government, such as the bureaucracy, is a political ___________ .

9. People who believe that they cannot influence politics have a low sense of political ___________ .

10. Most people of European abstraction who are not clearly identified with a racial or ethnic group are called ___________ .

MULTIPLE-CHOICE QUIZ

1. European immigration was a central fact of American life from the colonial period until the ___________ when Congress sharply cut off immigration.
   a. 1850s
   b. 1920s
   c. 1950s
   d. 1990s

2. Immigration from eastern and central Europe came primarily in the period of:
   a. 1800 to 1840.
   b. 1880 to 1890.
   c. 1890 to 1910.
   d. 1910 to 1925.

3. The purpose of a political machine was to:
   a. control local politics.
   b. encourage Irish and Italian immigration.
   c. keep immigrants from becoming citizens.
   d. operate schools in native languages.

4. Voting rights for black males were guaranteed by the:
   a. Bill of Rights.
   b. Thirteenth Amendment.
   c. Fourteenth Amendment.
   d. Fifteenth Amendment.

5. What was Tammany Hall?
   a. Where the first national Congress met in New York City
   b. The official residency of the mayor of New York City

c. A famous museum containing national government documents located in New York City
d. The most important political machine in New York City

6. After the Civil War and during Reconstruction, most black citizens found a home in the:
   a. Democratic Party.
   b. Greenback Party.
   c. Republican Party.
   d. Progressive Party.

7. This famous African American argued for "self-help," and not the struggle for political rights, as the most appropriate approach blacks should pursue in their quest for equality.
   a. W.E.B. DuBois
   b. Booker T. Washington
   c. Malcolm X
   d. Marcus Garvey

8. The largest Latino group in the United States today is of ____________ extraction.
   a. Puerto Rican
   b. Cuban
   c. Mexican
   d. Caribbean

9. Which group has the lowest citizenship rates?
   a. Mexican Americans
   b. Vietnamese
   c. Native Americans
   d. Japanese Americans

10. In 1968, Dennis Bank cofounded this Native American political movement.
    a. Native Americans for Equality (NAE)
    b. National Association for American Indian Rights (NAAIR)
    c. American Indian Movement (AIM)
    d. American Indian Peace Organization (AMPO)

11. This state was the first to grant full suffrage to women.
    a. Texas
    b. Wyoming
    c. New York
    d. Connecticut

12. Compared to most modern European nations,
    a. the United States is more ethnically and racially homogeneous.
    b. the United States is more ethnically and racially heterogeneous.
    c. the United States has fewer racial and ethnic groups.
    d. ethnic and racial groups have little political significance in the United States.

13. Currently, whites comprise about ____________ percent of the U.S. population.
    a. 25
    b. 50
    c. 75
    d. 95

14. This so-called "Civil War Amendment" to the U.S. Constitution guarantees equal protection under the law.
    a. Tenth
    b. Thirteenth
    c. Fourteenth
    d. Fifteenth

15. Which of the following is not one of the "broad strategies" African Americans have used in their quest for equality?
    a. self-improvement
    b. changing public policy by controlling state legislatures
    c. black nationalism
    d. protest

16. According to the text, great legislative victories, the end of legal segregation, and the beginning of black political power in the United States came with:
    a. the Civil Rights Act of 1964.
    b. the Voting Rights Act of 1965.
    c. the Nineteenth Amendment.
    d. all of the above.
    e. both a and b.

17. Which of the following statements is true?
    a. Democratic hostility to affirmative action and other programs of racial preference is likely to sharply check any large-scale black migration to the Democratic Party.
    b. Since the 1960s, blacks have overwhelmingly chosen Republican candidates.
    c. For the most part, racial segregation in the United States has been eliminated.
    d. Public opinion and voting evidence indicate that African Americans continue to vote as a bloc despite their economic differences.

18. Based on polls, voting data, etc., which of the following groups is least likely to be politically cohesive?
    a. Asians
    b. African Americans
    c. Hispanics
    d. all of the above groups are politically cohesive.

19. With respect to "class-based consciousness" in the United States, most Americans say they are:
    a. part of the middle class.
    b. part of the upper class.
    c. blue-collar workers.
    d. members of labor unions.

20. This U.S. Constitutional amendment ratified in 1920 guaranteed women the right to vote.
    a. Nineteenth
    b. Twentieth
    c. Twenty-first
    d. Twenty-second

21. A distinctive pattern of male and female voting patterns in electoral politics is the definition of:
    a. the "war of the sexes."
    b. sexism.
    c. gender gap.
    d. the "normal vote."

22. Disputes about racial, ethnic, and gender discrimination reveal that:
    a. America is a classless society.
    b. Americans believe in economic equity but not social equity.
    c. Americans hold conflicting perspectives about how to reconcile the values of liberty, equality, and democracy with a history of discrimination and political exclusion.
    d. Americans believe more in "equality of results" than "equality of opportunity."

23. What has been the result of expanding the American political community to include women and minorities?
    a. The provisions of the Fifth Amendment to the U.S. Constitution finally have been realized.
    b. Conflicts over their inclusion have tested Americans' understanding of equality, liberty, and democracy.
    c. Political conflict has been reduced.
    d. The power of state and local governments has grown at the expense of national government power.

24. Which of the following would policy makers most likely use if they wanted to control who immigrated into the United States?
    a. open immigration
    b. free trade agreements
    c. formal recognition of a nation by the United Nations
    d. a quota system based on national origin

25. Most Cuban Americans came to the United States in the early 1960s as refugees. As a result,
    a. they are resolutely anti-Communist.
    b. they favor the Democratic Party.
    c. most were very poor.
    d. they favor an"isolationist" foreign policy.

26. Many political analysts have called the Hispanic vote "the sleeping giant" because:
    a. Hispanics now account for 25 percent of the U.S. population.
    b. the Hispanic population has not yet realized its potential influence.
    c. Hispanic voter registration is very high as a group, but they do not vote.
    d. if Hispanics vote, their vote usually decides who wins an election.

27. Which of the following reasons best explains the lack of support for socialism in the United States?
    a. lack of a class consciousness
    b. lack of a history of working-class activity in the United States
    c. the absence of labor unions in America
    d. the absence of a violent labor history in the United States

28. Black churches were instrumental in the civil rights movement. On issues of economic inequality and social policy, the Catholic church often takes more liberal stands. In 1984, 80 percent of evangelical Christians voted for Ronald Reagan. The above statements illustrate which of the following points?
    a. Thomas Jefferson's "wall of separation" between church and state
    b. religion has always played an important role in American politics and public life
    c. the separation of church and state
    d. religion is unrelated to politics

29. Changes in civil rights, immigration, and gender laws have:
    a. lessened democracy.
    b. created a more exclusive society.
    c. resulted in less government.
    d. created a more inclusive citizenship.

QUESTIONS FOR DISCUSSION AND THOUGHT

1. Who immigrates to America and why? What does our nation represent that is not available to them in their own countries? Is it freedom? Wealth? Opportunity? Do you think these immigrants will find America to be all that they hoped for? If someone from another country consulted you about immigrating to America, what advice would you give? What could we do as a nation to help other countries around the world to improve their systems in order to relieve some of the immigration pressures on the United States? In what ways does the United States benefit from immigration? Do we, in fact, really want to reduce immigration? Would we be able to fill all the jobs in our labor market if we severely restricted immigration?

2. If the Equal Rights Amendment were proposed today, do you think it would be ratified? What, if anything, has changed in our political or economic systems since the 1970s that might affect ratification? Would you support ERA?

3. Is it true that girls are socialized differently from boys in our educational system? Why do girls do better than boys in math and science in the early grades, but then drop out of such classes by the time they get to high school? Do you think teachers treat boys and girls differently? If so, how?

4. Some people worry that the United States is becoming increasingly economically stratified, leading to even less economic and social equality. That is, the rich are getting richer and the poor are getting poorer, relative to the middle and upper classes. Others argue that even the poor in America have TV sets, VCRs, automobiles, and telephones; therefore, the poor here are not really that badly off. Do you see increasing stratification? What sort of economic future do you see for yourself? If stratification increases, what sort of America will we have in fifty years?

5. How powerful is the women's vote? Women's issues (child care, parental leave, education) are often given low priority in the United States, especially when compared to many other countries. Does this mean that the women's vote is not worth pursuing? What "women's issues" are of interest to you? To your representatives in Congress? To the general public?

THE CITIZEN'S ROLE

In this chapter, the authors note that "political and social institutions have ceased to mobilize an active citizenry," thus opening the door to "checkbook democracy," in which government responds to those with money and influence. Have you thought about your own involvement in society? Have you considered volunteering in a social or political organization? Contact a local volunteer organization such as the Boys or Girls Club, the YWCA, Special Olympics, the Red Cross, a community food bank or shelter or a political group, such as the College Democrats or Republicans, the Libertarian Student Club, Common Cause, or a state-wide student lobby group, and complete the table below.

Name of organization

Person interviewed

Purpose of organization

Number of paid staff

Number of volunteers

Number of volunteers needed

Qualifications for volunteers

Training for volunteers

Number of hours/week expected

---

1. Why did you pick this organization? Were you familiar with its programs?
2. Does the organization have trouble finding enough volunteers?
3. Have you ever volunteered with a social or political group? What did you gain from the experience?
4. Would you consider volunteering with this group? Explain.
5. What values do you see in volunteering? Do you think that American society is weakened by the reduction in volunteerism? Explain. Do you think that volunteering enhances a sense of political efficacy—that is, that individuals can influence the political system?

GOVERNMENT IN YOUR LIFE

Many people in the United States today worry that the "American way of life" is under attack because of shifts in social values, racial composition, and economic structure. One popular movement wants a constitutional amendment that would make English the official language. Using the form below, make a list of all of the advantages and disadvantages of such an amendment.

Advantages	Disadvantages

1. Which side, in your opinion, has the stronger arguments? Explain.
2. Do you think that making English the official language will stem the tide of cultural change in America? What changes are targeted by this amendment?
3. Suppose Puerto Rico, a Spanish-speaking territory of the United States, applied to become the fifty-first state of the United States. Would you support or oppose its joining the Union? Explain.
4. Do you support or oppose this amendment? Explain.
5. American society is becoming more diverse as more people from non-western countries enter and more groups in society gain equal rights. What sort of America do you envision fifty years from now? One hundred years? Is diversity America's strength or its weakness? Explain.

ANSWER KEY

Fill-in-the-Blank Quiz

1. poll tax, white primary
2. political machine
3. Gender gap
4. coalition, mobilization
5. socioeconomic status, participation
6. American political community
7. civic engagement
8. institution
9. efficacy
10. white ethnics

Multiple-Choice Quiz

1. b
2. c
3. a
4. d
5. d
6. c
7. b
8. c
9. a
10. c
11. b

12. b
13. c
14. c
15. b
16. e
17. d
18. a
19. a
20. a
21. c
22. c
23. b
24. d
25. a
26. b
27. a
28. b
29. d

CHAPTER 3 The Founding and the Constitution

THE CHAPTER IN BRIEF

Can you imagine living in a country where, even though you were a citizen and paid taxes, you were not allowed to vote for your own representatives? Where you were taxed but not allowed to vote on the taxation? Now suppose that you are a citizen of a country that owns vast lands overseas but where there are constant wars and uprisings and that the young men of your country must go to fight to protect those citizens. Shouldn't the people who are being defended have to help pay for their own defense? This was the genesis of the American Revolution.

Up until about 1750, the British colonists in the New World had been relatively quiet. But the increasing costs to Britain of fighting the French and Indian War and fending off the various Indian attacks meant that the British government was sending money and troops to America but receiving very little back in the way of taxes for support. So, they reasoned, let's put a few small taxes on the colonists as a way of raising money. Parliament passed the Stamp Act, the Sugar Act, and several other taxes on commerce in 1764. Immediately the colonists responded that they were being taxed without having any representation. The wealthy southern planters and New England merchants, who had been pro-British, joined with the lower classes to resist. Parliament repealed most of these taxes, but then did something else to anger the colonists. The East India Company was given a tea monopoly in the colonies, which led to another revolt, culminating in the Boston Tea Party in 1773.

Britain responded with harsh measures, including closing the port of Boston and limiting further colonization in the western lands. The Americans became mobilized again, and the radicals were gaining more public strength. In 1774, the colonies elected representatives to a Continental Congress held in Philadelphia, where they discussed asking for an American parliament or acquiring dominion status. But as messages were moving back and forth across the Atlantic, the colonials' resistance was growing. When the British troops fired on the minute men at Lexington and Concord, it was "the shot heard round the world."

A Second Continental Congress was called in 1775 and assembled a colonial army and navy. By 1776, it was clear that there would not be reconciliation with Britain, and the Congress directed Thomas Jefferson, Benjamin Franklin, Roger Sherman, John Adams, and Robert Livingston to write a statement declaring independence from British rule. The Declaration of Independence claimed that all men were entitled to certain natural rights, including "life, liberty, and the pursuit of happiness."

But now the colonials had no government. They were no longer British, and they had to quickly write a constitution. For almost twelve years, the states operated under the constitution called the Articles of Confederation. In a confederation, sovereignty (supreme political power) resides in the individual states; the national government is very weak. Congress was the central government. There was no executive branch and no judicial authority over national law. Because Congress lacked the power to regulate commerce between the states, competition between the states allowed foreign powers to play one state against another. Reform of the Articles was needed.

Another meeting was called, this time in Annapolis in 1786. Not much happened there, except that the delegates asked Congress to send commissioners to Philadelphia at some later time. The Philadelphia meeting might never have occurred if it had not been for the restive farmers in western Massachusetts, who, led by Daniel Shays, rebelled against the foreclosures occurring against their farms. The Congress had not been able to decide upon a course of action for resolving the crisis, and the leaders of the young nation realized that they had to act quickly to bolster their national government, lest internal strife undermine the nation's newly-won independence.

All the states except Rhode Island sent representatives to the Philadelphia Convention in 1787. Immediately the delegates decided they had to scrap the Articles entirely and write a new constitution, giving sovereignty to a central government. That's not what they were sent to do, so they held their meetings in secret. Conflicting views over commercial and property rights and ethical principles prompted several plans and compromises. The "Great Compromise" provided for a bicameral Congress of a House of Representatives (representing the people on a population basis) and a Senate where each state had two votes. The "Three-fifths Compromise" struck a bargain with the Southern states. They would support ratification if they could count three-fifths of the slaves for representation purposes.

Why didn't the delegates abolish slavery at that time? Many of them clearly had moral objections to slavery. But they had to make a choice: take a stand against slavery and risk the loss of the support of the South, or agree to a compromise which prohibited the importation of slaves after 1808.

The Constitution provided a framework for the new government, setting up major branches of government and delineating their powers and limitations. The

House was given the sole power to originate revenue bills (taxation), and its members are elected directly by the people. The House was to be directly responsible to the people to encourage popular consent for the new Constitution and new government. The Senate was given the sole power to ratify treaties and approve presidential appointments, and its members were originally appointed by the state legislatures. However, in 1913, the Seventeenth Amendment provided for direct election of senators by the people. Congress was assigned specific powers: to declare war, and to maintain an army and a navy. The national government did not have the authority to add to its powers except through a constitutional amendment. Lacking that, all power was reserved to the states (people).

The Constitution also set up the executive branch, or the presidency. The president has the unconditional power to accept ambassadors from other countries—meaning the ability to "recognize" other countries. The president also has the power to negotiate international treaties, which require Senate approval. The president can grant reprieves and pardons, appoint major departmental personnel, convene Congress in special session, and veto Congressional enactments. The veto power can be overridden by a two-thirds vote in both houses of Congress.

The third branch created in the new government was the judicial branch. The Supreme Court has the power to resolve conflicts between state and federal law. The Constitution established that national laws and treaties "shall be the supreme law of the land." In other words, if a federal law and state law are at odds, the state law is deemed invalid.

Article V of the Constitution established procedures for its own revision in the form of amendments, a difficult process at best. Since the Bill of Rights (the first ten amendments) was adopted in 1791, the Constitution has been amended only seventeen times, even though many more amendments have been proposed. The ratification process for the Constitution was established in Article VII, in which nine of the thirteen states would have to ratify, but the process was slowed by the issue of including a bill of rights.

The framers of the Constitution were the first Americans to confront the dilemma of freedom and power, and how to reconcile the two. To guard against the misuse of power, the framers incorporated two key principles into the Constitution: the separate branches of the government provided for checks and balances against each other; and federalism, or the system of two sovereigns (the states and the nation), provides limits on the power of both. The Bill of Rights gave further protection to citizens. The fight for ratification was between the Federalists, who wanted a strong central government, and the Antifederalists, who wanted the opposite. The issues were representation and tyranny by those in power. Compromise was reached with the inclusion of the Bill of Rights, and essentially the Federalists achieved their vision of a powerful national government that has endured for over two centuries.

The framers recognized the need for ongoing change and provided for the possibility of amendment, although the Constitution has proven extremely difficult to amend. For all practical purposes, only fifteen amendments have been added to the Constitution since 1791, not counting the Eighteenth and Twenty-first, which cancel each other out. Between 1789 and 1993, 9,746 amendments were formally offered in Congress, and 27 were ratified. The battle over the failed Equal Rights Amendment illustrates the difficulty of amending. Of the amendments that did succeed, we can see that their content is basically to further limit the powers of government, or to provide citizens with new rights.

The framers of the Constitution placed individual liberty ahead of all other political values, which led many of them to distrust both democracy and equality. As a result, the structure of the Constitution was designed to safeguard liberty as well as limit democracy and the threat of majority tyranny. By making liberty the number-one concern, the framers guaranteed the evolution of democracy and a measure of equality in the United States.

REVIEW QUESTIONS

1. What conflicts precipitated the First Continental Congress? What interests were represented?
2. What measures were pursued by this group? What was the Declaration of Independence? Who wrote it? What values were implicit in it? Whose interest did it represent? Support your answer to the last question with an argument.
3. Describe the Articles of Confederation. What did it say about the relationship between the national, state, and local governments? Why did the Articles fail?
4. What was the "second Founding"? Why is the term an appropriate description?
5. What was the Annapolis Convention? How did it differ from the Philadelphia Convention of 1787?
6. What contributions did Alexander Hamilton make to the Founding of the United States?
7. What was Shays's Rebellion? What social groups were in conflict? How was the conflict put to rest? What event did it lead to?
8. How and why did the framers of the Constitution avoid the issue of slavery? Why didn't they abolish the institution?
9. What was James Madison's contribution to the Founding of the United States?
10. What was Edmund Randolph's motion?
11. Why is the Connecticut Compromise called the Great Compromise?

12. What was the "Three-fifths Compromise"? What was its political significance?
13. Define the following key terms: bicameralism, checks and balances, indirect election, and federalism. How are they related?
14. What does Article I of the Constitution establish?
15. What branch of the national government was designed to be the most democratic and responsive to the people?
16. What does the doctrine of expressed powers do?
17. What constitutional provisions prevent states from interfering with commerce?
18. What powers does Article II of the Constitution grant the president?
19. What powers does Article III of the Constitution grant the Supreme Court? What power is not directly mentioned in the Constitution?
20. To what does the "supremacy clause" in Article VI of the Constitution refer?
21. How did the Constitution differ from the Articles of Confederation?
22. Describe the methods of amending the Constitution. How many amendments have been added to the Constitution since the Bill of Rights, and what do they have in common? What does this reveal about the Constitution in general?
23. Discuss the Bill of Rights. Note when it was adopted and how it relates to each of the three branches of the government.

KEY TERMS

Antifederalists
Articles of Confederation
Bill of Rights
checks and balances
confederation
elastic clause
electoral college
expressed powers
federalism
Federalist Papers
Federalists
Great Compromise
judicial review
limited government
New Jersey Plan
separation of powers
supremacy clause
Three-fifths Compromise
tyranny
Virginia Plan

FILL-IN-THE BLANK QUIZ

Use the key terms to complete the following sentences.

1. In a ____________, the supreme political power resides in the member states.
2. The ____________ Plan proposed a legislative body based on equal representation for all states.
3. The founders believed that unchecked power could lead to ____________.
4. The "necessary and proper" clause of Article I is often called the ____________.
5. The ____________ refused to ratify the Constitution unless a ____________ was added.
6. The first constitution of the United States was called the ____________.
7. The ____________ combined the New Jersey Plan with the ____________.
8. Technically, the president is elected by the ____________.
9. Supporters of a strong central government were known as ____________.
10. The phrase that establishes the sovereignty of the national government is the ____________.
11. The three basic principles of the Constitution are ____________, ____________, and ____________.
12. Because the South refused to ratify the Constitution if it abolished slavery, the Philadelphia Convention agreed to the ____________.
13. Those powers that are clearly stated in the Constitution are called the ____________.
14. The ____________ were written in support of ratification.
15. The purpose of a constitution is to provide ____________.
16. A gap in the original constitution that was filled by a decision of the Supreme Court was the need for some sort of ____________.

MULTIPLE-CHOICE QUIZ

1. The Stamp Act of ____________ created revenue stamps and required that they be affixed to all printed and legal documents, including newspapers, pamphlets, advertisements, notes and bonds, leases, deeds, and licenses.
   a. 1750

b. 1765
c. 1775
d. 1776

2. He was one of the major leaders (radicals) among the colonists who advocated an end to British rule. He also led the Boston Tea Party of 1773.
   a. John Adams
   b. Samuel Adams
   c. Daniel Shays
   d. George Washington Plunkitt

3. Who wrote the Declaration of Independence?
   a. Benjamin Franklin
   b. James Madison
   c. Alexander Hamilton
   d. Thomas Jefferson

4. Which state boycotted the Constitutional Convention?
   a. New York
   b. Virginia
   c. Georgia
   d. Rhode Island

5. This historian is famous for his "economic interpretation" of the Founders and the U.S. Constitution.
   a. Frederick Jackson Turner
   b. Charles Darwin
   c. Charles Beard
   d. Max Farrand

6. This French political theorist gave us the concept "separation of powers" in his classic book entitled, *The Spirit of the Laws.*
   a. Montesquieu
   b. Locke
   c. Hume
   d. Hobbes

7. Between 1789 and 1993, 9,746 amendments were formally offered in Congress. Of these, only ___________ were finally ratified by the states.
   a. 500
   b. 100
   c. 50
   d. 27

8. Prior to the twentieth century, most governments relied on ___________ for revenue.
   a. tariffs, duties, and other taxes on commerce
   b. local sales taxes
   c. a national sales tax
   d. a personal income tax

9. The First Continental Congress met in 1774. Which of the following actions did the delegates at the Congress take?
   a. They declared independence from Great Britain.
   b. They called for a total boycott of British goods.
   c. They elected George Washington as General of the Colonial Army.
   d. They wrote the pamphlet "Common Sense," which argued for independence from British rule.

10. The United States' first written constitution was:
    a. the U.S. Constitution.
    b. the Declaration of Independence.
    c. the League of States.
    d. the Articles of Confederation and Perpetual Union.

11. The Declaration of Independence and the Articles of Confederation were not sufficient to hold the new nation together as an independent and effective nation-state. Which of the following statements is not true?
    a. The central government under the Articles of Confederation was powerless to intervene to resolve and solve trade, economic, and political disputes among the states.
    b. Many of the pre- and post-Revolutionary "radicals"—small framers, artisans, and shopkeepers—wanted a strong national government in order to protect their economic interests.
    c. Many of the pre-Revolutionary colonial elite favored a stronger national government in order to protect their economic interests.
    d. Competition among the states for foreign commerce allowed the European powers to play the states against one another.

12. According to the authors, it is quite possible that the Constitutional Convention of 1787 in Philadelphia would never have taken place at all except for a single event that occurred during the winter following the Annapolis Convention. This event was:
    a. the battles of Lexington and Concord.
    b. the signing of the Declaration of Independence.
    c. Shays' Rebellion.
    d. the publication of Thomas Paine's "Common Sense."

13. This constitutional plan provided for a system of representation in a new national legislature based upon the population of each state or the proportion of each state's revenue contribution, or both.
    a. the Virginia Plan
    b. the New Jersey Plan
    c. the Connecticut Compromise
    d. the Electoral College

14. Which of the following statements is true about the "Three-fifths Compromise"?
    a. It settled the question of how many senators each state would get.
    b. It created a system to elect the president of the United States.
    c. Under this compromise, five slaves would count as three free persons in apportioning seats in the House of Representatives.
    d. Only "three-fifths" of all slaves were allowed to vote in national elections.

15. Under the original, unamended Constitution, the only person(s) elected directly by the people was/were:
    a. the president.
    b. Senators.
    c. Supreme Court judges.
    d. members of the House of Representatives.

16. One of the goals of the Founders was to create an active and powerful national government. Which of the following facilitated this goal?

a. expressed powers
b. necessary and proper clause
c. elastic clause
d. reserved powers
e. all of the above
f. only a, b, and c.

17. The concept "national supremacy," as defined in Article VI,
    a. allows state laws to be superior to conflicting national laws.
    b. provides the Supreme Court the power of judicial review.
    c. is also known as the "nullification act."
    d. allows national laws to be superior to conflicting state laws.

18. Since 1791, how many times has the U.S. Constitution been amended?
    a. 17
    b. 25
    c. 30
    d. 50

19. The president vetoes a bill passed by Congress. This action is an example of:
    a. checks and balances.
    b. separation of powers.
    c. executive order.
    d. executive privilege.

20. Which of the following statements is true about the Constitutional ratification process?
    a. Ratification of the Constitution was a speedy and noncontroversial process.
    b. The Constitution was ratified in state legislatures.
    c. The struggle for ratification was carried out in thirteen separate campaigns.
    d. The so-called Federalists opposed ratification of the U.S. Constitution.

21. What/Who were "Publius" and "Brutus"?
    a. Essays written defending (Publius) and attacking (Brutus) the proposed U.S. Constitution
    b. The nicknames given to Alexander Hamilton (Publius) and Aaron Burr (Brutus)
    c. Latin terms meaning Federalist (Publius) and Antifederalist (Brutus)
    d. None of the above

22. In general, it was the ___________ vision of America that triumphed.
    a. Federalist
    b. Antifederalist
    c. Jeffersonian
    d. Washingtonian

23. Most of the seventeen Constitutional amendments ratified since the Bill of Rights in 1791 have been directly or indirectly concerned with:
    a. due process of law.
    b. equal protection of the law.
    c. elections.
    d. civil liberties.

24. Which of the following statements is most accurate concerning the Constitution period?
    a. After fighting a revolutionary war, most Americans believed that a strong national government was needed to

raise a "national" army and navy.
b. The proposed new constitutional system faced considerable opposition.
c. The arguments offered by the Federalists for adoption of the U.S. Constitution were readily accepted by most Americans in the thirteen new states.
d. The Antifederalists strongly believed in a strong national government, but were opposed to a "bill of rights."

25. According to the text, the story of the founding is important because:
   a. it is a story about morality; the British were oppressive, and the Americans had the "moral" obligation to rebel.
   b. all students should learn the lessons of history.
   c. it was a story of political choices, and Americans continue today to make tough political choices.
   d. it illustrates that democracy is the only political choice for freedom-loving people.

26. Which of the following is most similar in structure to the United States under the Articles of Confederation?
   a. the current structure of the U.S. government
   b. a unitary system of government, like is found in France
   c. the United Nations
   d. a "pure democracy"

27. Which statement about Shays' Rebellion is true?
   a. Shays' Rebellion was widely supported and showed that the "propertyless masses" were in control of post-Revolutionary America.
   b. Shays' Rebellion showed that the Congress under the Articles of Confederation was too weak and that it was unable to act decisively.
   c. Shays' Rebellion was supported by the "landed gentry," such as Alexander Hamilton, as an expression of popular democracy in action.
   d. George Washington supported Shays' Rebellion since many of his former soldiers were among the protesters.

28. According to your text, which of the following statements best articulates the motives of the framers at the Constitutional Convention in Philadelphia?
   a. America's Founders were a collection of securities speculators and property owners whose main aim was self-interest and personal gain.
   b. The Founders' interests were reinforced by their principles.
   c. The framers were primarily interested in philosophical and ethical principles.
   d. The Founders were most concerned about the expansion of democracy to all new Americans.

29. The convention that drafted the American Constitution was chiefly organized by the New England merchants and southern planters. Why?

a. They were the people elected by members of the Continental Congress.
b. They were educated, well-known, respected, and had much vested, in terms of interest and principle, in the new nation.
c. They were the ones elected by "all free white men" in the thirteen new states.
d. They were the ones with the most to gain from a new nation and a new constitution.

30. Under the Great Compromise, small states were given an advantage in the:
    a. Senate.
    b. House of Representatives.
    c. Electoral College.
    d. Supreme Court.

31. The Founders created a "bicameral" legislative body. This two-chambered legislative body:
    a. elects all members of the House of Representatives every four years.
    b. elects one-half of the Senators every two years.
    c. allows for checks and balances.
    d. passes bills into law when either one-half the members of the House or the Senate vote accordingly.

32. According to the text, the Framers sought a new government that would serve the twin goals of:
    a. promoting commerce/protecting property and preventing "excessive democracy."
    b. expanding the right to vote and settling the issue of slavery.
    c. promoting commerce/protecting property and establishing "pure democracy."
    d. expanding the right to vote and protecting the civil rights of all Americans.

33. The power of judicial review:
    a. allows the Senate to confirm presidential judicial appointments.
    b. is defined in Article III of the U.S. Constitution.
    c. was assumed by the Supreme Court.
    d. was declared unconstitutional by Chief Justice John Marshall in *Marbury v. Madison.*

34. An important issue dividing Federalists and Antifederalists was the threat of "tyranny," meaning,
    a. generally, unjust rule by the group in power.
    b. from the Antifederalists' perspective, the fear of an aristocracy.
    c. from the Federalists' perspective, rule by the passions of the majority.
    d. all of the above.

35. Which of the following concepts best explains the underlying reason for the Bill of Rights?
    a. checks and balances
    b. separation of powers
    c. limited government
    d. rule by government

36. The amendment route to social change:
    a. is, and always will be, extremely limited.
    b. is very frequently followed.
    c. is hard, but has been used over fifty times in American history.
    d. has never been used in America.

37. The Constitution's framers placed ____________ ahead of all other political values.
    a. individual liberty
    b. democracy
    c. equality
    d. civil rights

QUESTIONS FOR DISCUSSION AND THOUGHT

1. Were the colonists fighting for liberty? Equality? Democracy? What was the basis of their opposition? Were the colonists justified in their rebellion against England? If you had been there, would you have sided with the colonial elite or with the radicals? Why?

2. Do you see the school prayer issue as a constitutional (legal) issue or as a moral issue? In a constitutional democracy which relies upon tolerance and rational discussion, is it ever proper for one religion to impose its morality and doctrine on another? Can you reconcile the need for tolerance with the demands of some religions to convert others to their beliefs? Or is this one of the contradictions we have to live with in order to sustain a democracy?

3. Explain this statement: "The Declaration of Independence is an extremely liberal document and the American Constitution is an extremely conservative document."

4. How might American history have been changed if:
    a. the colonists had lost the American Revolution?
    b. the Constitutional Convention of 1787 had never been held?
    c. the Constitution had never been ratified?
    d. we did not have a Bill of Rights in the federal Constitution?
    e. slavery had been abolished when the Constitution was adopted?

5. Suppose you wanted to change our government from a presidential to a parliamentary political system. What changes would be required in the Constitution? Do you see any advantages in a parliamentary system over a presidential one? Any disadvantages? How would American politics change?

6. Some people want to amend the Constitution to allow for initiative—that is, to allow voters to propose legislation and constitutional amendments, a process allowed in some state constitutions. Do you think this is a good idea? What advantages and disadvantages do you see in this?

THE CITIZEN'S ROLE

Do you think that the Equal Rights Amendment would have a better chance of being ratified today than it had in the 1970s? To determine popular support for ERA, circulate the petition below to get ten signatures. Then complete the following questions:

1. How many people did you ask to sign the petition? How many refused to sign?
2. How many people had heard of the Equal Rights Amendment?
3. What reasons did people give for signing or not signing?
4. Do you think that getting people to sign petitions is an effective way to get Congress to give serious consideration to a constitutional amendment? What other ways might be used to get the attention of Congress?

PETITION

The purpose of this petition is to ask Congress to consider a constitutional amendment that would guarantee equal rights to all persons, regardless of sex. The proposed amendment would read:

> Section 1. Equality of rights under the law shall not be denied or abridged by the United States or by any State on account of sex.
>
> Section 2. The Congress shall have the power to enforce, by appropriate legislation, the provisions of this article.
>
> Section 3. This amendment shall take effect two years after the date of ratification.

If you agree with this amendment, please print and sign your name below.

Name (printed)	Signature

GOVERNMENT IN YOUR LIFE

If you had been alive in 1789, would you have supported the proposed Constitution? Place yourself in the position of a New England merchant who supports ratification or a Southern farmer who opposes the new Constitution. Make a list of at least five arguments to support your position.

1. In what way would your position in the North or South affect your attitude about ratification?
2. In what way would your occupation affect your attitude?
3. Do you think your arguments would be persuasive to someone who is uncommitted?
4. Are you basing your arguments on your own self-interest or the nation as a whole?
5. Voting on the new Constitution was an awesome responsibility. Do you think that most Americans today would be qualified to debate, discuss, analyze, and vote on a new Constitution?

ANSWER KEY

Fill-in-the-Blank

1. confederation
2. New Jersey
3. tyranny
4. elastic clause
5. Antifederalists, Bill of Rights
6. Articles of Confederation
7. Great Compromise, Virginia Plan
8. electoral college
9. Federalists
10. supremacy clause
11. separation of powers, federalism, checks and balances (in any order)
12. Three-fifths Compromise
13. expressed powers
14. Federalist Papers
15. limited government
16. judicial review

Multiple-Choice Quiz

1. b
2. b
3. d
4. d
5. c
6. a
7. d
8. a
9. b
10. d
11. c
12. c
13. a
14. c
15. d
16. e
17. d
18. a
19. a

20. c
21. a
22. a
23. c
24. b
25. c
26. c
27. b
28. b
29. b
30. a
31. c
32. a
33. c
34. d
35. c
36. a
37. a

CHAPTER 4 Federalism

THE CHAPTER IN BRIEF

Imagine yourself back in the time of the American Revolution. Thirteen colonies, with quite different histories, came together to fight the British and to establish a new government. No state wanted to give up its identity to blend anonymously into one large nation. The nations of western Europe were, in fact, unitary; that is, they possessed a central government that had undivided authority over the entire nation. But that was not an acceptable choice in the new United States. How would you resolve the conflict between the need for some state autonomy and some national control?

At first the new states formed a confederation, a loose union of states wherein the states retained sovereignty (supreme political power), under the Articles of Confederation. But, as we saw in the last chapter, a confederation is inherently weak and ultimately it fell apart, leading to the new constitution. The solution in the Constitution of 1787 was to divide power *geographically* between the states and the federal government, with sovereignty placed at the national level. This was an ingenious solution which has been copied by many other nations since, such as Brazil, Canada, and Mexico. But it also has its complications because there is no real answer to the question: who should do what?

The Constitution gives only the bare outlines of a federal system. Article I, Section 8 lists "expressed" powers granted to the federal government, such as collecting taxes, coining money, declaring war, and regulating commerce between the states. In addition, it includes an ambiguous phrase that says that Congress shall "make all laws which shall be necessary and proper for carrying into execution the foregoing powers," often called the "elastic clause" because it can be stretched in many directions.

The Tenth Amendment attempted to strengthen the role of the states by stating that all powers not delegated to the national government or prohibited to the states are "reserved to the states respectively, or to the people." This "reserved powers" clause was intended to satisfy the concerns of the Antifederalists that the national government might become too powerful.

In turn, states must recognize that the acts of other states are legal in all states (the "full faith and credit" clause), treat all citizens equally (the "privileges and immunities" clause), and recognize the supremacy of the national government.

Local governments possess no constitutional standing at the federal level. In effect, the states are unitary governments that can grant or withdraw powers as they wish from their local governments. Most states allow larger cities to operate with greater independence through home rule charters, but this does not create mini-federalism.

A major battle over the definition of federalism came in the case of *McCulloch v. Maryland,* which dealt with the two important questions of federalism. The first was whether the federal government could charter a national bank—something that was not listed specifically as a federal power. The Federalist Chief Justice John Marshall ruled that the implied powers clause could be used to justify this action. The second issue was whether a state could tax an entity of the federal government; Marshall ruled that the federal government was supreme over the states and that Maryland had exceeded its authority.

The *McCulloch* case was followed several years later by *Gibbons v. Ogden,* in which Marshall proclaimed that Congress' power to regulate interstate commerce meant that New York could not regulate commerce between New York State and New Jersey. Thus, it would appear that the Federalists' version of a strong central government was the winner.

Appearances can be deceiving. The federal government, in fact, remained small and relatively insignificant, compared to the states. Even then, the South became increasingly concerned that the federal government might attempt to outlaw slavery, and thus they embarked on an attempt to withdraw from the union, claiming that states' rights were being infringed. In the late nineteenth century, the Supreme Court drew such a narrow definition of interstate commerce that it virtually prohibited any federal actions. In reality, the states dominated the federal system for most of our nation's history. Not until 1937, in the New Deal, did the nation change its views about federal powers, and then only because it was apparent that the states would never be able to fight the Depression on their own.

The New Deal ushered in an era of cooperative federalism (often called marble-cake federalism), in which the federal government, its power to act directly limited by the constitution, offered "carrots" to the states if they agreed to carry out the will of Congress. These carrots were in the form of grants-in-aid, money given to the states (often with a matching amount required) to do everything from offer a welfare program to build an interstate highway system. The first grants were given for a specific category, and are called categorical grants. Later, under President Nixon, many categorical grants were combined into larger block grants that offered greater flexibility in the use of the money. The Nixon administration also developed another method of sharing funding that was not tied to any specific programs. Revenue sharing was federal grants to states given on a complicated formula basis. The problem with revenue sharing was that, under President Reagan, the federal government didn't have any extra money to share; in fact, the government went deeply into debt, and revenue sharing died.

The result of federal grants has been to redistribute money across the nation on a more equitable basis, to devolve more authority down to the state level, and to move the actual program administration from the federal to the state levels. Governors frequently complain that there are too many strings attached to federal aid, but the federal government's response is that states have to be held accountable somehow, and that because some states have had notorious corruption in their governments in the past or have not treated all citizens fairly, they cannot be trusted completely.

A few years ago most political scientists accepted the cooperative federalism model as the most appropriate for our system. In the early 1990s, a conservative reaction to the increasing dominance of the federal government, especially its use of unfunded mandates, led to renewed interest in the Tenth Amendment. The conservative Republicans elected to Congress in 1994 have tried to send more powers back to the states, as, for example, in the welfare reform law. It is too soon to know if states will be competent enough to carry out this complicated reform, if they will truly be "laboratories of democracy," or will simply "race to the bottom" in an effort to save money. There will always be a seesawing action going on between state and federal powers, because there simply is no clear answer to the question: who should do what?

REVIEW QUESTIONS

1. Why are states called "laboratories of democracy"?
2. Compare dual federalism with cooperative federalism.
3. Why did the United States adopt a federal system instead of borrowing the unitary system common in Europe?
4. What factors might influence a nation in selecting a federalist system?
5. Where in the Constitution is federalism mentioned?
6. Define the "necessary and proper" clause. Why is it so important to the understanding of federalism?
7. Why did the Antifederalists support the Tenth Amendment?
8. Explain why states might not have to recognize gay marriages from other states in spite of the "full faith and credit" clause.
9. What is the comity clause? Does requiring out-of-state students to pay higher tuition rates at a state university violate this clause? Why or why not?

10. Compare the relationship between the federal government and the states to that of the states and local governments.
11. Which more closely approximates what the Founders had in mind: dual federalism or cooperative federalism? Why?
12. Explain the police powers of the states.
13. Why was *McCulloch v. Maryland* such an important case in the development of federalism?
14. What sort of power was extended to Congress through *Gibbons v. Ogden*?
15. Why is *United States v. Lopez* important in the study of federalism? What does it say about the attitude of the Supreme Court today regarding federalism?
16. Why was dual federalism replaced by cooperative federalism?
17. Compare categorical grants with block grants and revenue sharing. If you were a governor, which grant would you prefer? Why?
18. What is the difference between a project grant and a formula grant?
19. Why does the federal government mistrust the states? How does it attempt to overcome its suspicions?
20. Explain preemption and unfunded mandates. Are these unconstitutional power grabs by Congress or legitimate policies necessary for governing the entire nation fairly?
21. How did the welfare reform law change the federal-state relationships?
22. Which do you think protects your liberties more successfully—the states or the national government? Why?
23. Which do you think is more concerned with ensuring equality—the states or the national government? Why?
24. How have state legislatures become more democratic in the last forty years?

KEY TERMS

block grants
categorical grants
commerce clause
cooperative federalism
devolution
dual federalism
federalism
federalist
formula grants
grants-in-aid
home rule
implied powers
necessary and proper clause
New Federalism

preemption
project grants
redistributive programs
regulated federalism
reserved powers
revenue sharing
states' rights
unfunded mandates
unitary system

FILL-IN-THE-BLANK QUIZ

Use the key terms to complete the following sentences.

1. The federal grant created by President Nixon that provided unrestricted funds to states was the ____________ program.
2. Local governments are sometimes given ____________ to allow greater autonomy.
3. When power is distributed geographically throughout a nation, it is a system of ____________; when it is concentrated in one location, it is a ____________ system.
4. Two concerns that governors have about the increasing number of federal laws are ____________ and ____________.
5. Federal programs that take money from wealthier states to give to poorer states are engaged in ____________.
6. Originally, grants-in-aid were given on the basis of ____________ grants, but today most grants are competitive, or ____________ grants.
7. Governors prefer grants that consolidate several programs, also known as ____________ grants, to those that allow only a single program, or ____________ grants.
8. In *Gibbons v. Ogden,* the Supreme Court enlarged the meaning of the ____________ clause of the Constitution.
9. The constitutional provision that allows Congress to stretch its powers beyond those listed is known as the ____________ clause, and also as the ____________ clause.
10. The Tenth Amendment specified that those powers not specifically granted to the federal government were ____________ of the states or resided with the people.
11. Nations that have wide diversity of culture or language should probably become ____________ systems.
12. Nineteenth-century federalism was replaced during the New Deal with ____________.

13. A renewed emphasis on the Tenth Amendment could possibly return the nation to the nineteenth-century system of ____________.

14. When the federal government passes down programs to the states to administer, it is practicing ____________.

15. President Nixon's revenue sharing was part of his program of ____________.

16. The Clean Air Act, which requires states to meet federal standards of air pollution, is an example of ____________ federalism.

17. The technique used by President Franklin Roosevelt to extend federal powers was the ____________.

18. The principle espoused by the southern states that they could rebuff federal power was the ____________ principle.

MULTIPLE-CHOICE QUIZ

1. The New Deal of the __________ signaled the rise of a more active national government.
   a. 1920s
   b. 1930s
   c. 1940s
   d. 1960s

2. By the year 1932, ____________ percent of the American workforce was unemployed.
   a. 10
   b. 15
   c. 20
   d. 25

3. When President ____________ took office in 1932, he energetically threw the federal government into the business of fighting the Great Depression.
   a. Woodrow Wilson
   b. Herbert Hoover
   c. Franklin Roosevelt
   d. Theodore Roosevelt

4. The "New Federalism" was begun by President Nixon in the:
   a. 1950s.
   b. 1960s.
   c. 1970s.
   d. 1980s.

5. Most of the rules and regulations Americans face in their daily lives are set by:
   a. state and local governments.
   b. the federal government.
   c. regulatory commissions.
   d. the U.S. Supreme Court.

6. Especially since the New Deal in the 1930s, ____________ has/have played a much more prominent role in protecting liberty and promoting equality.
   a. the national government
   b. state governments
   c. county governments
   d. city governments

7. Which of the following statements best captures the meaning of the concept "devolution of authority"?
   a. State governments have given the federal government more of their powers over time.

b. State governments have "devolved" to the point where they exercise very little power in the federal system.
c. City governments are now the premiere power brokers in national politics.
d. The national government grants the states more authority over a range of policies.

8. The division of powers and functions between the national government and state governments is the definition of:
   a. confederation.
   b. intergovernmental relations.
   c. expressed powers.
   d. federalism.

9. Specific powers provided to the national government in the U.S. Constitution are called ____________ powers.
   a. expressed
   b. reserved
   c. concurrent
   d. defined

10. Federalism that limits national government power by creating two sovereigns—the national government and state governments—is called:
    a. "marble-cake" federalism.
    b. national-state sovereignty.
    c. dual federalism.
    d. feudal federalism.

11. For three-quarters of American history, ____________ has/have done most of the fundamental governing.
    a. state governments
    b. local governments
    c. the national government
    d. the people directly

12. The first and most important case favoring national power over the economy was:
    a. *Marbury v. Maryland.*
    b. *Brown v. Board of Education.*
    c. *Gibbons v. Ogden.*
    d. *McCulloch v. Maryland.*

13. G*ibbons v. Ogden* in 1824 was important because:
    a. the decision established the supremacy of the national government in all matters affecting interstate commerce.
    b. it established the principle of judicial review.
    c. it declared that interstate commerce was to be regulated by state governments.
    d. the decision established the principle of "no fees on exports."

14. One way in which the framers sought to preserve a strong role for the states was through the ____________ Amendment to the Constitution.
    a. First
    b. Fifth
    c. Tenth
    d. Fifteenth

15. "States' rights" advocates argue that:
    a. state governments' rights are subordinate to national government policies.
    b. the elastic clause allows for expansion of "states' rights."
    c. only the national government can amend the U.S. Constitution.
    d. they do not have to submit to national laws when they believe the national government exceeds it authority.

16. This provision allows cities a guarantee of noninterference in various local affairs by state governments.
    a. home rule
    b. referendum
    c. initiative
    d. the merit system

17. What is a "grant-in-aid"?
    a. money provided by cities to state governments
    b. money appropriated by the national Congress to state and local governments
    c. the major source of revenue for the national government
    d. what the Department of War uses to fund "military operations"

18. In contrast to the "dual federalism" that defined America until the 1930s, since the New Deal, ____________ federalism has prevailed.
    a. cooperative
    b. layer-cake
    c. traditional
    d. conflicting

19. When the federal government takes over areas of regulation formerly overseen by state and local governments, the process is called____________.
    a. preemption
    b. conditions on aid
    c. "hostile takeover"
    d. an unfunded mandate

20. Regulations or new conditions for receiving grants that impose costs on state and local governments for which they are not reimbursed by the national government is the definition of:
    a. preemption.
    b. unfunded mandates.
    c. fiscal federalism.
    d. dual federalism.

21. Which of the following types of grants give state and local governments the most leeway in spending federal grants-in-aid?
    a. block grants
    b. project grants
    c. formula grants
    d. categorical grants

22. Programs that are primarily for the benefit of the poor are called ____________ programs.
    a. distributive
    b. redistributive
    c. constituent
    d. regulative

23. Which of the following statements about federalism is true?
    a. Federalism is the most widely used method to divide powers among governmental units in the democracies of the world.
    b. The American system of federalism allows substantial inequalities to exist across the country.
    c. Federalism and democracy are synonymous concepts.
    d. The United States is the only federal system in the world.

24. "State governments experiment with different policies to find measures that best meet the needs and desires of their citizens." This quote from your text best reflects which of these statements?
    a. Unlike the federal government, state governments really never know which policies to pursue.

b. Unlike the federal government, state governments always seem to make the "right" policy decisions.
c. State governments can be viewed as "laboratories of democracy."
d. The federal government makes policies that apply equally to all state governments.

25. Which of the following statements is NOT true?
    a. For most of American history, the national government was quite small by comparison both to state governments and to the governments of other Western nations.
    b. For most of American history, virtually all of the functions of the national government were aimed at assisting commerce.
    c. For most of American history, virtually none of the national government's policies directly coerced citizens.
    d. For most of American history, the national government followed a strict interpretation of "interstate commerce."

26. "Implied powers" or the "necessary and proper clause" allows:
    a. state governments to "nullify" national government laws.
    b. the national government to interpret its delegated powers expansively.
    c. for "judicial review."
    d. the national government to "reserve" powers to state governments.

27. Which statement is true?
    a. The powers of local government are defined in Article I of the U.S. Constitution.
    b. The powers of local government are defined in Article II of the U.S. Constitution.
    c. The powers of local government are defined in Article III of the U.S. Constitution.
    d. Local government has no status in the American Constitution.

28. Which type of grant provides more control to federal agencies in the distribution of federal grants-in-aid?
    a. formula
    b. project
    c. revenue sharing
    d. block

29. Which of the following statements best captures the meaning of the concept "regulated federalism"?
    a. State governments "regulate" how much personal income tax revenue they send to the national government.
    b. In recent years the national government has created a large number of regulatory commissions primarily to monitor the policy performance of state governments.
    c. The national government sets standards of conduct and/or requires the states to set standards that meet national guidelines.
    d. The states act as watchdogs and "regulate" federal government grants-in-aid.

QUESTIONS FOR DISCUSSION AND THOUGHT

1. The diversity of state laws and procedures creates an unfair situation for many citizens. For instance, the average felony conviction leads to thirteen months in jail in South Dakota, compared to almost five years in Massachusetts. Connecticut spends twice as much on public education as does Mississippi. Should the federal government have more power to require greater uniformity in policy amongs the states?
2. World Federalists are people who believe that the entire world should become a single political system, with each nation a state under a single international federal-style government, such as the United Nations. What advantages and disadvantages do you see in this idea? Would you support world federalism?
3. If you have lived in another state, compare that state's political culture with this state. Have you observed differences in public services? Quality of public education? Quality of politicians? In your opinion, which state has better government? Why? How can you explain the differences?
4. The nullification efforts of the 1830s were unsuccessful, but it has been said that informal nullification goes on all the time, when unpopular federal laws or court rulings are disobeyed. Can we ever achieve complete obedience to the federal government?
5. Why did President Lincoln claim that the Union could not be dissolved? Do states give up all power to withdraw when they join the Union, or do they still retain some control over their fate?
6. As noted in the chapter's policy debate, the welfare reform legislation has devolved power to the states, in keeping with the theory of dual federalism. Given the variation in welfare services among the states, do you think that devolution will create greater inequalities? Or will it, by forcing more people to work, actually work in the other direction by increasing incomes at the lower levels?

THE CITIZEN'S ROLE

What issues are important to you? The table below lists several organizations and their concerns. Select one of these organizations and find out if your area has a local chapter by checking the Internet, local newspaper, telephone book, and the local Chamber of Commerce. Then contact the organization to get more information and, if possible, attend a meeting.

Issue	Organizations
Environment	Sierra Club, Wilderness Society, Ducks Unlimited
Public interest	Common Cause, Amnesty International, Concord Coalition
Voter education	League of Women Voters
Civil rights	ACLU, NAACP, National Organization for Women, American Indian Movement
Education/Children	Phi Delta Kappa, PTA, Children's Defense Fund
Agriculture	Farm Bureau, National Farmers Organization

1. Why did you select this issue?
2. What is the purpose of the organization you chose?
3. Does the organization have local meetings and programs? If so, give examples.
4. Would you consider joining this organization? Why or why not?
5. Do you think that local organizations such as these can influence national policy? Explain.

GOVERNMENT IN YOUR LIFE

Federalism allows states to run their programs with a great deal of independence and diversity. The table below shows how much money the states and their local governments spent on education (elementary, secondary, and higher) in 1992–93. Study the table carefully and then answer the questions below

Per Capita Expenditures for Education, 1992–93, by State[1]

Alabama	1060.70	Arkansas	1151.93
Alaska	2443.96	California	1263.19
Arizona	1303.18	Colorado	1383.94

[1] *Digest of Educational Statistics,* 1993.

Connecticut	1448.21	Maine	1303.65
Delaware	1656.86	Maryland	1335.17
District of Columbia	1244.05	Massachusetts	1106.92
Florida	1087.70	Michigan	1562.94
Montana	1366.02	Minnesota	1592.45
Nebraska	1473.44	Mississippi	1052.79
Nevada	1170.67	Missouri	1052.79
New Hampshire	1227.49	Oklahoma	1224.08
New Jersey	1607.71	Oregon	1478.85
New Mexico	1420.30	Pennsylvania	1402.93
New York	1665.12	Rhode Island	1337.95
North Carolina	1235.90	South Carolina	1192.27
North Dakota	1516.13	South Dakota	1214.45
Ohio	1253.43	Tennessee	955.86
Georgia	1157.24	Texas	1338.71
Hawaii	1234.67	Utah	1429.69
Idaho	1165.51	Vermont	1540.41
Illinois	1241.48	Virginia	1280.34
Indiana	1308.98	Washington	1630.78
Iowa	1448.41	West Virginia	1323.61
Kansas	1428.26	Wisconsin	1590.24
Kentucky	1100.46	Wyoming	1873.80
Louisiana	1150.41	United States (average for all states)	1327.16

1. How does your state compare to three neighboring states?
2. How much does your state vary from the national average?
3. Which three states spend the most for education? The least? What is the difference between the highest- and the lowest-spending states?
4. Compute the average of three southern states and compare them with the average of three New England states. What did you find?
5. What did you learn about federalism and diversity from this exercise?

ANSWER KEY

Fill-in-the-Blank Quiz

1. revenue sharing
2. home rule
3. federalism, unitary
4. unfunded mandates, preemption
5. redistributive programs
6. formula, project
7. block, categorical
8. commerce

9. necessary and proper, implied powers
10. reserved powers
11. federalist
12. cooperative federalism
13. dual federalism
14. devolution
15. New Federalism
16. regulated
17. grants-in-aid
18. states' rights

Multiple-Choice Quiz

1. b
2. d
3. c
4. c
5. a
6. a
7. d
8. d
9. a
10. c
11. a
12. d
13. a
14. c
15. d
16. a
17. b
18. a
19. a
20. b
21. a
22. b
23. b
24. c
25. d
26. b
27. d
28. b
29. c

CHAPTER 5 Civil Liberties

THE CHAPTER IN BRIEF

Back in Chapter 3 you learned that the Antifederalists refused to support the new Constitution unless individual rights were protected through a Bill of Rights. Once this was added in the form of ten amendments, the Constitution was ratified. Looking back, that was the easy part. What has been hard has been the constant struggle throughout American history to protect those very liberties that are given to us in the Bill of Rights. Even today, some people want to take away or limit our rights. Thomas Jefferson wrote, "I have sworn upon the altar of God eternal hostility against every form of tyranny over the mind of man." That's what the Bill of Rights is about: the freedom to express your own opinions, worship in your own way, be protected in your home, and be treated fairly by the government.

The Bill of Rights was ratified on December 15, 1791, after a long struggle with the Federalists, led by Alexander Hamilton, who felt such a document was unnecessary. It could have been called the Bill of Liberties instead. Civil liberties are protections of citizens from improper government action, a protection that Thomas Jefferson felt people were entitled to against every government on earth. The Bill of Rights is a series of restraints imposed on government. Some of these restraints are substantive, putting limits on what the government may or may not do, and some are procedural, dealing with how the government is supposed to act. The various amendments in the Bill of Rights deal specifically with limits on Congress, the executive branch, the judiciary, and the national government as a whole. By contrast, civil rights refers to the government's obligation to take positive action to protect citizens from illegal actions by government agencies or private citizens.

Until 1868, the Bill of Rights did not protect citizens at the state level because every American was said to be a citizen of the national government and separately a citizen of his or her state of residence. That was known as dual citizenship. In 1868, the Fourteenth Amendment was ratified with the purpose of nationalizing the Bill of Rights, making it apply at the state level. However, nationalization was a slow process. For sixty years the only nationalized portion was the property protection of the Fifth Amendment. In the 1920s, the Supreme Court began making decisions that nationalized bits and pieces of the Bill of Rights, but it wasn't until the 1960s that the Court began actively pursuing its nationalization.

Civil liberties in the 1990s require constant re-interpretation, since ensuring liberty for some requires restraining the liberty of others. Every provision in the Bill of Rights is subject to interpretation, generally by the Supreme Court, and in response to a question of the infringement of someone's liberty by someone else.

One topic dealt with in the First Amendment is religious freedom. The "establishment clause" has been interpreted to mean the strict separation of church and state. The "free exercise clause" protects the right to believe and to practice whatever religion one chooses; it also involves protection of the right to be a nonbeliever. Many cases involving diverse interpretations of the two clauses have come before the federal courts since the 1940s. Once they reach the Supreme Court, new precedents are set in law, but some cases are very complex because they involve both religious clauses. The Supreme Court has drawn up some guidelines on when the government can become involved with a religious activity. Known as the *Lemon* test, there are three requirements: government aid must have a secular (not religious) purpose, its effect on religion must be neutral (it neither aids nor hinders religion), and government and religion must not be entangled in each other's activities. For example, federal student loans are given to students who attend church-related colleges, because the loans aid the students and not the church, and they do not promote a particular religion. Furthermore, giving these loans does not give the government the right to tell the school what to teach.

Another issue that has been involved in many federal court cases, and which is also in the First Amendment, is the freedom of speech and of the press. Among the forms of speech that are absolutely protected are the truth, political speech, symbolic speech, and "speech plus," which is speech plus a physical activity such as picketing. The forms of speech that are currently only conditionally protected include libel and slander; obscenity and pornography; fighting words; and commercial speech. Despite the differences in criteria for protected speech and for unprotected speech, there are many fine lines that get crossed, and when there are disputes, the courts must consider the dispute and interpret the law.

The other amendments in the Bill of Rights are also under scrutiny all the time. A good example is the Second Amendment and the right to bear arms. When the amendment was written it was relevant to the time in history, and was associated with participation in a state militia. The right has been extended to individuals for self-defense, but it can be regulated by both state and federal law. Many of the problems with today's interpretations concern the types of weapons that private citizens own, ostensibly for self-defense. Many of them are automatic assault weapons, handy in war, but contributing to the problem of violence in nonmilitary society.

Amendments Four through Eight are procedural amendments. The Fourth Amendment protects against unreasonable searches and seizures; from this has been derived a right to privacy. The Fifth Amendment requires a grand jury for most crimes, protects against double jeopardy, and provides that you cannot be forced to testify against yourself. The Sixth Amendment requires a speedy trial and the right to witnesses and counsel. The Seventh Amendment requires a jury trial for all civil cases in which the value in controversy is over twenty dollars, and stipulates that the common law shall be used in any court in the United States. Finally, the Eighth Amendment prohibits cruel and unusual punishment.

Former chief justice Warren Burger became known as a judicial activist when he began allowing the use of the courts to extend and protect forms of privacy not given in the Constitution, such as homosexuality, intimate behavior, and abortion. Chief Justice William Rehnquist, on the other hand, is a leading critic of judicial activism with regard to the Bill of Rights, and is leading the Court in a more conservative, denationalizing direction. Narrower interpretations of earlier decisions have been made, but as yet, none have been literally reversed.

The Bill of Rights is integral to our democracy as it stands, but the process of interpretation will continue as our country becomes more diverse.

REVIEW QUESTIONS

1. What are civil liberties?
2. Why is the "nationalization" of the Bill of Rights important?
3. Explain the expansions of civil liberties in the twentieth century.
4. What did *Palko v. Connecticut* (1937) demonstrate with respect to the Bill of Rights and actions by the states?
5. Explain how the Fourteenth Amendment affected the guarantee of civil liberties.
6. What was the only change in civil liberties in the sixty years following the adoption of the Fourteenth Amendment?
7. Explain the establishment and free exercise clauses of the First Amendment. Why was religion so important to the Founders?
8. What did *Lemon v. Kurtzman* (1971) establish concerning the "wall of separation"?
9. Why is freedom of speech vital in a democracy? At what point does speech become unprotected by the First Amendment and why is it difficult to prove?
10. Explain the significance of *Reno v. ACLU*.

11. Compare absolutely protected with conditionally protected speech. Give examples.
12. Explain symbolic speech and speech plus. Give examples.
13. How does the Supreme Court define pornography? Why is this area of speech so unsettled?
14. What was the framers' original purpose for including a right to bear arms in the Bill of Rights? Why are restrictions placed on this freedom?
15. What restraints did the Supreme Court decisions in *Mapp v. Ohio* (1961), *Miranda v. Arizona* (1966), and *Gideon v. Wainwright* (1963) impose on the police?
16. What protections are granted in the Bill of Rights to the criminally accused?
17. What has the Supreme Court said about capital punishment? How has the current Court treated appeals in capital cases?
18. How has the right to privacy been interpreted as part of the Constitution and the Bill of Rights?
19. Discuss the implications of *Roe v. Wade* (1973) with respect to abortion and the right to privacy. Have there been any changes to that decision? If so, what are they based on?
20. Discuss the impact of the Rehnquist Court on civil liberties.
21. Why are civil liberties important in a democracy? What sort of government would try to limit the people's civil liberties? Why?

KEY TERMS

Bill of Rights
bill of attainder
burden of proof
civil liberties
civil rights
clear and present danger
double jeopardy
due process of law
eminent domain
establishment clause
exclusionary rule
ex post facto law
fighting words
free exercise clause
grand jury
habeas corpus
Lemon test
libel
Miranda rule
procedural liberties
right to privacy
selective incorporation
slander
speech plus
strict scrutiny
substantive liberties

FILL-IN-THE-BLANK QUIZ

Use the key terms to complete the following sentences.

1. Yesterday it wasn't a crime; today it is, and the legislature passes a law to arrest people who committed the act before it was a crime. The legislature has passed a(n) ____________ law.

2. An amendment that limits how government can treat its citizens deals with ____________ liberties, while one that limits what government can do deals with ____________ liberties.

3. In the United States, only a court can punish a person. If a legislature passed a law punishing an individual, the legislature would be guilty of passing a(n) ____________.

4. The checklist that the Supreme Court devised to prevent excessive entanglement between religion and government is the ____________.

5. The two different sides of the freedom of religion clause are the ____________ and the ____________.

6. A secret meeting of people who hear evidence to decide if there is reason to indict someone for a crime is a ____________.

7. In civil rights cases, the Supreme Court applies the ____________ test which places the burden of proof on the government and not on the challengers.

8. Anyone arrested in America today should be read the ____________ rule.

9. The first ten amendments to the Constitution are called the ____________.

10. In civil cases, the ____________ is on the challenger, while in criminal cases it is on the prosecution.

11. Symbolic speech, also known as ____________, is more protected than either ____________, ____________, or ____________.

12. Legal or moral claims for equality are called civil ____________, while areas of freedom where government may not enter are called civil ____________.

13. Illegally obtained evidence may not be presented in court under the ____________ rule.

14. The city used its power of ____________ to purchase your house to make room for a new highway.

15. Not all of the Bill of Rights have been applied to the states because the Supreme Court has used a policy of ____________.

16. The Supreme Court has found an implied ____________ in the Fourth Amendment.

17. The Supreme Court uses the ____________ rule to determine if speech is protected or not.

18. If you cannot be tried twice for the same crime, you are protected from ____________.

19. The government must treat everyone fairly according to a given set of rules. This procedural fairness is called ____________.

20. Under the right of ____________, everyone has a right to be brought into court to be told why he or she is being held.

MULTIPLE-CHOICE QUIZ

1. The first U.S. Congress met in late April:
   a. 1775.
   b. 1776.
   c. 1787.
   d. 1789.

2. In 1789 the House of Representatives adopted seventeen amendments, the Senate adopted twelve of these, and in 1791 the states ratified _________ of the amendments. From the start, these amendments were called the Bill of Rights.
   a. five
   b. eight
   c. ten
   d. twelve

3. These acts passed in 1798 made it a crime to say or publish anything that might tend to defame or bring into dispute the government of the United States.
   a. the Alien and Sedition Acts
   b. the Stamp Acts
   c. the North Tea Acts
   d. the Pinkerton Acts

4. In ____________ (1964) the Supreme Court ruled that to be deemed libelous, a story about a public official not only had to be untrue, but also had to result from "actual malice" or "reckless disregard."
   a. *Masson v. New Yorker Magazine*
   b. *New York Times v. Sullivan*
   c. *Moral Majority v. Hustler Magazine*
   d. *Miller v. California*

5. The Supreme Court did not address the issue of obscenity until the year:
   a. 1909.
   b. 1937.
   c. 1957.
   d. 1964.

6. The Supreme Court case of *Mapp v. Ohio* established:
   a. the "clear and present danger" doctrine.
   b. the *Lemon* test.
   c. the exclusionary rule.
   d. the standard by which obscenity is defined.

7. Protections of citizens from improper government action is the definition of:
   a. civil liberties.
   b. civil rights.
   c. civil liabilities.
   d. civil "tort" claims.

8. Which of the following places restraints on how the government is supposed to act?
   a. substantive liberties
   b. procedural liberties
   c. due process of law
   d. both b and c

9. ____________ refers to the obligations imposed on government to take positive action to protect citizens from any illegal actions of government agencies as well as of other private citizens.
   a. Civil liberties
   b. Civil obligations
   c. Civil rights
   d. Civil law

10. The first civil liberty "selectively incorporated" into the Fourteenth Amendment as a limitation on state government power was for:
    a. property protection.
    b. freedom of speech.
    c. freedom of the press.
    d. freedom of assembly.

11. This 1937 Supreme Court case established the principle of selective incorporation.
    a. *New York Times v. Sullivan*
    b. *Miller v. California*
    c. *Mapp v. Ohio*
    d. *Palko v. Connecticut*

12. The ____________ has been interpreted quite strictly to mean that a virtual "wall of separation" exists between church and state.
    a. free exercise clause
    b. freedom of religion
    c. establishment clause
    d. necessary and proper

13. The so-called *Lemon* test, which came from the court case *Lemon v. Kurtzman,* concerns the issue of:
    a. school desegregation.
    b. aid to religious schools.
    c. prayer in school.
    d. obscenity.

14. The First Amendment's ____________ protects the right to believe in and practice one's religion of choice.
    a. free exercise clause
    b. establishment clause
    c. freedom of assembly clause
    d. the "wall of separation" clause

15. Civil rights became part of the Constitution in 1868 with the adoption of the ____________ Amendment.
    a. Thirteenth
    b. Fourteenth
    c. Fifteenth
    d. Sixteenth

16. This Amendment provides for freedom of religion.
    a. First
    b. Second
    c. Fifth
    d. Tenth

17. Freedom of speech and freedom of the press are guaranteed in the ____________ Amendment.
    a. First
    b. Second
    c. Fifth
    d. Tenth

18. An example of speech plus would be:
    a. burning the American flag.
    b. giving a speech that is critical of American foreign policy.
    c. giving a speech against abortion and then distributing informational leaflets.
    d. a march on Congress in Washington, D.C.

19. As the text notes, four forms of speech fall outside the absolute guarantees of the First Amendment and therefore outside the realm of absolute protection. Which of the following is not a "conditionally protected" form of speech?
    a. political speech
    b. libel and slander
    c. obscenity and pornography
    d. fighting words
    e. commercial speech

20. The Supreme Court upheld a state university ban on Tupperware parties in college dormitories; declared as constitutional laws prohibiting the electronic media from carrying cigarette advertising; and upheld a Puerto Rico statute restricting the advertising of casino gambling. These are examples of restrictions on:
    a. libel and slander.
    b. fighting words.
    c. symbolic speech.
    d. commercial speech.

21. The Second Amendment concerns:
    a. the rights of the criminally accused.
    b. searches and seizures.
    c. the right to bear arms.
    d. the right to counsel.

22. The Fourth, Fifth, Sixth, and Eighth Amendments, taken together, define:
    a. due process of law.
    b. free speech.
    c. the right to bear arms.
    d. civil rights of minorities.

23. The Fourth Amendment concerns:
    a. the rights of the criminally accused.
    b. searches and seizures.
    c. the right to bear arms.
    d. the right to counsel.

24. The Fifth Amendment concerns:
    a. grand juries.
    b. double jeopardy.
    c. self-incrimination.
    d. eminent domain.
    e. all of the above.

25. "*Miranda* rights" concern:
    a. double jeopardy.
    b. self-incrimination.
    c. eminent domain.
    d. all of the above.

26. Taking private property for public use is covered under the provision of:
    a. eminent domain.
    b. the Second Amendment.
    c. the Sixth Amendment.
    d. *Palko v. Connecticut.*

27. The Eighth Amendment concerns:
    a. the rights of the criminally accused.
    b. searches and seizures.
    c. cruel and unusual punishment.
    d. the right to counsel.

28. Which of the following statements best reflects the nature of the Bill of Rights?
    a. The rights guaranteed to all in the Bill of Rights are self-executing.
    b. The Bill of Rights is not easy to use.
    c. Historically, the Bill of Rights has applied equally to both the federal and state governments.
    d. All of the above.

29. In essence for more than 170 years the Bill of Rights:
    a. applied only to state governments.
    b. was not used to limit government.
    c. did not really affect most Americans.
    d. settled the issue of slavery.

30. Which of the following was not an argument the Federalists used at the Philadelphia Convention against a "bill of rights"?
    a. A bill of rights was anti-democratic.
    b. Because the federal government has only delegated powers, a bill of rights is not needed.
    c. The U.S. Constitution is a bill of rights in itself.
    d. Adding a bill of rights might be dangerous since putting restraints on powers which are not granted might provide a pretext for the national government to claim more powers than it was given.

31. The government cannot establish an "official" state religion. This is an example of:
    a. due process of law.
    b. equal protection of the laws.
    c. restraints on substantive liberties.
    d. restraints on procedural liberties.

32. The concept of "selective incorporation" means:
    a. only some civil liberties are granted to state governments.
    b. all civil liberties in the Bill of Rights apply only to the national government, and not to state governments.
    c. amendments are added to the U.S. Constitution very slowly over time.
    d. only some of the liberties in the Bill of Rights are applied to the states.

33. According to the text, which of the statements below best expresses why the general status of civil liberties can never be considered fixed and permanent?
    a. Liberty for some requires restraining the liberty of others.
    b. The Bill of Rights restricts only national government actions.
    c. The Bill of Rights restricts only state government actions.
    d. By definition the protection of civil rights takes away civil liberties.

34. Ordinarily, when the constitutionality of a law is in question, the "burden of proof" is:

a. on the person making the complaint.
b. on the government.
c. settled by the Supreme Court.
d. really not an issue because the Supreme Court almost always rules in favor of the plaintiff.

35. Strict scrutiny implies:
a. that freedom of religion is relative and not absolute.
b. that the Court will examine the facts of a case very carefully.
c. that the civil liberty in question will be protected almost absolutely.
d. that the case will be heard by an appeals court.

36. As the text notes, a surprising new alliance has formed between conservative groups in America and a number of leading feminists that seek to limit freedom of speech defined as "obscene" or "pornographic." Why is this a "surprising" alliance?
a. Historically, conservative groups and feminists have not agreed on many issues.
b. Feminists usually do not focus on obscenity and pornography issues.
c. Historically, conservatives and feminists have agreed on most issues except those dealing with obscenity and pornography.
d. Conservative groups usually do not challenge First Amendment issues.

37. In recent years, a result of trying to limit the use of "fighting words" under "conditionally protected" speech has been:
a. the "political correctness" movement.
b. the development of so-called "hate crime" legislation.
c. the development of a doctrine known as "clear and present danger."
d. all of the above.

38. American citizens unquestionably have a right to bear arms, but the exercise of this right can be regulated by:
a. state law.
b. federal law.
c. the National Rifle Association.
d. both a and b.

39. Which of the following statements is not true?
a. Double jeopardy means being tried more than once for the same crime.
b. In *Palko v. Connecticut* the Court ruled that double jeopardy was not one of the provisions of the Bill of Rights incorporated in the Fourteenth Amendment.
c. In *Palko v. Connecticut* the Court ruled that double jeopardy was one of the provisions of the Bill of Rights incorporated in the Fourteenth Amendment.
d. The issue of double jeopardy led the Court to issue the so-called "*Miranda* rights."

40. The Supreme Court's decision in *Roe v. Wade* was based on:
a. the First Amendment.
b. the right to privacy.
c. the due process clause of the Fourteenth Amendment.
d. the Fifth Amendment.

QUESTIONS FOR DISCUSSION AND THOUGHT

1. Did you attend a public school where you had Bible readings, prayers, religious assemblies, or other religious acts? Who organized these activities? Were you ever in a school choir or band that performed religious music? Did you ever have a coach who prayed before games or suggested you join the Fellowship of Christian Athletes? If any of these occurred in your school, how did you feel about them? Did it ever occur to you that your principal and/or teachers might be violating a Supreme Court ruling? Do you consider religious exercises in public schools to be an infringement on other people's freedom?

2. How much free speech do you think we should allow in the United States? Would you want a follower of Louis Farrakhan to give a speech on your campus? A member of the freemen's militia? A neo-Nazi? A white racist?

3. Have you ever been called for jury duty? Explain the process. How did you feel about this? Did you try to get out of jury duty? What if everyone tried to evade jury duty?

4. The Christian Coalition is pushing for a "Religious Freedom Amendment" to the Constitution which reads:

   > "To secure the people's right to acknowledge God according to the dictates of conscience, neither the United States nor any State shall establish any official religion, but the people's right to pray and to recognize their religious beliefs, heritage, or traditions on public property including schools, shall not be infringed. Neither the United States nor any state shall require persons to join in prayer or other religious activity, prescribe school prayers, discriminate against religion, or deny equal access to a benefit on account of religion."

   Would you support such an amendment? Do you see this as an infringement of the First Amendment, or a logical result of it? If school prayers were allowed, who should write the prayers? Should different religious groups be allowed to rotate, that is, have a Protestant prayer on Monday, a Catholic prayer on Tuesday, Orthodox on Wednesday, Jewish on Thursday, Muslim on Friday? How would you accommodate different religious beliefs? Suppose someone chose to pray to "Our Heavenly Mother." Would that be acceptable? If not, what conception of a Supreme Being is acceptable to you for use in public schools?

5. Most of the democratic countries of the world have abolished capital punishment. Why do you think the United States still uses execution? If other countries had our crime rate, do you think they would want capital punishment? A Texas legislator recently introduced a bill allowing ten-year-olds to be executed. List arguments for and against capital punishment for juveniles. Do we draw the line according to age or severity of crime?

THE CITIZEN'S ROLE

To illustrate how individuals use the courts to protect their rights, select an important case from this chapter, such as *Brown v. Board of Education* or *Gideon v. Wainwright* and research the case from sources in the Internet. Both "Oyez Oyez Oyez" (http://oyez.nwu.edu) and "LawFind" (http://caselaw.findlaw.com) provide extensive information about Supreme Court cases. After you have read the case, answer the questions below.

1. Give a brief summary in your own words of the facts of the case.
2. Who was the plaintiff? The defendant?
3. Were any *amici curiae* briefs filed? If so, by whom? What is the significance of these briefs?
4. What was the Court's ruling? Why was the ruling significant?
5. What did you learn about Supreme Court processes and rulings from this exercise?

GOVERNMENT IN YOUR LIFE

A proposed constitutional amendment reads: "The Congress shall have power to prohibit the physical desecration of the flag of the United States."

1. Make a list of all of the reasons why this amendment should be passed.
2. Make a second list of reasons why this amendment should not be passed.
3. What, in your opinion, would constitute flag desecration?
4. Would you support this amendment? Explain.
5. If this amendment were passed, it would be the first time in over two hundred years that the First Amendment had been altered in any way. What, in your opinion, would be some possible consequences of amending the First Amendment?

ANSWER KEY

Fill-in-the Blank Quiz

1. *ex post facto*
2. procedural, substantive
3. bill of attainder
4. *Lemon* test
5. establishment clause, free exercise clause
6. grand jury
7. strict scrutiny
8. *Miranda*
9. bill of rights

10. burden of proof
11. speech plus, slander, libel, fighting words
12. rights, liberties
13. exclusionary
14. eminent domain
15. selective incorporation
16. right to privacy
17. clear and present danger
18. double jeopardy
19. due process of law
20. habeas corpus

Multiple-Choice Quiz

1. d
2. c
3. a
4. b
5. c
6. c
7. a
8. d
9. c
10. a
11. d
12. c
13. b
14. a
15. b
16. a
17. a
18. c
19. a
20. d
21. c
22. a
23. b
24. e
25. b
26. a
27. c
28. b
29. c
30. a
31. c
32. d
33. a
34. a
35. c
36. a
37. a
38. d
39. b
40. b

CHAPTER 6 Civil Rights

THE CHAPTER IN BRIEF

As America continually strives to reach its ideal of a democratic society, it must constantly face the reality of the inequalities that exist in the nation. The most agonizing of these inequalities has been our history of racial discrimination. We even fought a civil war over this issue in the nineteenth century.

After the Civil War, three constitutional amendments were passed that were designed to bring about racial equality, at least before the law. The Thirteenth Amendment abolished slavery; the Fourteenth guaranteed due process to all persons, and the Fifteenth gave black men the right to vote. On the surface, that would seem to enshrine in the highest law of the land the principle of fairness.

But it didn't work that way. The Supreme Court, in the late nineteenth century, turned increasingly conservative and declared the Civil Rights Act of 1875 unconstitutional. In 1896, the Court upheld a Louisiana law that required segregation in public facilities (*Plessy v. Ferguson)*. The Court claimed that the Fourteenth Amendment was not violated as long as the segregated facilities were equal—the "separate but equal rule." In fact, there was much separation but little equality.

The hypocrisy of America's position on race was made evident by World War II, the war to defeat fascism, in which thousands of black men served honorably but in segregated forces. President Truman desegregated the forces by executive order in 1948. Earlier, in 1946, he had appointed a civil rights commission which recommended desegregation, although it was unclear what federal authority could be used to accomplish this.

In the meantime, the Supreme Court moved from its early conservative stands on race and began to issue rulings that picked away at the practices of discrimination. Texas and Missouri were ordered to integrate some of their educational institutions because they did not offer "separate but equal" alternatives. Also prohibited were white primaries and restrictive covenants. Finally, in 1954, in *Brown v. Board of Education of Topeka*, the Court ruled that segregated schools were unconstitutional, a ruling that reversed the 1986 *Plessy* case. This was the capstone case for the NAACP, which had filed many lawsuits in the previous two decades aimed at striking down segregated facilities. The case was argued by Thurgood Marshall, who later became the first black to serve on the Supreme Court.

The nation as a whole did not welcome school desegregation. The southern states developed strategies of "massive resistance," such as subsidizing white "academies," delaying techniques, and even, in Arkansas, mobilizing the national guard to prohibit integration at Little Rock Central High School. President Eisenhower was finally forced to respond by sending in the U.S. military and federal marshals.

The northern states, which had *de facto* segregation, also resisted school integration. The nation sat riveted to the television news watching riots in Boston, as parents opposed forced busing. Even today, schools in America are still highly segregated, mostly because of housing patterns, but the Supreme Court has allowed school systems to end federal supervision if they can show that they have made an effort at desegregation.

The *Brown* case only involved schools, but the implication was that all public facilities would also be desegregated. That did not happen until Congress, ten years later, passed the Civil Rights Act of 1964. This landmark legislation dealt with four areas. First, it stated that a sixth-grade education was sufficient literacy for voting purposes. Next, it barred discrimination in public accommodations, defined as restaurants, hotels, service stations, theaters, and stores. Third, it gave the attorney general authority to sue for compliance and allowed federal aid to be withheld from segregated schools. The final provision outlawed discrimination on the basis of race, religion, or sex in employment.

The next year, Congress continued its assault on discrimination with the Voting Rights Act of 1965, which allowed the federal government to oversee local elections where there had been a pattern of discrimination. In 1968, another Civil Rights Act barred discrimination in the sale and rental of housing. Several amendments were added to these bills in 1975, 1978, and 1982. In 1990, discrimination against the disabled was attacked with the passage of the Americans With Disabilities Act, which required that public transportation and public services be accessible to those with physical handicaps. Finally, in 1991, another Civil Rights Act reversed several Supreme Court rulings which had the effect of making it harder for women and minorities to prove job discrimination.

The Civil Rights Act of 1964 also dealt with job discrimination, requiring all employers of fifteen or more employees to eliminate all forms of inequality. This provision built on the Equal Pay Act, passed a year earlier, which had outlawed pay discrepancies based on gender. The Department of Justice and the Equal Employment Opportunity Commission were empowered to investigate complaints.

Voting rights were further strengthened by a 1965 law that forbade literacy tests and provided for federal registrars in some counties. The Twenty-Fourth

Amendment was passed in 1964, which outlawed the poll tax, and a 1975 law mandated bilingual ballots in certain situations. Today, black voters have forced southern politicians to recognize their voting strength and to eliminate their traditional race-based appeals.

One of the most difficult problems of segregation is that of segregated housing patterns. As we mentioned above, public schools today are highly segregated, not by law, but because of the residential housing patterns. Minorities tend to live in inner cities, while whites live in the suburbs. Some lending institutions refused to make mortgages in minority areas, a practice known as redlining. This was attacked through the 1977 Community Reinvestment Act, which required banks to lend money in neighborhoods where they do business.

The success of black Americans in achieving their legal rights (which, remember, had actually been guaranteed to them one hundred years earlier) encouraged some other groups in America to pursue their own strategies for civil rights. Women had already achieved the Equal Pay Act. Groups such as the National Organization for Women (NOW) filed lawsuits against gender discrimination. The high point of the movement was the effort to win ratification of the Equal Rights Amendment to the Constitution, but the final vote was short by three states.

The Supreme Court over the years developed several tests to apply to cases of discrimination. The traditional rules of evidence require that the burden of proof be on the plaintiff (the one who makes the complaint). In racial discrimination cases, the Court applied the "strict scrutiny" test, which shifted the burden of proof to the defendant. In gender cases, an "intermediate scrutiny" test splits the difference. Part of the burden is placed on the government and part on the plaintiff. In other words, the Court considers racial discrimination to be the worst form, while gender discrimination is of lesser importance (although not unimportant).

Seeing the success of the NAACP's Legal Defense Fund, Latinos, Asian Americans, and Native Americans organized similar organizations. In recent years, gay and lesbian rights groups have organized political action committees. While the gay rights movement claims that it also deserves political protection as a discriminated group, several states and localities have passed laws and ordinances that specifically prohibit special protections for homosexuals. The Supreme Court, in *Romer v. Evans* (1996), struck down a constitutional amendment in Colorado that prohibited local governments from passing gay rights laws, thus affirming in federal law the civil rights of homosexuals.

This review of the laws striking down discrimination demonstrates that Americans are concerned about guaranteeing liberty and equality to all individuals. But laws are not enough. If we want to have true equality of opportunity, how do we compensate for the effects of two centuries of discrimination? The effects are real. They appear in the form of inferior schools in minority areas, the psychological costs of facing daily slights of discrimination, the effects of poverty, which is higher in minority groups. The race cannot be fair if some people must start behind the starting line. Americans agree with that statement. But how do we get everyone to the starting line? Americans have wide disagreements on the public policy designed to compensate for the effects of past discrimination. That policy is affirmative action.

In theory, affirmative action is a way of enlarging the pool of potential employees by taking aggressive actions in recruitment. An organization would set a goal for minority recruitment and then, for example, advertise its openings in a Spanish-language newspaper. Where a minority who is hired is more qualified than a white person, there is no issue of discrimination. If two people are of equal qualifications, the choice may be made with race in mind, but absolute quotas are not to be used. If a person of lesser qualifications is chosen over one more qualified, there may be an issue of reverse discrimination. This is what Allan Bakke charged when he was denied entrance at the University of California Medical School. The Supreme Court agreed that the university had discriminated against him. Race could be one factor among several, the Court ruled, but there cannot be rigid quotas. A similar case was heard by the Fifth District Court of Appeals in 1996, involving the University of Texas Law School (*Hopwood*). Many observers believe that the Supreme Court is softening its stand on affirmative action and that it may even be banned in the future.

It is true that many people are uncomfortable with the idea of racial preferences, especially because those least disadvantaged are often the ones who are most likely to be given preference. On the other hand, Americans also recognize that racism and discrimination are a sordid part of our history and that we have a moral obligation to erase its effects. Just how that is done, though, will be a problem for our nation for many years to come.

REVIEW QUESTIONS

1. What, according to the text, does the end of segregation mean? With all of the civil rights legislation that has been enacted since the 1960s, has the end of segregation, in your opinion, been achieved? Why or why not?
2. How did the case of *Plessy v. Ferguson* uphold legal segregation? What were the problems inherent in that decision?
3. Who was the first president actually to begin pushing for racial integration? What was the catalyst for his actions?
4. What pre-1954 Court case paved the way for the eventual integration of residential neighborhoods? How did that occur?
5. In the case of *Brown v. Board of Education,* what previous Court precedent was overturned? Did school desegregation immediately take place? If not, why not?

6. What historic incident was marked by the deployment of U.S. troops against the National Guard? Was the outcome positive for civil rights?
7. In the Civil Rights Act of 1964, what interest group beside blacks was included as a victim of discrimination? Do you think that the inclusion of this second group prompted much of the ensuing civil rights protests of the following year?
8. How did the 1964 Civil Rights Act implement enforcement of school desegregation nationwide?
9. What power did the EEOC have that would ensure nondiscriminatory actions by private companies?
10. How has the shape of American politics been altered by the passage of the Voting Rights Act? How did the act strengthen and protect voting rights, and for whom?
11. What specific act of discrimination was outlawed by the 1968 Civil Rights Act? How effective was it in attaining its goal? What additional acts were passed?
12. How did the conservative Burger Court make it easier for plaintiffs to file and win suits on the basis of gender discrimination?
13. In your opinion, should the Equal Rights Amendment have been ratified as worded, or do you think its opponents were correct in anticipating social disruption had it passed?
14. Why did Asian Americans and Latinos oppose the Immigration Reform and Control Act of 1986? Why did legal immigrants fear its effects? Were their fears justified? What organizations have arisen to challenge discrimination of Asian Americans and Latinos?
15. What civil rights have Native Americans enjoyed since 1975? What did the Supreme Court do for Native Americans in 1987? How have they benefited?
16. How did the case of *Regents of the University of California v. Bakke* (1978) introduce the concept of "reverse discrimination"? What effect did it have on existing affirmative action policies?
17. How have affirmative action efforts polarized the politics of civil rights?
18. The text emphasizes the themes of liberty, equality, and democracy. Explain why there is always a tension between liberty and equality. Is it possible to have democracy without both liberty and equality?

KEY TERMS

affirmative action
Brown v. Board of Education
civil rights
de facto
de jure
discrimination
equal protection clause
intermediate scrutiny
redlining
"separate but equal" rule
strict scrutiny

FILL-IN-THE-BLANK QUIZ

Use the key terms to complete the following sentences.

1. The historic court case that outlawed school segregation was ______.
2. Public schools today are still segregated as a result of ______ segregation.
3. The ______ test puts the burden of proof on the government instead of the challengers in cases of racial discrimination.
4. When a pizza company refuses to deliver in certain neighborhoods because of its fear of crime, the company may be guilty of ______.
5. The ______ clause of the Fourteenth Amendment was designed to prevent ______.
6. When the Supreme Court approved the ______ rule, it was allowing ______ segregation.
7. The Supreme Court uses the ______ rule when it takes up cases of gender discrimination.
8. Equality under the law for all people, regardless of race, religion, or sex, is called ______.
9. ______ is a government policy designed to compensate for past discrimination.

MULTIPLE-CHOICE QUIZ

1. In 1946, in order to bring civil rights to the attention of the American people and to bring the problem to the White House, President ______ appointed the President's Commission on Civil Rights.
   a. Roosevelt
   b. Truman
   c. Eisenhower
   d. Kennedy

2. This decision by the Court ruled against the widespread practice of "restrictive covenants."
   a. *Palko v. Connecticut*
   b. *Mapp v. Ohio*
   c. *Shelley v. Kraemer*
   d. *Baker v. Carr*

3. This organization was formed in 1909 to fight discrimination against blacks.
   a. The American Civil Liberties Union
   b. The Urban League
   c. The Southern Leadership Conference
   d. The National Association for the Advancement of Colored People

4. Ten years after the *Brown* decision, about ____________ percent of black school-age children in the Deep South were attending schools with whites.
   a. 1
   b. 10
   c. 25
   d. 50

5. By far the most important piece of legislation passed by Congress fostering equal opportunity in the United States was the:
   a. Dred Scott law.
   b. Equal Pay Act of 1963.
   c. Civil Rights Act of 1964.
   d. Civil Rights Act of 1991.

6. In ______ Congress passed legislation outlawing literacy tests in all fifty states and mandating bilingual ballots.
   a. 1964
   b. 1965
   c. 1969
   d. 1975

7. According to the authors of the text, today, the existence of a powerful women's movement derives in large measure from the enactment of Title VII of the Civil Rights Act of 1964 and from the ____________ Court's vital steps in applying that law to protect women.
   a. Warren
   b. Burger
   c. Rehnquist
   d. O'Connor

8. With the adoption of the ____________ Amendment in 1868, civil rights became part of the Constitution, guaranteed to each citizen through "____________."
   a. Fourteenth, equal protection of the laws
   b. Fourteenth, due process of law
   c. Fifteenth, equal protection of the laws
   d. Fifteenth, due process of law

9. This constitutional amendment abolished slavery.
   a. Tenth
   b. Thirteenth
   c. Fourteenth
   d. Fifteenth

10. This constitutional amendment guaranteed voting rights for black men.
    a. Tenth
    b. Thirteenth
    c. Fourteenth
    d. Fifteenth

11. ___________ refers to the use of any unreasonable and unjust criterion of exclusion.
    a. Due process of law
    b. Exclusionary rule
    c. Discrimination
    d. Equal protection of the laws

12. This court decision established the principle of "separate but equal."
    a. Dred Scott
    b. *Brown v. Board of Education*
    c. The Slaughterhouse Cases
    d. *Plessy v. Ferguson*

13. Legal segregation is called ___________ segregation.
    a. de jure
    b. de facto
    c. state-sanctioned
    d. discrimination

14. The Civil Rights Act of 1964:
    a. prohibited discrimination in public accommodations.
    b. prohibited school segregation.
    c. prohibited employment discrimination.
    d. all of the above

15. The constitutional basis of the Civil Rights Act of 1964 was the:
    a. Fourteenth Amendment.
    b. full faith and credit clause.
    c. supremacy clause.
    d. Thirteenth Amendment.

16. In 1964 the states ratified the ___________ Amendment, which abolished the poll tax.
    a. Fifteenth
    b. Nineteenth
    c. Twenty-fourth
    d. Twenty-sixth

17. In 1968 Congress passed this law prohibiting discrimination in the sale or rental of most housing—eventually covering nearly all the nation's housing.
    a. Fair Housing Act
    b. Civil Rights Housing Act
    c. Urban Renewal Act
    d. Model Housing Act

18. The practice of financial institutions refusing to lend money for housing mortgages for entire neighborhoods is called:
    a. exclusionary zoning.
    b. financial zoning.
    c. restrictive lending.
    d. redlining.

19. "Equality of rights under the law shall not be denied or abridged by the United States or by any State on account of sex." This is the wording of the:
    a. due process clause of the Fourteenth Amendment.
    b. equal protection of the laws clause of the Fourteenth Amendment.
    c. anti-gender discrimination clause of the Civil Rights Act of 1964.
    d. proposed Equal Rights Amendment.

20. What decision was rendered in the Supreme Court case of *Lau v. Nichols*?
    a. Private schools must be desegregated.
    b. The busing of students for the purpose of integration was permissible.
    c. Schools districts must provide education to students whose English is limited.
    d. all of the above

21. ____________ is defined as compensatory action to overcome the consequences of past discrimination.
    a. Affirmative action
    b. Reverse discrimination
    c. Compensatory damages
    d. Punitive damages

22. The Supreme Court decision in *Plessy v. Ferguson*:
    a. required the desegregation of schools.
    b. allowed segregation of the races.
    c. allowed busing of children to desegregate schools.
    d. was invalidated after passage of the Fourteenth Amendment.

23. What is the practice of "restrictive covenants"?
    a. a practice of requiring separate public facilities for blacks and whites
    b. a type of literacy exam used in the South to keep blacks from voting
    c. the seller of a home adds a clause to the sales contract requiring the buyer to agree not to sell the home later to a black, Jew, etc.
    d. a type of "poll tax"

24. How did the *Brown v. Board of Education* decision alter the constitutional framework?
    a. After the decision the states no longer had the power to use race as a criterion of discrimination in law.
    b. After the decision the federal government had the power to intervene with strict regulatory policies against the discriminatory policies of state and local governments.
    c. After the decision the Court no longer needed the Fourteenth Amendment to invalidate state and local laws.
    d. only b and c
    e. only a and b

25. In cases of racial discrimination, the Supreme Court uses the ____________ test.
    a. *Lemon*
    b. community standards
    c. strict scrutiny
    d. intermediate scrutiny

26. Which of the following statements best captures the impact of what the authors call "Phase One of School Desegregation" following the decision of the Court in *Brown v. Board of Education*?
    a. There was immediate desegregation in the North, but not in the South.
    b. There was immediate desegregation in the South, but not in the North.
    c. There was massive resistance to desegregation in the South.
    d. The Office for Civil Rights immediately began the process of cutting off federal funds for noncompliance.

27. According to the authors of the text, what is the current status of school desegregation?
    a. Additional progress is likely to be extremely slow unless the Supreme Court decides to permit federal action against de facto segregation and

against the varieties of private schools and academies that have sprung up for the purpose of avoiding integration.
b. As a result of the Civil Rights Act of 1964, school desegregation efforts have been largely achieved.
c. Schools in the South have been desegregated, but due to the courts' reluctance to impose remedies for de facto segregation, schools in the North remain segregated.
d. Once again it seems that the Court, under the leadership of Chief Justice Rehnquist, is ready to start the so-called "third-wave" of desegregation efforts.

28. To make it easier for minorities and women to get to court and make their cases concerning discrimination, they must show that the employer's hiring practices:
    a. had the "effect" of exclusion.
    b. had the "intent" of exclusion.
    c. were blatantly discriminatory.
    d. were for "business necessity."

29. When hearing gender-related discrimination cases, the Court uses the doctrine of:
    a. absolute scrutiny.
    b. strict scrutiny.
    c. intermediate scrutiny.
    d. any of the above, depending on the case.

QUESTIONS FOR DISCUSSION AND THOUGHT

1. In their book *Failing at Fairness*, authors Myra and David Sadker asked this question of hundreds of students across the country: "Suppose you woke up tomorrow and found you were a member of the other sex. How would your life be different?" How would you answer this question? What does your answer tell you about privileges that one group in society might have that are often denied other groups? Now change the question: "Suppose you woke up tomorrow and found you were a member of another race. How would your life be different?" Does this give you any insight into your own attitudes and beliefs about other races?

2. Why have most of the advances in civil rights come through the federal courts and not through our legislatures? What does this say about our democratic system? Which would you rather have: judges who believe in judicial restraint when it comes to civil rights, or judges who are activists?

3. Thirty years ago, most people assumed that we were "all the same underneath"—that is, everyone wanted to assimilate and become part of a homogeneous group. Today, we talk about "valuing differences" and searching for diversity. What "differences" can minorities bring to the

workplace? To politics? Are there any disadvantages to diversity? Do you think you are able to accept people who are different?

4. Some white males today claim that "reverse discrimination" has kept them from getting jobs for which they were qualified. Yet, when ABC's "PrimeTime Live" sent both a man and a woman to apply for a job, the man was offered the management position while the woman was offered a job as a receptionist. The reporters also discovered that women were charged more for having a suit cleaned than were men, the man got a teetime at a golf course when the woman was told there were no openings, and the man was quoted a lower price for a new car than was the woman. How serious a problem is reverse discrimination? What has been your experience with discrimination?

5. The college admissions lawsuits have brought out another form of discrimination against Asians and Asian Americans who have been restricted entry because of a quota system at some highly ranked schools. Substitute "Jews" for "Asians" and "Asian Americans" and you have replicated a policy that was common in many universities only a few decades ago. Why have these two groups been restricted entry? Should universities try to build their student bodies on the basis of proportionate representation? Does that mean if 10 percent of Americans are of Scandinavian extraction, that they should have 10 percent of the slots at competitive schools? Is there ever any basis for schools to discriminate in enrollment? If so, what is/are legitimate discriminating factors? Age? Standardized test scores? Quality of high school attended? Letters of recommendation?

6. In Pasadena, California, in 1985, the Armenian American population (about 13,000 out of a population of 130,000) requested that the city council designate them a "protected class" under Pasadena's affirmative action policies. The council agreed that Armenians had been subject to discrimination and voted to include, not only them, but any immigrant who had lived in the United States for less than fifteen years. How far should we go in providing affirmative action for disadvantaged groups in the United States?

THE CITIZEN'S ROLE

In 1996 the Fifth Circuit Court of Appeals ruled in the case of *Hopwood v. Texas* that the University of Texas Law School could not use race as a factor for admissions, financial aid, or retention. The Supreme Court refused to hear the case, which means that the lower court ruling stands. It is important to note, however, that the Fifth Circuit covers only Texas, Louisiana, and Mississippi and thus is not controlling in the rest of the nation. The American Council on Education has argued that the *Bakke* case, which held that race could be one factor in admissions although not the sole factor, was still controlling in the rest of the nation. However, many other institutions have changed their minority admissions procedures to conform with *Hopwood.*

In the table below, list all the arguments you can think of to support affirmative action in higher education. Then, playing the "devil's advocate" role, list opposing arguments.

Arguments supporting affirmative action	Arguments opposing affirmative action

1. Does your institution use race as a factor in admissions?
2. Is your institution within the jurisdiction of the Fifth Circuit Court of Appeals?
3. When you were constructing your arguments for and against, which side of the issue was harder for you to deal with? Explain.
4. Which side, in your opinion, has the stronger argument?
5. If race cannot be used as a factor in admissions, financial aid, or retention programs, what factors should be used? Explain.

GOVERNMENT IN YOUR LIFE

Contact the athletic department at your school to determine how much equality there is between men's and women's sports. Answer the questions below.

1. List the men's sports at your school and their budgets.

2. List the women's sports at your school and their budgets.
3. How do the two compare in terms of number of sports? How do the budgets compare?
4. Do you think your institution is doing an adequate job in trying to achieve parity between the sports? Explain.
5. If you were the athletic director, what changes would you make, if any, in the distribution of the sports? Explain.

ANSWER KEY

Fill-in-the-Blank Quiz

1. *Brown v. Board of Education*
2. de facto
3. strict scrutiny
4. redlining
5. equal protection, discrimination
6. separate but equal, de jure
7. intermediate scrutiny
8. civil rights
9. Affirmative action

Multiple-Choice Quiz

1. b
2. c
3. d
4. a
5. c
6. d
7. b
8. a
9. b
10. d
11. c
12. d
13. a
14. d
15. a
16. c
17. a
18. d
19. d
20. c
21. a
22. b
23. c
24. e
25. c
26. c
27. a
28. a
29. c

CHAPTER 7 Public Opinion

THE CHAPTER IN BRIEF

"Public opinion" is the term used to denote the beliefs and attitudes that people have about issues, events, and personalities. Those who have opinions are those who care enough about politics and public life to stay informed. We often think in terms of differences of opinion, but it is most important to remember the fundamental values on which most Americans agree—matters such as equality of opportunity, individual liberty, and democracy. Americans tend to agree on these because there was never a rigid class structure or a strong Communist or Socialist party in this country. These principles have not always been put into practice (for example, many Americans once kept slaves), but the strength of the principle ultimately helped to overcome practices that deviated from it.

There are many issues, of course, on which people disagree: issues such as economics, foreign and social policy, race relations, environmental affairs, and many others. Differences of political opinion are associated with such variables as income, education, occupation, race, gender, ethnicity, age, religion, and region. For example, social welfare programs are supported more by the poor than by the wealthy, and civil rights issues are supported more by blacks than by whites. Because of the diversity of people in America, we have a great diversity in opinion.

Our own political beliefs and attitudes are socialized into us beginning at an early age by our families. As we grow, involuntary groups such as gender, race, and age shape our experience, and later, voluntary groupings such as political parties, labor unions, and educational and occupational groups allow us to share our attitudes and perspective. Schools teach a common set of public values, and higher education seems to convince individuals of the importance of involvement in the nation's politics. As circumstances and the political climate change, so too can our views change. The proper efforts of the government to affect political opinion are called "civic education." When it is carried too far it is called "indoctrination," which is the sort of thing that caught the Germans up in the Nazi movement.

An ideology is a complete set of underlying orientations, ideas, and beliefs through which individuals come to understand and interpret politics. Out of the many political ideologies in the world, two major ones are embraced in the United States: modern liberalism and modern conservatism. What these two ideologies support is the basis of most of the differing opinions in this country today. Liberals typically support political and social reform; extensive government intervention in the economy; expansion of federal social services; more vigorous efforts on behalf of the poor, minorities, and women; greater concern for consumers and the environment; abortion rights; criminals' rights; arms control; aid to poor nations; and support for the United Nations. Liberals typically oppose state involvement in religion, nuclear testing, and the use of American troops to influence the domestic affairs of developing nations.

By contrast, conservatives typically support the social and economic status quo, school prayer, traditional family arrangements, and the maintenance of American military power, and typically show more concern for crime victims rather than for perpetrators. They oppose large and powerful government, governmental activity in social and economic programs (believing that the private sector could do a better job), government regulation of business, the legalization of abortion, and school busing. With the two factions holding such opposite views, it is a credit to the democratic process that Americans still feel that the United States is the best place to be and that everyone's basic liberties are protected.

Political beliefs are sometimes inconsistent. Most people, in fact, don't have strongly held opinions on most political issues. These people are the ones most likely to be influenced by others and change their opinions. Individuals who possess political knowledge are more likely to vote and participate in politics in other ways, which enhances their sense of political efficacy. Those who have little interest in politics, on the other hand, are also the ones who are most likely to feel that they cannot influence government.

Political issues become a commodity in the "marketplace of ideas" as competing forces attempt to persuade as many Americans as possible to accept their positions on the events of the day. Ideas must be vigorously promoted in order to become widely known and accepted, much like the ad campaigns for a new product. Government public relations is only one source of information and evaluation. Private groups also shape public opinion, as we can see with religious leaders and the "right to life" campaign, for example. Groups with access to financial resources market their ideas most effectively. The promotion of political themes is known in corporate circles as "issues management." Liberals have access to the media and the support of public interest groups, as well as "think tanks" and universities, to market their ideas. Upper-income groups dominate the idea market and are best able to promote their ideas because they have the most access to government power.

Politicians had direct exposure to public opinion in the past, because political debate usually took place in public, but now that the media separate leaders from the public, there are other methods for measuring public opinion. Opinion is sometimes interpreted from mass behavior such as consumer behavior, and sometimes is gotten directly from the public in polls and surveys.

It is important to understand how a poll is constructed so that you can determine its validity. First, a sample is chosen which is representative of the total population. Pollsters speak of "random selection," but they don't mean chaotic. Random, in this case, means that everyone in the population has an equal chance of being selected. The size of the sample is important because size affects reliability. Most polls are around 1,200 to 1,500 people, which yields the smallest margin of error possible at an economical cost. Remember, there will always be some error, and at some point pollsters trade off error margin for costs.

Secondly, the questions must be clear and unbiased. A bias in the question will yield different results than an unbiased question. Push polls, which are nothing more than loaded questions, have become popular in recent years, although the morality of these is certainly suspect.

Polls are also often used in place of news. Journalists are frequently guilty of reporting polls instead of content stories, which can create a bandwagon effect. Being ahead in the polls is money in the bank for a politician, as the front runners find it easier to raise money when they look like winners.

Public opinion is very important in a democracy. History has shown that changes in public opinion have been followed, in many cases, by changes in government policy consistent with shifts in popular mood. Sometimes a lack of consistency between opinion and government policy can be due to a nominal majority not being as intensely committed to an issue as the opposing majority. Or it could be due to the structure of American government; an appointed judiciary can produce policy decisions contrary to popular sentiment. All in all, though, government actions do not remain out of line with public sentiment for long, and that is a sign of a vital and thriving democracy.

REVIEW QUESTIONS

1. Is it true that college students are among the least politically active Americans? Why?
2. How do most Americans feel about affirmative action policies as they relate to equality of opportunity?
3. What types of issues do modern liberals support and what do they oppose?
4. List some beliefs of modern conservatives.
5. According to the text, why might women be more likely than men to vote for Democratic candidates in national and local elections?

6. How do social groupings attempt to influence their members' political views?
7. What is the major difference between civic education and indoctrination?
8. How does property ownership elicit support for government?
9. How has the government used the public school system to orient students toward national needs?
10. Are new political ideas marketed most effectively by "oppressed" minorities, by the elite, or by other groups?
11. How do most political issues evolve?
12. How does the media sometimes act against government public relations in the shaping of public opinion?
13. What is the role of the media in reducing differences of opinion among the public?
14. In writing questions used in opinion polls, what are some of the problems that can seriously compromise the validity of the poll?
15. Why is it important in a democracy for government leaders to remain partially ignorant of true public opinion?

KEY TERMS

agencies of socialization
attitude
bandwagon effect
conservative
democracy
equality of opportunity
gender gap
ideology
illusion of saliency
liberal
liberty
marketplace of ideas
political socialization
public opinion
public opinion polls
push polls
salient interests
sample
value

FILL-IN-THE-BLANK QUIZ

Use the key terms to complete the following sentences.

1. A person who is a ____________ has a core value of equality, while one who is a ____________ values liberty.
2. Public opinion is measured scientifically by ____________.

3. The size of the ____________ is important in evaluating the reliability of a poll.
4. The voting differences between men and women are called the ____________.
5. "How would you vote if you knew that Congressman Jones kicked his dog?" This is an example of a ____________.
6. Societies use many ____________ to inculcate the core values of the nation into each generation.
7. Core values in the American ideology are ____________, ____________, and ____________.
8. A poll that gives the impression that an issue is important to the public, when it really is not, is creating a(n) ____________.
9. The process of acquiring our political attitudes is called ____________.
10. The public forum in which political ideas are discussed and debated is the ____________.
11. Politicians like to have several polls showing that they are ahead because of the ____________ this is likely to cause.
12. One's basic orientation to politics is a ____________, while one's ____________ is a more specific view about a particular issue.
13. The attitudes of the citizenry in general are called ____________, while those issues that are important to you are called ____________.
14. Individual perceptions about politics, such as beliefs about what government should do and how it should be done, are called a(n) ____________.

MULTIPLE-CHOICE QUIZ

1. The GOP stands for:
   a. Good Ole Party.
   b. Grand Old Party.
   c. Good and Original Party.
   d. Great Omnipotent Party.
2. The term used to denote the beliefs and attitudes that people have about issues, events, and personalities is:
   a. public opinion.
   b. political socialization.
   c. democracy.
   d. political culture.
3. What is the so-called "gender gap"?
   a. refers to different "agents of socialization" for men (boys) and women (girls)
   b. political differences between men and women
   c. the difference between the number of men and women in

political institutions, such as Congress

d. a term used in the military noting that in general women, unlike men, cannot serve in combat positions

4. Which of the following is not a core/fundamental American value?
   a. individual liberty
   b. democracy
   c. big government
   d. equality of opportunity

5. Which of the following variables is likely to affect public opinion?
   a. income
   b. race
   c. education
   d. gender
   e. all of the above

6. The processes through which underlying political beliefs and values are formed are collectively called:
   a. political socialization.
   b. public opinion.
   c. survey research.
   d. political learning.

7. Which of the following is not one of the four most important agents of socialization?
   a. partisanship
   b. family
   c. membership in social groups
   d. prevailing political conditions

8. James Madison and other framers of the Constitution thought that ____________ would always be the most important source of conflict in political life.
   a. race
   b. the inherent gulf between the rich and poor
   c. religion
   d. education level

9. The set of underlying orientations, ideas, and beliefs through which individuals come to understand and interpret politics is called:
   a. liberalism.
   b. conservatism.
   c. public opinion.
   d. ideology.

10. The belief that people who occupy the same territory have something important in common that makes them separate from and superior to other people is the definition of the concept called:
    a. political culture.
    b. public opinion.
    c. political efficacy.
    d. nationalism.

11. Above all, a public opinion sample must:
    a. be representative.
    b. be nonrandom.
    c. consist of 10 percent of the population group.
    d. be administered in person-to-person interviews.

12. According to the text, which type of equality is most prominent in the United States?
    a. equality of results
    b. output equality
    c. market equity
    d. equality of opportunity

13. "Agreement on fundamental political values, though certainly not absolute, is probably more widespread in the United States

than anywhere else in the Western world." Why?
a. Unlike most European nations, socialist movements in the United States were more prominent and successful.
b. Unlike most European nations, social class distinctions in the United States are more prominent.
c. Unlike many European nations, America has never been socially or economically homogeneous.
d. Unlike the typical European nation, race is not an important factor in American politics.

14. Which of the following agents of socialization provide people with their initial orientation to politics?
a. family
b. peers
c. church
d. education

15. Which of the following is an example of a social group?
a. being female
b. a labor union
c. a political party
d. none of the above
e. all of the above

16. Blacks and whites and men and women have important differences of opinion on a number of political issues. Which of the following statements is true about these differences?
a. Women tend to be more militaristic than men.
b. Whites are more likely than blacks to support the federal government providing more services, even if it means higher taxes.
c. Men are more likely than women to favor measures to protect the environment.
d. Blacks are less likely than whites to believe that racism is a big problem in our society today.
e. None of the above is true.

17. In many respects schooling in the United States:
a. helps determine a person's success in life.
b. is a great equalizer.
c. teaches children a common set of civic values.
d. all of the above.

18. One of the major differences between college graduates and other Americans can be seen in levels of:
a. political tolerance, college graduates have less political tolerance than Americans with less education.
b. religion, college graduates are more religious than Americans with less education.
c. political participation, college graduates participate more in politics than Americans with less education.
d. all of the above.

19. "The South's move from the Democratic to the Republican camp took place because of white southern opposition to the Democratic Party's racial policies." According to the authors, this statement illustrates:
a. how political conditions affect political beliefs.

b. how political socialization does not always work.
c. the transitory nature of political culture.
d. why the Democrats have not won a southern state (except Arkansas) in a presidential election since 1964.

20. I support political and social change, government intervention in the economy, the expansion of federal social services, and more vigorous efforts on behalf of the poor, women, and minorities. I am most likely a:
    a. liberal.
    b. conservative.
    c. libertarian.
    d. none of the above

21. I support the social and political status quo and I am suspicious of efforts to introduce new political formulae and economic arrangements. I am most likely a:
    a. liberal.
    b. conservative.
    c. libertarian.
    d. none of the above

22. Although political ideologies color our political perspectives, they seldom fully determine our views. Why?
    a. Most people have at least some conflicting underlying attitudes.
    b. Individuals may have difficulty linking particular issues of personalities to their own underlying beliefs.
    c. Most individuals' ideologies contain internal contradictions.
    d. all of the above

23. The ____________ is the interplay of opinions and views that takes place as competing forces attempt to persuade as many people as possible to accept a particular position on a particular event.
    a. economic marketplace
    b. marketplace of ideas
    c. political marketplace
    d. marketplace of demographics

24. According to the authors of your text, lowering the voting age to eighteen is a classic example of the concept called:
    a. capture.
    b. subsystem politics.
    c. co-optation.
    d. political pacification.

25. People are more likely to change their opinions when they:
    a. are presented with a well-reasoned argument.
    b. are well-informed on the issue.
    c. don't have any strong feelings about the issue.
    d. are regular voters.

26. Which of the following is not important in determining the reliability of a poll?
    a. the size of the population
    b. the size of the sample
    c. the wording of the questions
    d. the margin of error

QUESTIONS FOR DISCUSSION AND THOUGHT

1. What is the first political event you can remember? Do you know the party identification of your parents? Did your family encourage political discussion? How did their opinions and attitudes about politics affect your own political opinions? What people influenced your opinions about politics?
2. What effect has college had on your political attitudes? Why does it have this effect? Are college faculty effective at indoctrinating students, either consciously or unconsciously? Why or why not?
3. What is your opinion on same-sex marriages? What is the basis for your opinion: legal, social, religious? Has your opinion changed or evolved in any way over the last year or so? If so, why?
4. George Gallup originally designed polls to help make the democratic system more responsive to the people. Did he succeed? Is the system too responsive to public opinion? If someone from the Gallup Poll called to ask you how you planned to vote for president in an upcoming election, would you tell the truth? If Peter Jennings stopped you outside the polling place and asked you how you had voted, would you tell him the truth? Do you think most people lie to pollsters?
5. Do you think you are informed enough about such issues as health care reform, tax code revision, or foreign trade to make an intelligent decision at the polls? Can democracy work if people are not well informed enough to understand these complex issues?
6. Does advertising manipulate public opinion about issues and candidates? Is this any different from advertising a consumer product? If political attitudes are the result of manipulation, does this make a mockery of free elections? If citizens' preferences are not freely chosen, what does this mean for democracy?

THE CITIZEN'S ROLE

Public opinion is influenced by the news media and how they report important news stories. How fair are the news media? Are you getting the whole story? A good way to determine the answer is to compare the way in which several media sources treat the same story. Select a major news story of the last two weeks and locate the story in each of the following sources:

1. A national newspaper such as the *New York Times*
2. A local newspaper

3. A newsmagazine such as *Newsweek*
4. A public radio program (NPR's "Morning Edition" or "All Things Considered")[1]
5. CNN
6. A network evening news program such as Tom Brokaw's on NBC

Compare the stories by answering the questions below.

1. How many column inches were used on the story in the national newspaper? The local? The newsmagazine?
2. How many minutes were spent on the story on public radio, compared to network television?
3. Which stories provided the most information? The least?
4. Were the stories slanted in different directions? Explain.
5. After doing this exercise, which news source do you think is the most reliable? Why?

GOVERNMENT IN YOUR LIFE

Does what children see on television influence their behavior? To test this question, watch one hour of children's cartoons, preferably with a small child. Count the number of acts of violence, such as hitting, killing, verbal assault, and so on.

1. What cartoons did you watch? How many acts of violence did you count?
2. If you watched the cartoons with a child, what was his or her response?
3. Do you think cartoons are more violent today than when you were younger? If so, why?
4. In your opinion, is there a linkage between what children see on television and their social behavior?
5. Should the government control children's viewing? Explain.

[1]If you do not have public radio available, select a second TV network source.

ANSWER KEY

Fill-in-the-Blank Quiz

1. liberal, conservative
2. public opinion polls
3. sample
4. gender gap
5. push poll
6. agencies of socialization
7. democracy, liberty, equality of opportunity
8. illusion of saliency
9. political socialization
10. marketplace of ideas
11. bandwagon effect
12. value, attitude
13. public opinion, salient interests
14. ideology

Multiple-Choice Quiz

1. b
2. a
3. b
4. c
5. e
6. a
7. a
8. b
9. d
10. d
11. a
12. d
13. c
14. a
15. e
16. e
17. d
18. c
19. a
20. a
21. b
22. d
23. b
24. c
25. c
26. a

CHAPTER 8 The Media

THE CHAPTER IN BRIEF

Suppose you lived in a nation where the news media were controlled by the government. What sort of news do you think would be reported? Would you be able to trust what you heard or read? How would you be able to form political opinions if only one side of an issue were presented?

This is why a free press is so important to a democracy. Our system relies upon rational discussion of public policy. That discussion cannot take place unless many opinions are voiced and heard by others. The First Amendment guarantees a free press so that we can live in a democracy. But do Americans actually hear a variety of opinions? Is the public discussion open to all? Are there some opinions that are heard more than others?

If we truly want to hear many different opinions, we must have a variety of news sources available to us. Unfortunately, one of the trends of the last fifty years has been the "nationalization" of the media. Even though we have many sources of news available to us, all too often the original sources of the news are few. Most stories can be traced back to a few news organizations, usually the Associated Press, the *New York Times*, the *Washington Post*, and the *Wall Street Journal,* and the three major news magazines (*Newsweek, Time,* and *U.S. News and World Report*). Most radio and television news stories are derived from the print media. This leads to a homogenization of the news; that is, the same stories are recycled in slightly different forms.

Most people get their news from television, although TV news is brief and shallow. Radio news is similar, although an exception is National Public Radio's news programs ("Morning Edition" and "All Things Considered") which do original stories in depth. However, the newspaper is still the best source for news because it can provide more stories, go into greater detail, and is produced daily. A rising source is the Internet, which can supplement the regular newscasts and daily papers with current stories and a variety of interpretations.

A major reason for the nationalization of the news is that so many media outlets are owned by so few corporations. Over 75 percent of the daily newspapers in America are owned by large conglomerates, which also own many radio and TV stations. Even the television networks are part of these consolidated companies; ABC, for example, is owned by Walt Disney.

Nationalization of the news has the effect of making all major political issues known across the nation, rather than locally, as in the past.

As a reaction to the homogenization of the news, in recent years we have seen the development of several "news enclaves," or alternative news sources. Examples are black radio, Spanish-language television, religious channels, and conservative talk shows.

Because of the First Amendment, newspapers and other print media in the United States do not have to obtain a government license or permission before going into business. Broadcast media, however, are required to receive a license from the Federal Communications Commission, an independent regulatory agency. Licenses are required because of the physical limits of the airwaves; without regulation, there would be chaos on the airwaves. Stations are required to broadcast their call letters every hour so that the FCC can monitor for pirate stations—those that are broadcasting without a license.

Generally speaking, the FCC does not regulate content of radio and television. However, Congress attempted to regulate content on the Internet in 1996 when it passed the Communications Decency Act, which made it illegal for anyone to post obscene material on the Net. This was overturned by the Supreme Court in *Reno v. ACLU*, but it shows that there are always attacks on the free press.

In fact, the press is not entirely free. The government is prohibited from censorship ("prior restraint"), but it may be allowed in wartime. The government argued in the famous Pentagon Papers case that national security was involved and thus the documents should not be published. The Court found that there was nothing in the papers that compromised national security at that time and ruled against the government. Another limit is through libel laws, although it is difficult to win a libel case against a newspaper unless one can prove that the story was published with "actual malice" intended.

While the free press is vital to a democracy, we must also understand that journalists are not value-free. In fact, they bring to their jobs their own personal backgrounds, interests, values, and political attitudes. Several studies have shown that, at least at the national level, journalists are liberal. Today there is a conservative media complex that has risen to challenge the mainstream press. If there is a bias in the news, it tends today to be more of a selection, or commercial, bias. That is, stories are selected that appeal to the consumers' and advertisers' tastes and interests in order to sell papers and increase market share.

Where do journalists get their news? Politicians are usually good sources, as they want to get free media coverage and get their ideas and opinions exposed to the public. Most politicians today hire media consultants occasionally or employ one on their staff. However, politicians' stories are no longer taken at face value; there is usually someone—perhaps another politician—who offers a response, which, of course, is also covered by the media.

The selection bias mentioned above needs to be explored further. The bias is clearly in favor of the more educated and affluent public, the "upscale" audience. This public reads newspapers and magazines, which in turn draws advertisers. The topics that are covered are those of greatest interest to these consumers, while the interests of the working class are rarely discussed.

Groups that cannot afford to hire media consultants and cannot attract the attention of the journalists may use protest and even violence to gain attention. The civil rights movement of the 1960s and the anti-Vietnam war movement reached national attention when they were covered on the daily television news. Both received favorable coverage from the press, in contrast to the militia movement, which is seen as a group of alienated working-class individuals and thus marginalized until they do something to force national attention, such as take hostages.

It should be clear by now that the media and the public have a symbiotic relationship—they need each other. Still, the media in recent years have acquired a great deal of power over public opinion. First, the media help set the agenda for public discussion. Frequent stories on the problems surrounding health maintenance organizations, for example, force the public and especially legislators to take notice. Secondly, the media can "frame" or interpret the issue. The same day that the Monica Lewinsky story broke, several prominent journalists began talking about impeaching President Clinton, even though the general public was probably not ready to jump to that conclusion.

Finally, the media can shape our opinions of politicians. For example, prior to the 1996 presidential campaign, Bob Dole's chances of winning were portrayed as slim, even from the outset of his campaign, and Ross Perot was frequently portrayed as a political curiosity rather than as a viable candidate. The media portrayal of a politician is important because it affects his or her "momentum," or illusion of growing popularity. Politicians try to wrest image-making away from the media by going directly to the public, through debates, town meetings, and even appearances on "The Tonight Show."

Even though we know that today's journalism is often biased, it is still better than it used to be. In the nineteenth century, newspapers were partisan organs and often sensationalized the news to sell newspapers. As journalism developed, the print media tried to become more balanced, and were generally respectful of the president. The Vietnam war altered this relationship, when the press discovered that Americans wanted more critical coverage; the Watergate affair soon after accelerated this change, so that today newspapers are much more skeptical about politicians.

Our free press gives the media enormous power, and with that power there exists the potential for abuse. We must be prepared to take the risk of occasional abuse, however, because the forms of governmental control that would prevent the misuse of power would also destroy our freedom.

REVIEW QUESTIONS

1. Why are the media so influential?
2. Explain how TV has reduced regional differences. What impact might this have on American politics?
3. Describe the role of the media during the nineteenth century. Why has the emergence of a national media enhanced the power of the presidency?
4. What is the doctrine of "no prior restraint" and what case established it?
5. Explain how writers, producers, news sources, and audiences determine what is news.
6. What type of tactics are used by groups in gaining media access? Explain a recent event when each tactic was used. Focus on the way the media reported and interpreted the event.
7. What is freedom of the press? Does everyone favor press freedom? What groups are most supportive of freedom of the press?
8. Does the existence of many newspapers, radio stations, and TV stations in the United States mean that Americans receive many versions of the national news? What term describes the alternative to the mainstream media?
9. What federal agency regulates the broadcast media? Explain two regulations this agency imposes.
10. Which presidents have made the most effective use of the media? What were their media strategies?
11. How important is a free press to the preservation of democracy?
12. Discuss the role of the media in the following major events of the last twenty years: the Vietnam War, the civil rights movement, and Watergate.
13. Why does an issue lose its chance of producing a meaningful policy if it has lost media attention?
14. What factors determine the news coverage a particular story receives?
15. Explain how advances in mass communications technology changed the power of the presidency as an institution.
16. Explain the significance of *Reno v. ACLU.*

KEY TERMS

agenda setting
equal time rule
fairness doctrine
framing
news
news enclave
prior restraint
right of rebuttal

FILL-IN-THE-BLANK QUIZ

Use the key terms to complete the following sentences.

1. A television channel that runs religious programs and talk shows that feature discussions of politics from a religious point of view is an example of a(n) ____________.
2. Another term for censorship of the press is ____________.
3. The leading story of a newscast and the front-page story are placement decisions that help the media contribute to ____________.
4. "Bill, as the reporter on the scene, tell us just what this story means." "Well, Dan, this means that the candidate is in serious trouble." This is an example of ____________ an issue.
5. If an individual has been personally attacked on a radio program, he or she can exercise the FCC's ____________.
6. In the last few years, the Internet has emerged as an alternative ____________ source.
7. The Reagan administration abolished the FCC rule that required radio and television stations to provide equal time to the opponents of a controversial program. The rule that was rescinded was the ____________.
8. Stations are still required to abide by the ____________, which requires them to treat all political candidates for the same office equally.

MULTIPLE-CHOICE QUIZ

1. More than ____________ of the daily newspapers in the United States are owned by large conglomerates such as the Hearst or Gannett corporations.
   a. one-quarter
   b. one-half
   c. three-quarters
   d. 90 percent
2. In the United States there are only three truly national newspapers. Which of the following is not one of the newspapers?
   a. the *Wall Street Journal*

b. the *Christian Science Monitor*
c. *USA Today*
d. the *Washington Post*

3. Which of the following is not part of the "conservative media complex" that has emerged in opposition to the liberal media?
a. the *Washington Post*
b. the *Wall Street Journal*
c. the *Washington Times*
d. the *American Spectator*

4. Who is the leader of the Christian Coalition?
a. Pat Buchanan
b. Pat Robertson
c. Pat Cadell
d. Jesse Jackson

5. American radio and television are regulated by:
a. state governments.
b. the Federal Communications Commission.
c. local governments.
d. all of the above.

6. Broadcasters must provide candidates for the same political office equal opportunities to communicate their messages to the public. This is the:
a. equal time rule.
b. right to rebuttal rule.
c. fairness doctrine.
d. equal access rule.

7. Unlike the broadcast media, the print media are not subject to:
a. strict government censorship.
b. federal regulation.
c. libel laws.
d. provisions of the First and Fourteenth Amendments.

8. The interpretation or "spin" a new story receives from the news media is influenced by certain major and minor factors. Which of the following is not one of those factors?
a. corporate sponsors
b. journalists
c. the sources or topics of the news
d. the audience of the news.

9. In general, survey research suggests that journalists, who have a good deal of discretion or freedom to interpret the news:
a. have a conservative bias.
b. have a liberal bias.
c. are apolitical.
d. never let their political ideology affect their stories.

10. According to the authors, which of the following is probably NOT a major source of government news?
a. politicians
b. political candidates
c. interest groups
d. political parties

11. Which of the following events do the authors not use to illustrate the power of the media in American politics?
a. the civil rights movement
b. ending American involvement in the Vietnam War
c. Watergate
d. the savings and loan scandal

12. A form of journalism in which the media adopt an adversarial posture toward the government and public officials is called:
a. objective journalism.

b. "yellow journalism."
c. investigative journalism.
d. "fighting words" journalism.

13. What effect does the organization of the media have on politics?
    a. In general, news in America has been nationalized.
    b. It provides for wide diversity in the issues covered and editorial opinions.
    c. It allows for "small voices" to be heard over the corporate news giants.
    d. National news becomes more important than local news.

14. What does the concept "nationalization of the news" mean?
    a. National issues are more important to people than local news.
    b. National news media cover more or less the same sets of events, present similar information, and emphasize similar issues and problems.
    c. Unlike for most of the nineteenth century, today news travels across the nation very quickly and efficiently.
    d. The media are owned and controlled by government.

15. Some African Americans rely upon newspapers and radio stations that aim their coverage primarily at black audiences. This is an example of:
    a. media bias.
    b. ethnocentrism.
    c. news enclaves.
    d. discrimination.

16. According to the authors of the text, today most publishers:
    a. are most concerned with editorial content.
    b. are business people and are more concerned with business operations than editorial content.
    c. dictate a particular political bias that the media should promulgate.
    d. have a liberal political ideology.

17. "Although they represent only a small percentage of the population, individuals under the age of fifty whose family income is in the 80th percentile or better account for nearly 50 percent of the retail dollars spent on consumer goods in the United States." This statement supports the authors' contention that:
    a. that the print and broadcast media cater to the preferences of consumers.
    b. that the media cater to the "upscale" segments of their audiences.
    c. that the media attempt to understand the tastes and preferences of consumers.
    d. all of the above

18. According to the authors, the media have generally treated the white, working-class, "militia" movement as a dangerous and irrational development. Why?
    a. The social forces to which the media are most responsive are in general not sympathetic to the "militia" movement.

b. The media almost never provide positive coverage of social movements.
c. Journalists do not understand the goals and objectives of the movement.
d. Positive media coverage would automatically "legitimize" the movement.

19. According to the authors of your text, what is an important purpose of presidential candidates such as Bill Clinton, Bob Dole, and Ross Perot appearing at town hall meetings and on television talk shows?
    a. to get "free" media exposure
    b. to take away control of the image-making process from journalists and media executives
    c. these places seem to be the only "stage" to address public policy concerns
    d. to raise money from individuals and interest groups

20. Several studies have indicated that during the course of the 1992 Bush/Clinton presidential contest the media tended to be more critical of George Bush and more supportive of Bill Clinton. According to the authors of the text, these findings support:
    a. a conspiracy theory among the media, interest groups, and government officials.
    b. a de facto alliance that developed over a number of years between the media and liberal forces.
    c. a growing conservatism in the United States.
    d. the need for greater insistence on the "fairness doctrine."

QUESTIONS FOR DISCUSSION AND THOUGHT

1. How many hours a week do you watch television? How do you think television has affected your thinking about government and politics? About social justice? About crime? About the economy? If you turned off your television for a month, would it bother you?
2. Do you read a newspaper or news magazine regularly? Do you think you should? Are you more interested in local, state, national, or international news? Which has more impact on your daily life?
3. If you decided to run for public office, would you be willing to release your income tax records? Your medical records? If there were something in your past that you would not want revealed, would you lie to cover it up if the press found out about it?
4. The U.S. government has been highly criticized for restricting media coverage of the Persian Gulf War. Can we have a free press in wartime? What problems do you see with allowing the press to cover whatever they want in a war zone?

5. The intent of the Communications Decency Act was to prevent children from obtaining obscene or pornographic material from the Internet. Do you think this is a big problem? If so, how would you go about preventing your child from obtaining such material? Would you support broad censorship of the Internet to protect your child? Whose responsibility is it to protect children from offensive materials?
6. Why is a free press essential to democracy? If there were no free press, how would you get your information? If you couldn't trust the information, what effect would that have on your political attitudes? Can we maintain a democracy when most Americans pay little attention to political events?

THE CITIZEN'S ROLE

Express your opinion on a political subject by writing a letter to the editor of either a local newspaper or your school paper. The letter should be typed on white paper, and be short and clear to the reader. Use the following format for a business letter, and be sure to use the spell-checking and grammar-checking tools on the computer.

Street address
City, State, ZIP
Date

Name of newspaper
Address of newspaper

Dear Editor:

[Text of letter: State the issue, your opinion, what action you think should be taken.]

Sincerely,
[Your signature]
Your name, typed

1. Why did you select this issue?
2. Did writing the letter help you form an opinion on the issue?
3. Will you send this letter? Why or why not?

4. Does expressing a political opinion make you uncomfortable? Explain.
5. Do you think most Americans know enough about the issues so that they can form opinions based on rational thought? Explain.

GOVERNMENT IN YOUR LIFE

An emerging area of conflict over the free press revolves around the Internet. Many people support the Communications Decency Act because they believe that it is appropriate to limit children's access to pornographic sites. According to the Electronic Freedom Foundation and similar sources, though, many nonpornographic sites would also be eliminated. Examples of sites are: the Sistine chapel, the King James Bible, The Prolife News, the National Alliance of Breast Cancer Organizations, online medical textbooks, lyrics of many rock groups, even the Starr report on President Clinton. Check out the EFF site at http://www.eff.org/blueribbon to learn more about this issue.

1. Do you believe that your freedom of the press would be limited by the Communications Decency Act? Explain.
2. Do you see any way that children's access to pornographic sites can be controlled? If so, how?
3. Would you support Senator John McCain's bill to force federally funded libraries to use software filters to censor access "to protect children from inappropriate material"?
4. The Electronic Freedom Foundation and other groups have created a "blue ribbon campaign," in which they ask supporters of free speech and free press to wear a blue ribbon. Would you be willing to wear a blue ribbon to school for one day? How many students do you think have heard of the Blue Ribbon Campaign?
5. First Amendment freedoms are constantly under attack. Do you think that you can do anything to protect these basic freedoms? If so, what?

ANSWER KEY

Fill-in-the-Blank Quiz

1. news enclave
2. prior restraint
3. agenda setting
4. framing
5. right of rebuttal
6. news
7. fairness doctrine
8. equal time rule

Multiple-Choice Quiz

1. c
2. d
3. a

4. b
5. b
6. a
7. b
8. a
9. b
10. c
11. d
12. c
13. a
14. b
15. c
16. b
17. d
18. a
19. b
20. b

CHAPTER 9 Political Parties

THE CHAPTER IN BRIEF

When eighteen-year-olds gained the right to vote through the Twenty-Sixth Amendment to the Constitution, many people predicted that young people would become a potent political force, but that has not happened. Apart from the Vietnam War protests, America's youth have been relatively quiet. They have weak attachments to political parties and are generally indifferent to party politics. One reason for this inertia may be that American college students look forward to becoming part of the system and are less likely to want to destroy what they see as their route to success in the future.

Political parties have been used by many groups throughout American history as a way to influence the political system. But governments *also* use political parties to influence groups.

The Constitution does not mention political parties because they barely existed in 1789. Madison, however, spoke of "factions" and Washington, in his Farewell Address, warned of the "baneful effects of the spirit of party." The Federalists, who controlled the federal government in the early years, tried to outlaw their Jeffersonian Republican opponents through the Alien and Sedition Acts. Today we recognize political parties as necessary for the organization of elections, the formulation of policy alternatives, and the organization of personal political values.

Political parties in America have formed in two ways. The first is the "internal mobilization" process, which occurs in times of conflict. Government officials and competing factions organize popular support for their programs. The Jeffersonians and the Federalists, the first parties, were internal mobilization parties. The second process is "external mobilization," in which groups outside of the formal governmental system organize their own parties and overtake the existing parties. The Republican Party of today was externally mobilized.

Of the two major parties today, the Democrats are the older, stemming from the old Jeffersonian party which split in 1824. Andrew Jackson led one of the four factions to its new incarnation as the Democratic party, the party of the common man. From 1828 to 1860, the Democrats were the dominant American party, controlling the White House for all but eight years and the Congress for twenty-four years. The Democrats believed in a narrow interpretation of the Constitution, states' rights, and a small federal government.

In 1860, the Democrats split into northern and southern factions over the issue of slavery, and as a result the party lost its control of the nation until Franklin Roosevelt's election in 1932. The new Democratic coalition (post-New Deal) was a coalition of liberals, labor, Catholics, Jews, and blacks. The southern Democrats were conservative and more attuned to the Republican party, although they did not align themselves with the Republicans until the 1980s. Since then, the Democrats have maintained their political base among government employees, labor, and liberals, but this was not enough to allow them to retain control of Congress in 1994.

The Republicans formed from the remnants of older political groups, such as the Whigs, Know-Nothings, and antislavery Democrats in 1854, as a response to the Kansas-Nebraska Act, which allowed each new state to decide if it would allow slavery. Besides being antislavery, the Republicans represented the interests of the growing business class. From 1860 to the New Deal in 1932, the Republicans dominated American politics. In recent years, the party has attracted more blue-collar workers and conservative religious groups (the "religious right").

At least five party realignments have occurred in American history. The first was around 1800, when the Jeffersonian Republicans replaced the Federalists; the second was the 1828 election of Andrew Jackson, which brought about the long era of Jacksonian Democracy. The third realignment was the rise of the Republican Party in 1860, followed by the fourth alignment after the election of 1896, in which Republicans regained hegemony which had been weakening. The fifth realignment was from 1932 to 1936, when Franklin Roosevelt's New Deal Democrats established their control, lasting until the 1960s. Realignment occurs when an economic or political crisis brings new leadership to the fore and causes people to reexamine their political loyalties.

Although we speak of the United States as a two-party system, we have always had minor parties that articulate the protests of those who feel unrepresented. The populists, the progressives, and, most recently, Ross Perot's Reform Party have made major impacts on government even though they have never captured the presidency. This is because the major parties coopt the ideas of the minor parties and incorporate them into their own programs, thus depriving the minor parties of their issues. Sometimes, too, these are regional parties that are unable to draw nationwide attention, such as George Wallace's 1968 campaign in the deep South.

Why does the United States have a two-party system and not a multiparty system such as France? Political scientists believe that the single-member-district plurality system of election encourages two parties. Think of it this way. If only one person can be elected from a district, how can that person maximize his or her chances of election? Obviously, by being the only candidate. But democracy demands opposition, and so the next best chance is by having only two candidates. More parties merely splinter the vote even further, making it very difficult for anyone to win with a clear mandate. Many European countries have multiple-member districts, in which several persons are elected from the district instead of just one, thus encouraging more small parties to organize and get on the ballot. The European system of proportional representation awards seats according to the relative size of the party vote. (This is explained further in Chapter 10.)

Party organization in the United States is based on having a party organization at every level of government. At the highest level, the parties hold a national convention every four years, where they nominate candidates for president and vice president, approve the party platform, and revise the party's rules. Since 1972 the Democrats have apportioned their convention representation according to proportional representation and have required states to include women and minorities. The platform is an important document because it states what the party stands for and what it hopes to accomplish if elected.

In between conventions, the Democratic and Republican National Committees run the parties and, most importantly, raise money for the next election. The president chooses the national chair for his party. Parties also have congressional campaign committees to raise funds for congressional candidates. Both parties also have state central committees, county committees, and in some cases, committees at the lowest levels such as precincts.

For many years, political parties could build support by offering patronage through their political machines, especially in urban areas. However, civil service reform took many of the government jobs out of the hands of the party officials, thus depriving them of important sources of power. In recent years, parties have turned to "soft money" funds to promote party building activities such as voter registration drives and campaign funds for candidates. As a result of this fund-raising process, state and local committees are now tied more closely to national parties than ever before.

Party identification in America does not require formal membership and obligations, merely the statement that one "is" a Democrat or a Republican—a psychological tie. Today about one-third of Americans consider themselves Democrats, one-third Republicans, and one-third Independents. Those whose sense of identification is strongest are most likely to become party activists. Blacks tend to be Democrats, as are women, Jews, the working class, liberals, and those who live in the Northeast. Republicans tend to be male, Protestant, conservative, upper-income and live in the West and Southwest. The Latino vote is split: Cuban Americans are generally Republicans, while Puerto Ricans and Mexican Americans are Democrats.

Political parties are very important in the electoral process. Each year, parties work hard to recruit candidates for public office. Parties can no longer count on large numbers of volunteers to help out with campaigns and must instead raise money to pay for pollsters, media specialists, phone banks, direct mail, and professional public relations. Politics has gone from "labor-intensive to capital-intensive." This shifts the balance of power from groups such as labor unions that can turn out large numbers of workers to groups with money to hire professionals. Special interests become the new powers as they provide the necessary funds to both parties.

American parties are not strongly ideological, although there is some evidence that parties are lining up more along a liberal/conservative continuum. Parties both reflect the interests of their constituents and mold public opinion in their roles as "policy entrepreneurs."

Congress depends on political parties for its basic organization. Both congressional leaders and committee members are chosen by party affiliation, with each committee having a quota of Democrats and Republicans. The majority party will always have the majority of the seats on a committee. At one time, these assignments were made according to seniority, but today seniority is no longer automatic. The president heads his own political party and depends on his party in Congress to support his legislative agenda.

Healthy political parties are essential for democracy. They provide competition for elections, protect our basic First Amendment liberties, promote voter turnout, and simply make democratic government possible. American parties are not "responsible" parties such as found in a parliamentary system, but our system would not survive without them. For that reason, we need to strengthen our parties and encourage the public to take their party affiliations seriously.

REVIEW QUESTIONS

1. Why are political parties important in a democracy? Is it possible to have a democracy without political parties?
2. What is the reason that social forces unite into an organized political party?
3. In the early years of our nation, were political parties seen as essential to the social order? Why or why not?
4. Both political parties and interest groups seek influence over the government. What is the major difference in the way that political parties and interest groups pursue that goal?
5. What criteria for party membership, if any, exist in the United States?
6. Does a presidential nominee consider the party's platform as a set of promises to keep if the nominee is elected? Do voters take the platforms seriously?
7. What are the functions of the national committees?

8. How is the function of a congressional campaign committee different from the function of a party's national committee? Do the two committees always correlate their activities? What might prevent them from doing so?
9. What was the origin of the Democratic Party? State a major difference between the nineteenth-century Democratic Party and the Democratic Party of today in regard to its view of the federal government.
10. What was the main social force behind the creation of the Republican Party in the 1850s? What other issues were on the early Republican agenda?
11. Historically, when and why do realignments occur?
12. What are the major differences between what each party supports today? What do these differences reflect?
13. How are third-party candidates hampered by America's single-member-district plurality election system? Theoretically, how could this hurt the two-party system?
14. What do a party's principal efforts and energy go into?
15. How did the creation of an opposition party in the early years of our nation serve to prevent rebellion against the government?
16. How does the party system prevent powerful people from controlling the government?
17. Why is it important to the Republicans that they block Clinton's legislative reform proposals?

KEY TERMS

caucus (political)
divided government
machines
majority party
minority party
multiple-member district
national convention
nomination
party activists
party identification
party organization
patronage
platforms
plurality system
policy entrepreneur
political parties
proportional representation
responsible party government
single-member district
soft money
third parties
two-party system

FILL-IN-THE-BLANK QUIZ

Use the key terms to complete the following sentences.

1. The party philosophy and positions on issues that are used as campaign documents are ____________.
2. Historically the two major parties have caused the death of most ____________ because they appropriate the major issues for themselves.
3. Even though the United States occasionally has a minor party develop, it is still considered to be a ____________ system.
4. The presidential candidate is chosen at a party's ____________.
5. Most Americans identify with a political party, even though the tie may be weak. This psychological tie is called ____________.
6. Local party organizations have received a boost in recent years because the national parties have funneled ____________ to the lower levels.
7. When we elect someone to Congress, we can vote for only one person and only one person is elected. This is a ____________ system.
8. A parliamentary system offers ____________, while a presidential system sometimes has ____________ because the executive and legislative branches may be held by different parties.
9. A voting system which allows candidates to be elected if they have more votes than anyone else, but not a majority, is a ____________.
10. In 1992, Ross Perot identified the budget deficit as a major crisis and brought the issue to the attention of the American public so successfully that the two major parties were forced to face the budget issue. You could say that Ross Perot was a ____________.
11. The party with the most votes in the House of Representatives is the ____________ party, while the other party is the ____________ party.
12. Prior to civil service, political parties and political machines offered jobs to loyal voters. This practice, known as ____________, has been severely curtailed today.
13. The ballot in front of you lists twelve people running for the same office, and the instructions tell you to vote for five. You are voting in a ____________ system.
14. Once every four years, political parties hold conventions at which the major goal is the ____________ of a candidate for the presidency.
15. Presidential candidates flock to Iowa to campaign in the presidential pri-

maries because Iowa holds early closed-party meetings at the precinct level, known as ____________.

16. Proportional representation differs from single-member districts because it is based upon a ____________.

17. The formal structure of a political party is known as its ____________; those who are involved in it are called ____________.

18. The terms "realignment" and "dealignment" refer to the changing strength of ____________.

19. "Bosses" who controlled the local political process were managers of political ____________.

MULTIPLE-CHOICE QUIZ

1. What was the first American political party?
   a. Jeffersonian Republicans
   b. Federalists
   c. Antifederalists
   d. Democrats

2. When the Jeffersonian Party splintered in 1824, Andrew Jackson emerged as the leader of one of its four factions. In 1830, Jackson's group became the:
   a. Republican Party.
   b. Suffrage Party.
   c. Democratic Party.
   d. Whig Party.

3. The ____________ gave each territory the right to decide whether or not to permit slavery.
   a. Compromise of 1850
   b. The Missouri Compromise of 1820
   c. The Kansas-Nebraska Act of 1854
   d. Three-fifths Compromise of 1860

4. In the United States, party politics has followed a fascinating pattern. Typically, during the course of American political history, the national electoral arena has been dominated by one party for a period of roughly ____________ years.
   a. ten
   b. twenty
   c. thirty
   d. fifty

5. According to the authors of your textbook, it seems today, unlike the 1960s, college students are much more aligned with the ____________ Party.
   a. Republican
   b. Democratic
   c. Libertarian
   d. Reform

6. At the national level, the party's most important institution is the quadrennial:
   a. election of members of the House of Representatives.
   b. election of U.S. Senators.

c. meeting of the Party State Caucuses.
d. national convention.

7. Which of the following takes place at the national party convention?
a. At least since post-World War II, after several ballots (roll call votes of the states) the party's presidential candidate is finally selected.
b. The convention must choose a vice president from among the losing presidential candidates.
c. The party decides its rules of procedures and writes a party platform.
d. All of the above.

8. Which of the following is often argued to be a positive benefit of the use of a "proportional representation" voting system?
a. Representatives chosen by the voting system are more representative of various groups in society.
b. The voting system ensures that only Democrats and Republicans are elected.
c. The voting system discourages the rise of third parties.
d. Unlike the single-member district voting method, the proportional plan has not been declared unconstitutional by the U.S. Supreme Court.

9. According to the authors, party platforms should be viewed as:
a. binding documents by which political parties are evaluated.
b. essentially superficial and frivolous documents.
c. internal party documents.
d. all of the above.

10. Which of the following is a task(s) of the Democratic and Republican National Committees?
a. nominating the president and vice president
b. raising campaign funds
c. writing party platforms
d. helping the president select cabinet members

11. Which of the following is true about congressional campaign committees?
a. They raise funds for the presidential candidate representing their party.
b. They raise funds for House and Senate campaign races and always coordinate fund-raising efforts with national committee fund-raising activities.
c. In recent years Republicans have sought to coordinate the fund-raising activities of all its committees, whereas the Democrats have been slower to pursue such coordination efforts.
d. All of the above.

12. What are legally defined subdivisions of wards that are used to register voters and set up ballot boxes or voting machines?
a. block captains
b. county districts
c. political machines
d. precincts

13. Historically, America has always been a ____________-party system.
a. one

b. two
c. three
d. four

14. From 1828 to 1860, the ____________ Party was the dominant force in American politics.
a. Democratic
b. Republican
c. Whig
d. Jeffersonian Republican

15. From 1896 to 1932, for the most part, the ____________ Party was the dominant force in American politics.
a. Democratic
b. Republican
c. Whig
d. Jeffersonian Republican

16. From 1932 to 1968, for the most part, the ____________ Party was the dominant force in American politics.
a. Democratic
b. Republican
c. Whig
d. Jeffersonian Republican

17. What is it called when the dominant party has been supplanted by a new party after a so-called "critical election"?
a. "shift of power"
b. dealignment
c. realignment
d. detente

18. In America, unlike many other western nations, the ____________ election system is used.
a. cumulative voting
b. single-member-district plurality
c. multiple-member district
d. proportional representational

19. The process by which a party selects a single candidate to run for each elective office is the definition of a:
a. caucus.
b. primary.
c. nomination.
d. general election.

20. A psychological tie to a political party is the definition of:
a. party identification.
b. political socialization.
c. caucus.
d. a party activist.

21. America's only national party(ies) is (are):
a. the Democratic Party.
b. the Republican Party.
c. the Independent Party.
d. all of the above.
e. only a and b.

22. Since the 1930s and the New Deal, African Americans have been overwhelmingly ____________ in their party identification; women are somewhat more likely to support ____________ candidates; and Jews are among the ____________ Party's most loyal constituent groups.
a. Democratic, Democratic, Democratic
b. Republican, Republican, Republican
c. Democratic, Republican, Democratic
d. Democratic, Republican, Republican

23. Upper-class Americans are considerably more likely to affiliate with the ___________ Party; conservatives are more likely to identify with the ___________ Party; and citizens living in the Northeast region are more likely to identify with the ___________ Party.
    a. Democratic, Democratic, Democratic
    b. Republican, Republican, Republican
    c. Republican, Democratic, Republican
    d. Republican, Republican, Democratic

24. According to the authors of the text, college students in the U.S., unlike many other nations of the world, have been a quiescent or even a conservative political force. What explanation is offered for this political orientation?
    a. College students simply do not understand the American political system.
    b. Higher education is probably the most important route of access to economic success and social status in the United States and students do not wish to participate in radical attacks upon a political and social order that promises to reward them.
    c. In the United States college students usually sympathize with extremist political groups, and such groups currently are not active in American politics.
    d. Since most college students are not eligible to vote, students as rational actors see little incentive to participate in politics.

25. In modern history, ___________ have been the chief points of contact between governments, on the one hand, and groups and forces in society, on the other.
    a. interest groups
    b. political parties
    c. presidents

26. Political parties can be distinguished from interest groups in that:
    a. unlike interest groups, political parties do not aggregate and articulate interests.
    b. membership in political parties requires paying fees or dues.
    c. political parties seek universal benefits for all Americans, whereas interest groups are only interested in seeking benefits for business corporations and/or professional groups.
    d. political parties seek to control the entire government by electing their members to office, thereby controlling the government's personnel. Interest groups usually accept government and its personnel as a given and try to influence government policies through them.

27. According to the authors of the text, political parties as they are known today developed along with the expansion of suffrage and can be understood only in the context of:

a. elections.
b. political culture.
c. social movements.
d. political realignments.

28. Compared with political parties in Europe, parties in the United States have always seemed:
 a. strong.
 b. centralized.
 c. weak.
 d. coherent.

29. Today political parties in the United States are weaker than in previous years and are less able to control:
 a. elections.
 b. nominations.
 c. congressional committees.
 d. the office of the presidency.

30. Historically, political parties form in one of two ways. ___________ occurs when conflicts break out and government officials and competing factions seek to mobilize popular support.
 a. "Internal Mobilization"
 b. "External Mobilization"
 c. "Micro-Mobilization"
 d. "Macro-Mobilization"

31. Historically, realignments happen:
 a. when the American people support the supremacy of foreign policy initiatives versus domestic policies.
 b. when a political party is rocked by scandal and political elites leave the party due to corruption.
 c. when new issues combined with economic or political crises persuade numbers of voters to reexamine their traditional loyalties and permanently shift their support from one party to another.
 d. all of the above

32. Typically, third parties in the United States:
 a. have represented the interests of the poor.
 b. have represented social and economic protests that were not given voice by the two major parties.
 c. have been very successful in capturing national political offices, but not state and local offices.
 d. have replaced one of the dominant parties of the time.

33. Which of the following reasons best explains the short lives of third parties?
 a. Their goals and objectives are too extreme for most Americans.
 b. They lack requisite resources (membership, money, organization, etc.) to survive.
 c. Third parties are organized to redistribute income; once new policies are in place, the parties disband.
 d. Their causes are usually eliminated by the ability of the major parties to absorb their programs and to draw their supporters into the mainstream.

34. Which of the following is not usually considered a function of political parties?
 a. nominating candidates
 b. getting out the vote

c. influencing voters' choices
d. lobbying

35. Until recent years at least, ___________ have been the principle agents responsible for giving citizens the motivation and incentive actually to vote.
    a. the major parties
    b. the media
    c. family and friends
    d. interest groups

36. The authors of the text are emphatic that one of the major factors responsible for the relatively low rates of voter turnout that characterize American national elections is:
    a. low levels of political efficacy.
    b. dissatisfaction with the political system.
    c. apathy.
    d. the decline of political parties.

37. According to the authors, weak political parties:
    a. give rise to strong interest groups.
    b. are inevitable in an electronic media age.
    c. have a neutral impact on American politics.
    d. are good for democracy.

QUESTIONS FOR DISCUSSION AND THOUGHT

1. How has your parents' party identification affected your choice of party? Is there a strong relationship between their party choices and your own? According to your religious affiliation, race, gender, residence, and social class, what party would you be expected to belong to? If you were to leave the party of your parents, would you go to the opposite party or become an independent? Why?

2. Should politicians be held to higher standards than "normal" people? Have you ever criticized a politician for doing something that you have done yourself? Do you hold politicians to a higher standard than you hold yourself? Is that okay?

3. Today many politicians are hiring private investigators to check out their opponents' credit reports, medical records, their high school and college grades, their neighbors where they grew up—in short, anything seems to be fair game. One politician was criticized for his wife's failure to renew a dog license on time! Does this sort of scrutiny drive off many good potential candidates? If so, what can be done about this gross invasion of privacy? Or is this just the price one pays for seeking public office today? Do we really need to know every little secret about a candidate and his or her family?

4. In the past, critics frequently charged that there were very few differences between the two major parties. Is that true today? What do you think the Republicans stood for in the 1996 presidential election? The Democrats? Social critic Jim Wallis claims that both parties have become "morally vacuous." He charges that the Democrats are obsessed with "radical

individualism," while the Republicans are absorbed with materialism. Would you agree?

5. We talk a lot about the need for campaign finance reform, but in fact few individuals give money to candidates, and there are restrictions at the federal level on that amount. Have you ever given money to a candidate? Would you, if asked? If individuals don't give, can you blame politicians for getting big money (and soft money) from special interests? Where else can they get the money they need? Personal wealth? But what if they have modest resources? Should only the rich run for office?

6. Can democracy be sustained when so few people are involved in the political system? Voter turnouts at local elections sometimes run less than ten percent, and yet local governments are the ones that affect people closely on a daily basis. Why don't more people vote?

THE CITIZEN'S ROLE

The basic building block of American political parties is the local organization. Look in your telephone book for the location of the county office of the party of your choice. Call the office to arrange a visit where you can learn what the local party does and how one can volunteer to help. You may choose to visit with your college campus' political party organizations instead.

1. Who runs this political party at the local level? Does it have a paid staff or volunteers?

2. What does the local office do between elections?

3. Did the local party officials encourage you to participate and volunteer your time?

4. What are the areas of greatest need for volunteers at this office?

5. Did you feel that you could participate in the local political party if you wanted to, or did you feel that it was a closed club? Explain.

GOVERNMENT IN YOUR LIFE

Visit the web site of one of these political parties: Democrats, Republicans, Libertarians, Greens, Peace and Freedom, Natural Law, Reform.

1. Did the site clearly explain the philosophy of the party? Explain its philosophy.

2. Did the site clearly explain the party's position on major issues? List the issues and give the party's position.

3. If this is a minor party, what was the basis for its separation from the two major parties? Does the minor party have any issues that might be taken over by one of the major parties? Explain.
4. If this is a major party, does the web site emphasize middle-of-the-road or more extremist policies? Explain.
5. Do political parties, in your opinion, want to discuss issues or personalities with the American public? Explain.

ANSWER KEY

Fill-in-the-Blank Quiz

1. platforms
2. third parties
3. two-party system
4. national convention
5. party identification
6. soft money
7. single-member district
8. responsible party government, divided government
9. plurality system
10. policy entrepreneur
11. majority, minority
12. patronage
13. proportional representation
14. nomination
15. caucuses
16. multiple-member district
17. party organization, party activists
18. political parties
19. machines

Multiple-Choice Quiz

1. b
2. c
3. c
4. c
5. a
6. d
7. c
8. a
9. c
10. b
11. c
12. d
13. b
14. a
15. b
16. a
17. c
18. b
19. c
20. a
21. e
22. a
23. d
24. b
25. b
26. d
27. a
28. c
29. b
30. a
31. c
32. b
33. d
34. d
35. a
36. d
37. a

CHAPTER 10 | Campaigns and Elections

THE CHAPTER IN BRIEF

Today in the United States, all native-born or naturalized citizens over the age of eighteen, with the exception of convicted felons, have the right to vote in all national and local elections. It was not always this way. Voting was restricted in the past in many states to white male property owners. In 1870, the adoption of the Fifteenth Amendment gave African Americans the right to vote, but many southern states blocked that right with the discriminatory use of poll taxes and literacy tests. Since most southern blacks were poor and illiterate, they could not vote until the 1965 Voting Rights Act removed those restrictions. Women won the right to vote in 1920 with the adoption of the Nineteenth Amendment. Women had lobbied for the vote for a half-century, but their cause was advanced by World War I, when the president and Congress felt that women would get behind the war effort if they had a say in politics. A final step in expanding the vote came when the voting age was lowered from twenty-one to eighteen in 1971 with the adoption of the Twenty-sixth Amendment. States now have limited, if any, power in determining who is eligible to vote.

Though virtually every American adult has the right to vote, American voter participation is very low compared to participation in European countries, but it is generally greater in presidential elections than in state and local elections. Registration requirements tend to diminish the size of the electorate. America's weak party system also contributes to lower voter turnout because party workers are not out mobilizing eligible voters. For that reason, the American electorate is smaller and more skewed toward the middle and upper classes.

Americans participate in three types of elections as well as other voting processes. Primary elections are used to select each party's candidates for the general election. In some states only the registered members of a political party may vote in a primary election to select that party's candidates. This is called a 'closed primary." Other states allow al registered voters to decide in which party's primary they will participate. This is called an "open primary." The general election that follows is the decisive electoral contest. The winner is elected to office for a specified term. In some southern states, the law specifies that if no candidate wins an absolute majority in the primary election, a runoff must be held between the two candidates with the largest numbers of votes. The referendum is a process that allows citizens to vote directly on proposed laws or other governmental actions. An election is an institution of representative government, and a referendum is an institution of direct democracy, where voters govern directly without intervention by government officials. The validity of referenda results, however, are subject to judicial action.

There are several criteria for winning an election. In a majority system, a candidate must receive 50 percent plus one of all the votes, with provisions for a runoff in the case of more than two candidates. In a plurality system, the winning candidate is the one who receives the largest number of votes. This system is used in virtually all general elections in the United States. Most European nations employ proportional representation, which awards legislative seats to competing political parties roughly in proportion to the actual percentage of the popular votes each received. Proportional representation is conducive to multiparty systems.

Electoral districts are redrawn every ten years in response to population changes determined by the decennial census. The character of district boundaries is influenced by federal court decisions. Gerrymandering is a term for the American parties' way of manipulating electoral outcomes by organizing electoral districts in their favor, despite judicial intervention. However, since 1993 the Supreme Court has undermined efforts to create "minority" districts.

Prior to the 1890s, voters cast ballots according to political parties. Because only one party's candidates appeared on a given ballot, voters had no way to cast anything other than a straight party vote. The advent of the neutral ballot, prepared and administered by the state rather than the parties, allowed voters to decide based on individual, rather than collective, merits of the parties' candidates. It decreased the chance that electoral decisions could lead to policy change and led to increasingly divided partisan control of government.

America's electoral college is composed of those designated to formally elect the president and vice president of the United States. It is a form of indirect voting and is a relic of the early days when it was assumed that ordinary citizens were not qualified and could not be trusted to choose their leaders directly, and so would elect representatives to cast intelligent votes on their behalf. Each state today is entitled to a number of electoral votes equal to the number of the state's senators and representatives combined, for a total of 535 electoral votes for the fifty states. In the event that no candidate receives a majority of all electoral votes, the names of the top three candidates are submitted to the House, where each state, regardless of size, is able to cast one vote. In the event of an election resulting in a discrepancy between the electoral and popular outcomes, there would be much political pressure to eliminate the electoral college and introduce direct popular election of the president.

Election campaigns are expensive, and a candidate's first step is to organize groups who will work to raise the necessary funds. The second step involves recruiting advisers and creating a formal campaign organization. Advisers include a campaign manager, a media consultant, a pollster, a financial adviser, a press spokesperson, and a staff director to coordinate the activities of thousands of volunteers and paid workers in order to mobilize support and raise funds. A campaign's third step is polling, in which surveys of voter opinion provide the basic information candidates and their staffs use to develop campaign strategies.

The next step in most campaigns (for all offices but the presidency) is the primary elections, which determine which candidates will receive the Democratic or Republican nomination. There are two types of primary campaigns. The personality clash is a competing effort by ambitious individuals to secure election to office. This type of campaign can enhance voter interest, producing a candidate with the capacity to win the general election. The ideological struggle occurs when one wing of a party decides that an incumbent is too willing to compromise or too moderate in his or her political views; this struggle can undermine a party's general election chances by producing a candidate that is too extreme to win in the general election.

Presidential nominations follow a different pattern from that for other offices. Ten states begin with a caucus, a form of nominating process that begins with precinct-level meetings throughout a state; the rest hold primaries. Both are an attempt by candidates to capture national convention delegates. Before a nomination is actually awarded, the national party convention is held for the purpose of formally certifying each party's presidential and vice presidential nominees. The conventions draft a party platform, which is a statement of party principles. In the first years of our nation's history, presidential nominations were controlled by each party's congressional caucus, but they failed to take into account the views of party members throughout the nation. Party conventions were devised in the 1830s as a way of allowing party leaders and activists throughout the nation to participate in selecting presidential candidates. Until World War II, national convention delegates were selected by state party leaders, and nomination required two-thirds of the convention delegates. In contemporary party conventions, nomination is determined by primary elections and local party caucuses and is ratified within the convention, where party rules are adopted and the platform is drafted.

Convention delegates are generally political activists with strong positions on social and economic issues. Republican delegates tend to be more liberal than Democratic voters. The primaries determine how a state's delegation will vote. Conventions last several days. First, there is the selection of party committees, then the convention chairperson is elected. Nomination speeches follow, and then a vote is taken. Television networks carry convention highlights to the public, and the parties are eager to receive as much media coverage as possible. After the nominations are formalized, there is a big celebration, and the presidential and vice presidential nominees deliver their acceptance speeches. (The vice presidential candidate is selected by the presidential nominee, and the choice is ratified by the convention.) The speeches are carefully designed to make a good impression on the general electorate.

The general election is the last step in the attainment of office. There are two types of general election campaign, the labor intensive and the capital intensive. Local and congressional campaigns are usually of the first type, labor intensive, depending on hard work designed to enhance the visibility of the candidates rather than on issues and policy proposals. Statewide campaigns, some congressional races, and the presidential race fall into the second category, capital intensive, which is media driven. The idea is to present to voters themes and issues that will induce them to support one candidate rather than the other.

Candidates use television in many ways, including the talk-show interview, the "electronic town hall meeting," the "infomercial," and debates. Television presents the candidates and the issues to more people than any other medium. It takes enormous amounts of money to fuel a media campaign. The money comes from various sources: direct mail contributions, large individual gifts, political action committees, candidates' personal or family resources, and political parties.

Campaign financing is regulated by the Federal Campaign Act of 1971. Interest groups provide money to campaigns in hopes that candidates will show support for their views and needs. A wide variety of interest groups finance political campaigns toward their own ends. However, not all interests are represented; many lack the money to contribute.

No matter who has the money and power, it is ultimately the voters who decide electoral outcomes. There are three main factors that influence voters' choices: partisan loyalty, or an identification with either the Democratic Party or the Republican Party; issues, where voters choose a candidate whose views are similar to their own; and candidate characteristics, where candidates' personal attributes, such as looks or personality, race or ethnicity, religion, gender, and social background, attract voters.

Voting has declined in this country, and it is not so much the voters' fault as it is the politicians' for failing to mobilize voters. Instead of engaging voters, opposing political forces use other methods such as congressional investigations, media revelations, and judicial proceedings to govern. It is not as if politicians don't know how to mobilize voters, it is that both sides prefer to compete for power without engaging in full-scale popular mobilization. Unfortunately, this is a political process with obvious class bias. Today's political process in America is less than democratic.

REVIEW QUESTIONS

1. What are the key principles of the election process?
2. Discuss the institutional developments that made it possible for African Americans and women to vote. What was the most recent expansion of suffrage in the United States?

3. What are the requirements to vote in the United States? What powers do states have in the election process?
4. Describe split-ticket voting.
5. How did the actions of the Progressives affect voter turnout? What recent bill has been passed to ease such restrictions?
6. Explain the different types of elections held in the United States. Describe the referendum voting process. Is it a election? Why or why not?
7. Define a plurality electoral system.
8. Define proportional representation. Whom does it generally benefit?
9. How are electoral districts determined? How have state legislatures sought to manipulate this process to their advantage? Has the Supreme Court upheld this?
10. Explain America's indirect election. Who are the electors? How do they determine for whom they will cast their vote? Is it always consistent with the popular vote?
11. Explain the role of advisers, polling, and primaries in a campaign.
12. What effect can an ideological struggle have on a political party?
13. Explain the presidential nomination process.
14. What was the "King Caucus"? Why did it fail?
15. In most states, how are delegates chosen? What are their duties?
16. What effect can media coverage of a convention have on a candidate?
17. How is campaign finance regulated? Is it necessary? Why or why not?
18. From what sources do candidates receive money for a political campaign? What types of interests do PACs represent?
19. What factors influence voter decisions?
20. Explain the ımpact on democracy from low voter turnout.
21. Can we really claim to be a nation that values equality if large numbers of people do not exercise their right to vote—the very essence of political equality?

KEY TERMS

benign gerrymandering
campaign
caucus (political)
closed caucus

closed primary
coattail effect
delegates
electoral college
gerrymandering
incumbent
infomercial
issues advocacy
majority system
midterm elections
minority district
open caucus
open primary
platform
plurality system
political action comı
poll tax
primary elections
proportional representation
prospective voting
referendum
retrospective voting
soft money
split-ticket voting
suffrage
superdelegates
town meeting
turnout
unit rule
winner-take-all system

FILL-IN-THE-BLANK QUIZ

Use the key terms to complete the following sentences.

1. An electoral system that declares the person with the most votes to be the winner is a ____________ system; one that requires the winner to have over 50 percent of the total vote is a ____________ system.
2. An internal party document outlining the political party's position on current issues is a ____________.
3. Drawing electoral districts in a way that benefits a certain party is ____________, but if it is done to achieve racial balance, it is called ____________.
4. A closed party meeting known as a(n) ____________ can allow anyone in (called a(n) ____________) or can be limited only to registered party members (a(n) ____________).
5. Offyear elections, also called ____________ elections, draw fewer voters than presidential elections.
6. A private group that raises funds for candidates is a ____________.
7. The ____________ was outlawed by the Twenty-fourth Amendment.
8. When Ross Perot bought thirty minutes of television time to explain why he believed the federal deficit should be cut, he was actually producing a(n) ____________.
9. Officially, the president and vice president are elected by the ____________.

10. Mary Hansen has never run for political office before, but you vote for her because you think she shows the potential to be a good senator. You have engaged in ____________ voting.
11. A synonym for the right to vote is ____________.
12. Funds given to conduct voter registration drives which are not accountable under the federal election laws are called ____________.
13. American voter ____________ is much lower than most other democratic nations.
14. In some states the voters are able to vote directly on legislation through a process called the ____________.
15. Another way to get around campaign finance laws is to provide commercials that do not directly name a candidate but make it clear which candidate they agree with. This is called ____________.
16. Voting for a candidate because you like what he did in his first term is ____________ voting.
17. If you can vote only in the primary election of the party you belong to, your state has a(n) ____________ primary; if you can choose the party ballot when you cast the vote, your states has a(n) ____________ primary.
18. The Democratic party selects delegates using two methods: ____________ and ____________.
19. If all political party convention delegates must vote according to the majority, the convention uses the ____________.
20. You vote for a Republican for president but a Democrat for Congress. You have engaged in ____________.
21. When Lyndon Johnson won by a large margin in 1964, the momentum carried many other Democrats into office as well. This is known as the ____________.
22. Political activists who are selected to attend the party's convention are called ____________.
23. All of your state's electoral votes go to the winning candidate. Your state uses the ____________ system of awarding votes.
24. An open forum in which candidates can answer questions from the audience, with no journalists as intermediaries, is a ____________.
25. You want to be governor, but first you must win support from donors, political activists, and voters. You have to ____________ for the office.

26. The person who already holds the office is the ___________ and has a significant advantage over the challengers.

27. Candidates for the general elections are chosen in ___________ elections.

28. The purpose of benign gerrymandering is to create a ___________.

MULTIPLE-CHOICE QUIZ

1. The most recent expansion of the suffrage in the United States took place in ___________, during the Vietnam War, when the Twenty-sixth Amendment was ratified, lowering the voting age from twenty-one to eighteen.
   a. 1964
   b. 1971
   c. 1975
   d. 1980

2. In America, slightly more than ___________ percent of those eligible participate in national presidential elections, while ___________ percent of those eligible vote in midterm congressional elections. The comparable national voter turnout in European countries is usually between 80 and 90 percent.
   a. 33, 20
   b. 33, 50
   c. 50, 33
   d. 66, 50

3. The boundaries for congressional and state legislative districts in the United States are redrawn by the states every ___________ years in response to population changes determined by the census.
   a. two
   b. ten
   c. twenty
   d. twenty-five

4. State legislators routinely seek to influence electoral outcomes by manipulating the organization of electoral districts. This strategy is called:
   a. reapportionment.
   b. the "one person, one vote" doctrine.
   c. gerrymandering.
   d. benign gerrymandering.

5. In this 1993 court case, the Supreme Court began to undermine efforts to create minority districts.
   a. *Shaw v. Reno*
   b. *Mapp v. Ohio*
   c. *Reno v. UCLA*
   d. *Baker v. Carr*

6. Traditionally, the first state to hold a presidential caucus is ___________, and the first state to hold a presidential primary is ___________.
   a. California, Maine
   b. Iowa, New Hampshire
   c. Maine, California
   d. Pennsylvania, Maine

7. Between the 1830s and World War II, national convention delegates were generally selected by:

a. a state's party leaders.
b. state legislatures.
c. primary elections.
d. direct primaries.

8. In 1996, political candidates spent a total of more than ____________ on election campaigns.
   a. one million dollars
   b. one billion dollars
   c. one trillion dollars
   d. none of the above; such data are not collected

9. Individuals may donate a maximum of ____________ to any single candidate, a political action committee can donate ____________ to each candidate.
   a. $500, $5,000
   b. $1,000, $5,000
   c. $10,000, $50,000
   d. $100,000, $500,000

10. This 1993 legislation requires all states to allow voters to register by mail when they renew their driver's licenses.
    a. the Voter Registration Act
    b. the "Rock the Vote" Act
    c. the Motor Voter Bill
    d. the State Voter Renewal Bill

11. Suffrage is another term for:
    a. what has happened to minority groups in the United States over time.
    b. the right to vote.
    c. democracy.
    d. party identification.

12. Congressional elections that do not coincide with presidential elections are sometimes called:
    a. midterm elections.
    b. unimportant.
    c. secondary elections.
    d. off-year elections.

13. In the American federal system, the responsibility for organizing elections:
    a. rests largely with Congress.
    b. is constitutionally defined.
    c. is defined in federal statutes.
    d. rests largely with state and local governments.

14. America's rate of voter participation, or turnout, is:
    a. low.
    b. very low.
    c. high.
    d. very high.

15. These are used to select each party's candidates for the general election.
    a. primary elections
    b. closed primaries
    c. open primaries
    d. all of the above

16. This type of election system is used in virtually all general elections in the United States.
    a. majority system
    b. plurality system
    c. proportional representation
    d. cumulative voting

17. An effort by political candidates and their supporters to win the backing of donors, political activists, and voters in their quest for political office is the authors' definition of:
    a. a campaign.
    b. incumbency.
    c. subsystem politics.
    d. interest group liberalism.

18. A current office-holder is called:
    a. a party official.
    b. a "partisan."
    c. an incumbent.
    d. all of the above.

19. In most states, how do independent and third-party candidates qualify for the general election ballot?
    a. by paying a small "filing fee" with a state's Secretary of State.
    b. by winning a primary election in which all independent and third-party candidates are on the ballot.
    c. by obtaining thousands of petition signatures.
    d. by qualifying automatically.

20. Most states use ____________ to choose national convention delegates.
    a. primary elections
    b. state legislatures
    c. general elections
    d. caucuses

21. The Democratic Party requires that state presidential primaries allocate delegates on the basis of:
    a. one person, one vote.
    b. the unit rule.
    c. winner-take-all.
    d. proportional representation.

22. What is a superdelegate?
    a. reserved slots at the Democratic national convention for elected Democratic officials
    b. reserved slots at the Republican national convention for elected Republican officials
    c. a delegate at a national party convention
    d. a delegate at a national party convention that has two votes

23. Ross Perot's thirty-minute TV programs are examples of:
    a. infomercials.
    b. spot advertisements.
    c. use of a media "visual."
    d. town meetings.

24. They are organizations established by corporations, labor unions, or interest groups to channel the contributions of their members into political campaigns.
    a. special interest groups
    b. political action committees
    c. congressional campaign committees
    d. so-called "soft money" cartels

25. According to the authors, which of the following is not one of the three types of factors that influence voters' decisions at the polls?
    a. partisanship
    b. issues
    c. candidate characteristics
    d. the electoral system used to select candidates

26. If you were to create a "democratic" electoral system, which characteristic would you value most highly?
    a. The electoral system uses proportional representation.
    b. The electoral system allows for opposition.
    c. The electoral system allows for the election of women and minorities.

   d. The electoral system does not allow the use of poll taxes and literacy exams.

27. Which of the following is a function of elections?
   a. They serve as institutions of legitimization.
   b. They serve as valves for social discontent.
   c. They promote leadership accountability.
   d. all of the above

28. Why were registration requirements instituted at the end of the nineteenth century?
   a. They were instituted to increase the number of eligible voters.
   b. The Democrats wanted to disenfranchise Republicans.
   c. They replaced poll taxes and literacy exams as requirements for voting.
   d. Progressives hoped to make voting more difficult both to reduce corruption and to reduce lower-class voting.

29. Which of the following is a result of registration requirements?
   a. The size of the electorate is diminished.
   b. Those who register are of higher education and income.
   c. Fewer minorities vote.
   d. all of the above

30. Which of the following helps explain low rates of voter turnout in the United States?
   a. the demise of political machines
   b. the absence of strong political parties
   c. the use of proportional representation electoral systems
   d. all of the above
   e. only a and b

31. In the general election you vote for the Democratic Party candidate for U.S. Senator, the Republican Party candidate for president, and an independent candidate for governor. This is an example of:
   a. straight-ticket voting.
   b. a blanket primary.
   c. a direct primary.
   d. split-ticket voting.

32. Straight-ticket voting occurs most often when a voter casts a ballot for a presidential candidate and then "automatically" votes for the remainder of the party's candidates. The result of this voting pattern is known as the:
   a. Hawthorne effect.
   b. "yellow dog" effect.
   c. "pull" effect.
   d. coattail effect.

33. The state of Oklahoma has six members in the U.S. House of Representatives. How many electoral votes does Oklahoma have?
   a. 2
   b. 6
   c. 8
   d. can't tell from this information

QUESTIONS FOR DISCUSSION AND THOUGHT

1. Do you think democracy is endangered by the need to raise huge amounts of money to run for public office? Is the need for big money leading to less democracy—that is, government by special interests? Would you support public financing of campaigns?

2. Should race be taken into account when congressional districts are redrawn after each census? If twenty percent of a state is African American, should twenty percent of the districts have an African American majority?

3. Do you think it is okay for someone with a lot of money but no political experience, like Ross Perot or Steve Forbes, to run for president of the United States? Which is more important for a candidate to have: ambition or experience? Candidates today like to define themselves as "outsiders"; do we want nonprofessional politicians in Washington?

4. When you vote, which is more important to you: a candidate's personality and character or his or her stand on the issues? Would you rather vote for a candidate with character problems but with a strong vision that you agree with, or a candidate with excellent personal character but who has little vision or sense of where he or she wants to take the nation? Do you vote for a candidate you really like, or for the candidate you dislike the least?

5. Our current campaign advertising system markets candidates just like we market automobiles and beverages. Should we require that no "fancy stuff" be allowed in their TV ads, that they should stand in front of the camera and explain their stands on the issues? Should candidates be forbidden to use "negative advertising"? Should television networks be mandated to provide free political advertising? What problems might occur in constructing and implementing such a rule?

6. Why is voter turnout so low in the United States? What are the consequences of low levels of voter turnout? Some European critics charge that the United States cannot claim to be a democracy when so few of its citizens actually vote. Is there any basis to this charge?

THE CITIZEN'S ROLE

Senator Phil Gramm once said that money was the "mother's milk" of politics. To see just how much money is going into campaigns, visit the web site for the Federal Election Commission or http://www.tray.com for a site that is easier to use. Select one member of the House of Representatives or the Senate and his or her opponent and analyze their sources of funding.

1. How much money did they raise last year?
2. How much money came from out-of-state donors?
3. How much difference was there between the two candidates in amount of money raised?
4. If one candidate was an incumbent, was there a clear difference between the fund-raising of the two candidates?
5. How important is money to the election process? Did the candidate with the most money win?

GOVERNMENT IN YOUR LIFE

Below are ten questions selected from a literacy test given by a southern state during the time of segregation.

1. A United States senator elected at the general election in November takes office the following year on what date? ____________
2. The Constitution limits the size of the District of Columbia to ____________.
3. The electoral vote for president is counted in the presence of two bodies. Name them. 1: ____________ 2: ____________
4. Of the original thirteen states, the one with the largest representation in the First Congress was ____________.
5. If election of the president becomes the duty of the United States House of Representatives and it fails to act, who becomes president and when? ____________
6. If a state is party to a case, the Constitution provides that original jurisdiction shall be in ____________.
7. If an effort to impeach the president of the United States is made, who presides at the trial? ____________
8. When the Constitution was approved by the original colonies, how many states had to ratify it in order for it to be in effect? ____________
9. Persons opposed to swearing in an oath may say instead, "I solemnly ____________."
10. If it were proposed to join Alabama and Mississippi to form one state, what groups would have to vote approval in order for this to be done? ____________

Answer the questions below.

1. Do you think that these questions were reasonable to ask potential voters?
2. What was your score (see answers below)? Do you think you can be an informed voter, even if your score was low? Explain.
3. What was the real purpose of this test?
4. Is there anything wrong in expecting voters to be informed about the Constitution?
5. Do you think most Americans could pass this test? What does that say about the state of constitutional knowledge?

Answers

1. January 3 at noon
2. Ten square miles
3. House of Representatives, Senate
4. Virginia
5. Vice president, January 20 at noon
6. United States Supreme Court
7. Chief Justice of the Supreme Court
8. Nine
9. Affirm
10. United States Congress and both state legislatures

ANSWER KEY

Fill-in-the-Blank Quiz

1. plurality, majority
2. platform
3. gerrymandering, benign gerrymandering
4. caucus, open caucus, closed caucus
5. midterm
6. political action committee
7. poll tax
8. infomercial
9. electoral college
10. prospective
11. suffrage
12. soft money
13. turnout
14. referendum
15. issues advocacy
16. retrospective
17. closed, open
18. proportional representation, superdelegates
19. unit rule
20. split-ticket voting
21. coattail effect
22. delegates
23. winner-take-all

24. town meeting
25. campaign
26. incumbent
27. primary
28. minority district

Multiple-Choice Quiz

1. b
2. c
3. b
4. c
5. a
6. b
7. a
8. b
9. b
10. c
11. b
12. a
13. d
14. b
15. a
16. b
17. a
18. c
19. c
20. a
21. d
22. a
23. a
24. b
25. d
26. b
27. d
28. d
29. d
30. e
31. d
32. d
33. c

CHAPTER 11 Groups and Interests

THE CHAPTER IN BRIEF

An interest group is a group of people drawn or acting together because of a common interest, concern, or purpose. Interest groups have been an important part of the American experience since the early days of the country. Citizens get together in voluntary associations and engage in politics long enough to put things right when a threat to their community or way of life is perceived. The Minutemen of the American Revolution were an early interest group. Trade and business associations were more permanent groups that evolved later against perceived threats from unions. In politics these groups came to be called "pressure groups," "lobbies," and "interest groups," but politics was only an occasional activity; basically, they were groups of people with shared interests. These groups are an extremely significant component of a free society. They exert influence over the political process wherever power exists, and since the 1930s such political activity has been primarily at the national level. Groups are important contributors to political candidates and parties in election campaigns. Organized groups with a lot of money have the power to influence legislators, but if governments were to interfere in any way in the political process, they would have the power to suppress freedom, so it is important that these groups have the freedom to compete for influence, and the outcome of this competition is compromise and moderation. The only flaw in this system is the class bias that occurs in favor of those with greater financial resources.

Groups are formed to increase the chance that their views will be heard and influence government decisions in their favor. There are many types of interest groups, such as business and agriculture groups, labor groups, professional associations, public interest groups, ideological groups, and government groups. Established groups generally have a strong organization, with leadership analogous to business leadership. They are organized by political entrepreneurs and generally have paid professional staffs. They get their money from membership dues, contributions, and the selling of ancillary services. Many have an agency or office, which can be a research organization, public relations office, or lobbying office, that carries on the group's tasks. All groups have members; in some groups, like the National Organization for Women, members serve on committees and engage in projects, while in others, like the Children's Defense Fund, a professional staff carries on the group's activities and members merely pay dues and make other contributions.

In order to recruit members, groups offer incentives to join. Selective benefits are available only to members, and could be in the form of special services or goods, or even money. Material benefits, such as insurance plans, are commonly used. Solidary, or psychological, benefits include friendship, networking opportunities, and consciousness-raising. Purposive benefits are those that appeal to the purpose of an interest group. Most groups face the "free rider" problem, which means that many nonmembers enjoy benefits of the efforts and contributions of others without effort on nonmembers' part. Such benefits are called "collective goods," or "public goods." An example is national defense, which benefits everyone regardless of the amount of taxes they pay or the support they give. In such situations, groups do not reduce their efforts, but try even harder to get free riders to join in their cause. Because the majority of members come from higher-income and highly educated groups, interest groups have a strong upper-class bias.

In the past twenty-five years there has been an enormous increase in the number of interest groups and in the extent of the influence. The expansion of the national government has led to interest-group activity that is a direct consequence of government action. For example, federal programs and court decisions on abortion and school prayer were stimuli for political action by fundamentalist religious groups. President Clinton's health care plan caused various groups of physicians, hospitals, and pharmaceutical and insurance companies to begin massive lobbying campaigns that presented their version of the public interest. Clinton knew that the Republicans opposed this effort (the health care plan) to expand the Democrats' political base, and the administration denounced all these special-interest activities.

The New Politics movement is a fairly new set of forces in American politics; a coalition of upper-middle-class professionals and intellectuals that formed during the 1960s in opposition to the Vietnam War and racial inequality. They called themselves "public interest" groups, and they focused on such issues as environmental protection, women's rights, and nuclear disarmament. They either constructed or strengthened Common Case, the Sierra Club, the Environmental Defense Fund, Physicians for Social Responsibility, the National Organization for Women, and Ralph Nader's consumer groups.

There are many strategies used by interest groups in their quest for political power. Going public is an attempt to mobilize the widest and most favorable climate of opinion. Institutional advertising places ads in magazines and newspapers to create positive associations between an organization and the community at large to muster support for future political campaigns. Social movements such as boycotts, mass rallies, and marches have been a very successful way of going public. In a grassroots lobbying campaign, a lobby group mobilizes its members and their families throughout the country to write or phone their group's representatives in support of the group's position.

Lobbying is an attempt by an individual or a group to influence the passage of legislation by exerting direct pressure on members of the legislature. There are several types of lobbyists: group members who go to Washington only for the duration of a campaign, professional lobbyists who live in Washington, and staff lobbyists—professionals who work full time for a particular interest group. All individuals lobbying the national government are required to register, and nonprofit organizations that receive federal grants or contracts are prohibited from using public funds to lobby the government. The lobbying industry consists of at least 1,800 associations in Washington, with new groups moving in all the time. Unions, commodity groups, trade associations, and business corporations keep representatives in Washington all the time. Besides lobbying the government, lobbies lobby one another, and Congress also brings pressure upon lobby groups to support particular courses of action.

Access is actual involvement in the decision-making process, and is usually a result of time and effort spent cultivating a position within the inner councils of government. This method of gaining access often requires the sacrifice of short-run influence. Corridoring is a term used for gaining access to the bureaucracy. One informal method is for private citizens to attend public hearings and take part in the discussions. Another method is participation as a member of an advisory committee of an agency, a method sometimes called "participatory democracy." "Influence peddling" is a negative term for the sale or rental of access by securing the services of certain important Washington lawyers and lobbyists.

Another strategy in the quest for political power is the use of the courts (litigation). This is used to affect public policy in at least three ways: by bringing suit directly on behalf of the group itself; by financing suits brought by individuals; and by filing a "friend of the court" (amicus) brief to an existing court case. The New Politics agenda was clearly visible in court decisions during the 1970s and 1980s. These decisions involved such things as environmental policy, consumer policy, civil rights policies, and antinuclear policy.

Interest groups frequently make use of electoral politics in gaining power. The most common way is by giving financial support to parties or to particular candidates. Groups also engage in campaign activism; interest groups work vigorously in election campaigns.

James Madison theorized on interest groups over two hundred years ago. He recognized that in a free society the organization and proliferation of interests is inevitable, and also, that to place limits on the organization of interests would be to limit liberty itself. What is true is that considerable competition exists among organized groups in the United States, and that interest-group politics is generally a form of political competition in which the rich and powerful are best able to engage. Also, interest groups more often represent relatively narrow, selfish interests. The dilemma: to regulate interest group politics is, as Madison warned, to limit freedom, and to expand governmental power. To not regulate interest group politics, on the other hand, may be to ignore equal justice. There is no ideal answer.

REVIEW QUESTIONS

1. What is the difference between a voluntary association and a pressure group or an interest group? Give examples.
2. How do special-interest contributions affect the behavior of United States legislators?
3. Compare ideological groups to public interest groups.
4. What is the difference between "membership associations" and "staff organizations"? What is the role of membership in both types of groups?
5. How does the "free rider" problem affect group involvement?
6. Explain why solidary benefits are also called psychological benefits, and give some examples.
7. How did the AARP overcome the "free rider" problem?
8. Why are interest groups controlled mainly by wealthier and better-educated citizens?
9. How is the expansion of government related to interest-group activity?
10. What public strategies were used by the Civil Rights groups in the 1950s and 1960s to influence government policy, and why were these strategies used rather than another type, such as lobbying?
11. Define lobbying. What is the origin of the term?
12. What is access, and how does an interest gain access to government?
13. Discuss the ways that interest groups can use the courts to affect public policy.
14. Why do business groups in particular see the courts as a means to effect policy changes?
15. How do organized groups seek influence in the context of electoral politics? How did the subject of abortion become such an important political issue?
16. What is the dilemma, as defined by James Madison, between liberty and equality as they apply to interest-group politics and government regulation?

17. Why is the statement that interest groups "speak with an upper-class accent" such a damning statement about democracy and equality? Do you see any way in which the rest of the people can organize and be effective in the political arena? Why or why not?

KEY TERMS

access
Astroturf lobbying
capture
collective good
corridoring
cross-lobbying
free rider
going public
grassroots lobbying
institutional advertising
iron triangle
issue network
lobbying
material benefits
membership associations
New Politics movement
pluralism
political action committee
public interest groups
reverse lobbying
soft money
solidary benefits
staff organization

FILL-IN-THE-BLANK QUIZ

Use the key terms to complete the following sentences.

1. The theory that the political system is dominated by interest groups that compete for political gain is called ____________.
2. The political movement that began in the 1960s and 1970s and formed public interest groups is the ____________ movement.
3. When a large group of the public becomes aroused by a political issue and send many letters and petitions to Congress, it is ____________ lobbying; when the letters and petitions are forged or faked by paid consultants, it is ____________.
4. Candidate Miller received a contribution of $5,000 from one source. That amount can only come from a ____________.
5. When one interest group tries to persuade another interest group to support its cause, it is engaging in ____________.
6. You are a government employee at the Department of Energy. A couple of times each week a lobbyist for the oil industry stops by to visit. She is probably ____________ at your agency. She is there because she is trying to develop ____________.

7. When many religious organizations work together to develop a strategy to overturn *Roe v. Wade*, they are forming a(n) ____________

8. I am very rich and I want to give lots of money to support my candidates. If I give money to my party to conduct voter registration drives, I am giving ____________.

9. The relationship between the Department of Education, the House Subcommittee on Education, and the National Education Association is a(n) ____________.

10. Many ____________ owe their vitality to the untiring efforts of Ralph Nader.

11. My college alumni association wants me to join so they are offering discounts on cruises and low rates on a Visa card. They are trying to tempt me to join by offering me ____________.

12. You are a lobbyist for the cotton growers, and a senator asks you for your support for an agriculture bill he wants to introduce. The senator is using ____________.

13. An ad in a magazine states that the Bull's-Eye stores give 5 percent of their after-tax profits to charity. The firm is using ____________ to enhance its image.

14. Joe refuses to join the teacher's union, but the union negotiates pay and benefits for all teachers, even nonmembers. Joe likes to get the advantages without paying the cost. Joe is a(n) ____________.

15. An interest group strategy that tries to mobilize public opinion in its support is called ____________.

16. If the farm programs at the Department of Agriculture reflect the interests and biases of the livestock producers to the virtual exclusion of all others, that agency has been ____________ by an interest group.

17. Clean air is a ____________ that is shared with anyone in the area, not just those who have paid to clean it up.

18. Organized interests that seek to gain influence in the legislative process are engaged in ____________.

19. I like to go to my AARP bridge club each week because I enjoy seeing my many friends in the organization. AARP is offering me ____________.

20. An interest group that asks little of its members beyond paying dues is probably a(n) ____________.

MULTIPLE-CHOICE QUIZ

1. This 33 million-member interest group is very powerful and represents the interests of older Americans.
   a. NOW
   b. NRA
   c. AARP
   d. AFL-CIO

2. In their box insert entitled, "Losing Money Left and Right," the authors tell the story of how this private sector firm was attacked by both the political left and right over the issue of gay and lesbian rights.
   a. Coca-Cola
   b. IBM
   c. Mobil Oil Company
   d. Coors Beer

3. General Motors is an example of a ___________ interest group, the AFL-CIO is an example of a ___________ interest group, and the American Bar Association is an example of a ___________ interest group.
   a. professional association, business, labor
   b. business, professional association, labor
   c. business, labor, professional association
   d. labor, professional association, business_

4. Common Cause is an example of a(n) ___________ interest group, the National Taxpayers Union is an example of a(n) ___________ interest group, and the Brookings Institution is an example of a(n) ___________ interest group.
   a. public-interest, ideological, public-sector
   b. ideological, public-interest, public-sector
   c. public-sector, public-interest, ideological
   d. ideological, public-sector, public-interest

5. According to the authors of the text, which of the following is *not* a key organizational component of interest groups?
   a. money
   b. members who are political officials
   c. leadership
   d. membership

6. Benefits that are broadly available and cannot be reasonably denied to others is the definition of:
   a. constituent goods.
   b. regulative goods.
   c. collective goods.
   d. universalistic goods.

7. What is a "free rider"?
   a. an interest group that files an *amicus curiae* brief
   b. a person who enjoys the benefits of an action or service without any effort on his/her part
   c. an economic term that means a person receives the services distributed by a monopoly
   d. a member of a "public-interest" group

8. Interest groups offer numerous incentives to members to join. Friendship would be an example of a(n):
   a. informational benefit.
   b. material benefit.
   c. solidary benefit.
   d. purposive benefit.

9. Over the past twenty-five years, the number of interest groups in America has:
   a. increased.
   b. increased enormously.
   c. decreased.
   d. decreased enormously.

10. An attempt by an individual or a group to influence the passage of legislation by exerting direct pressure on members of the legislature is the definition of:
    a. "strong-arm" tactics.
    b. lobbying.
    c. *amicus curiae.*
    d. subsystem politics.

11. Which of the following are the requisite parts of a so-called "iron triangle"?
    a. state, local, and federal governments
    b. the president, the secretary of defense, and the secretary of state
    c. an executive agency, a congressional committee or subcommittee, and an interest group
    d. an interest group, the president, and Congress

12. When an agency falls under the influence of an interest group it is said to be:
    a. "captured."
    b. "coopted."
    c. "wayward."
    d. "unresponsive."

13. The term "*amicus curiae*" means:
    a. send the records of a case up.
    b. national supremacy.
    c. friend of the court.
    d. mechanical jurisprudence.

14. A strategy that attempts to mobilize the widest and most favorable climate of opinion is the definition of:
    a. internal mobilization.
    b. direct intervention.
    c. external mobilization.
    d. going public.

15. Which of the following can be used by interest groups to "go public"?
    a. institutional advertising
    b. social movements
    c. grassroots mobilization
    d. all of the above

16. According to the authors of the text, by far the most common *electoral strategy* employed by interest groups is that of:
    a. staging protests aided by the media.
    b. giving money to political parties or to particular candidates.
    c. direct-mail advertising.
    d. lobbying Congress.

17. According to the authors of the text, forming PACs and contributing to the campaign coffers of candidates is basically a strategy of buying:
    a. access.
    b. votes.

c. Congresspeople.
d. information.

18. In the 1830s, Alexis de Tocqueville observed that Americans were not particularly civic-minded most of the time and were happy to go their individual ways seeking their fortunes as opportunity and imagination drove them. But, like the minutemen of the Revolution, when a threat to their community or way of life was perceived, Americans mobilized into:
    a. "voluntary associations."
    b. "involuntary associations."
    c. "permanent associations."
    d. "interest groups."

19. According to James Madison, a good constitution:
    a. prohibits the formation of interest groups or "factions."
    b. encourages multitudes of interests so that no single interest can ever tyrannize the others.
    c. should be silent on the issue of the formation of interest groups; such groups should not be regulated in a free society.
    d. should protect the rights of interest groups in a bill of rights.

20. Today, James Madison's interest group theory is called:
    a. subsystem politics.
    b. interest group liberalism.
    c. pluralism.
    d. interest group dynamics.

21. Which statement below best captures the essence of the following quote: "The flaw in the pluralist heaven is that the heavenly chorus sings with a strong upper-class accent"?
    a. Pluralism is biased in favor of those with greater financial resources.
    b. Only groups who have many resources capture the attention of policy makers.
    c. The upper-class feels obligated to pursue redistributive policies to correct market inequities.
    d. all of the above

22. According to the authors, in general, to obtain adequate political representation, forces from the bottom rungs of the socioeconomic ladder must be organized on the massive scale associated with:
    a. political parties.
    b. interest groups.
    c. charismatic leaders.
    d. "public" interest groups.

23. According to the authors, the explosion of interest-group activity in the United States has been the result of:
    a. the concomitant growth in the power of American political parties.
    b. the increasing importance of the election as a "linkage institution."
    c. the expansion of the role of government.
    d. the decline of "public interest" groups.

24. Which of the following is true about the so-called "New Politics" movement?

a. The movement is made up of the poor and lower socioeconomic strata of American society.
b. The membership seeks particular benefits for specific groups (e.g., prayer in school for religious members, a balanced budget for fiscal conservatives).
c. The movement is overwhelmingly supportive of the status quo and the political system.
d. The movement is made up of upper-middle-class professionals and intellectuals for whom the civil rights and antiwar movements were formative experiences.

25. What is meant by the concept "cross-lobbying"?
    a. It occurs when one lobby lobbies another lobby.
    b. It occurs when an interest group lobbies the legislative and executive branches simultaneously.
    c. It occurs when an interest group lobbies the courts.
    d. all of the above

26. If an interest group is "corridoring," it is trying to gain access to the:
    a. courts.
    b. president.
    c. Congress.
    d. bureaucracy.

27. In terms of the public policy process, what is the significance of the concept "iron triangle"?
    a. Policy is disproportionately made at the subsystem level.
    b. Policy is particularistic in nature rather than aimed at the "public interest."
    c. Policies made through iron triangle processes can lead to a runaway budget.
    d. all of the above

28. I run a Washington-based consulting firm. An interest group hires my firm to persuade Congress not to pass a particular bill. I use mailing lists and send to members of Congress thousands of letters showing "an outpouring of opposition to the bill." In many cases the individuals whose names were on the letters had no strong feelings or even no opinion about the bill. This process is called:
    a. deceptive advertising.
    b. Astroturf lobbying.
    c. direct-mail advertising.
    d. negative lobbying.

QUESTIONS FOR DISCUSSION AND THOUGHT

1. A continuing problem for interest groups is the "free-rider" problem. The free rider is one who receives the benefits of a group but does not join it. An example is a worker who does not join the labor union but still receives the union-negotiated wages, benefits, and vacations. Unions, of course, want anyone who receives the benefits to belong to the organization (this is called

a "closed shop"). Many states have passed "right to work" laws that forbid a closed shop. What do you think? Should people who enjoy the benefits of a union be required to join? Can a union be effective if people are not required to join?

2. The tobacco lobby has always been one of the largest and most powerful in Washington. Not only does it give money to strategic legislators, it has had the strong support of those who have tobacco farmers in their districts. But suddenly tobacco is on the defensive. It has lost some important cases in court and has paid huge settlements to some of the states. Why do you think the tobacco lobby lost its power? Does its loss of influence predict the fall of other powerful lobbies such as social security, education, national defense, etc.? Why or why not?

3. Some observers believe that interest groups in America are slowly eroding democracy—that is, most groups are interested only in personal gain, not the national interest. Countries like Japan and Germany have very few interest groups and are thus able to make decisions more quickly with a view toward the public interest. What arguments can you think of in favor of our pluralist (interest-group-driven) type of government? Now list all the ways you can think of in which interest groups impede democracy. Which system would you prefer: one with many groups or one with few?

4. What is the public interest? Do the public interest spokesmen, such as Ralph Nader, represent your own interests? For example, Nader has opposed the NAFTA treaty with Mexico, air bags, and nuclear power. He has also worked tirelessly for automobile safety, the right to get information from the government, and exposing scientific frauds. Is this the "public interest" or just the interests of another special group?

5. James Madison asserted that in a free society the clash among competing interests, each pursuing selfish goals, would result in policies that served the common good. Is free competition among competing interests actually the best way to promote the common good? Is such free competition typical in the United States today?

THE CITIZEN'S ROLE

To illustrate how interest groups work to gain members, compare two groups using their web sites. First, look at the AARP site (http://www.aarp.org) and then turn to the State Public Interest Research Groups' site at http://www.igc.apc.org/pirg. Then answer the following questions.

1. How much does it cost to join each group? How is the membership money spent?

2. What benefits (informational, material, solidary, or purposive) are offered by AARP?
3. What benefits are offered by the PIRGs?
4. What political issues are important to AARP? To the PIRGs?
5. By looking at their web sites, who do you think these groups are appealing to? Is there a socioeconomic bias in their presentations? If so, what is it?

GOVERNMENT IN YOUR LIFE

In 1998, the Congress considered a bill that was aimed at restricting tobacco use, especially among teenagers. The key provisions were: a $1.10 tax hike per pack over five years; giving the Food and Drug Administration the power to regulate tobacco as a drug; banning tobacco billboards near schools; prohibiting the use of color and cartoons in ads; placing penalties on companies for failing to achieve reductions in teen smoking; limiting smoking in public places because of the effects of second-hand smoke; and limiting the liability damages against the industry to $6.5 billion a year. The bill was killed after the tobacco industry spent $50 million on an ad campaign opposing the bill.

Analyze the bill by completing the chart below, identifying those groups or individuals in society who would have gained and those who would have lost if the bill had been passed.

Potential winners	Potential losers

1. Is the list unbalanced, or does one side have a greater advantage? Explain.
2. In terms of the general public, which side do you think would have gained the most?
3. In terms of narrow-focus interest groups, which side do you think would have gained the most?

4. In your opinion, which side has the stronger argument? Why? What is the basis of your opinion?

5. Does our political system operate on the basis of self-interest? Explain.

ANSWER KEY

Fill-in-the-Blank Quiz

1. pluralism
2. New Politics
3. grassroots, Astroturf
4. political action committee
5. cross-lobbying
6. corridoring, access
7. issue network
8. soft money
9. iron triangle
10. public interest groups
11. material benefits
12. reverse lobbying
13. institutional advertising
14. free rider
15. going public
16. captured
17. collective good
18. lobbying
19. solidary benefits
20. staff organization

Multiple-Choice Quiz

1. c
2. d
3. c
4. a
5. b
6. c
7. b
8. c
9. b
10. b
11. c
12. a
13. c
14. d
15. a
16. b
17. a
18. a
19. b
20. c
21. a
22. a
23. c
24. d
25. a
26. d
27. d
28. b

CHAPTER 12 Congress

THE CHAPTER IN BRIEF

Congress is central to our democracy because it serves as the voice of the American people in Washington and because it controls a formidable battery of powers that it uses to shape policies. The framers of the Constitution provided for a bicameral (or divided) legislature, consisting of two chambers, the House of Representatives and the Senate, to serve different constituencies. The Senate was to represent the elite members of society and be attuned more to issues of property than of population. The House was designed to be more representative of the common people. Today, members of both chambers are elected directly by the people. The Senate has 100 members, two from each state. It is the more deliberative of the two bodies, while the House is more centralized and organized. Senate rules give its leadership relatively little power and discourage specialization. The 435 members of the House are elected from districts apportioned according to population. House rules give House leaders more control over the legislative process and provide for House members to specialize in certain legislative areas.

Each member's primary responsibility is to the people who live in his or her district, not to the congressional leadership or to the member's political party. There are two types of representation, or circumstances under which a person is trusted to speak for another. Sociological representation occurs if two individuals are so similar in background, character, interests, and perspectives that anything said by one would very likely reflect the view of the other. These attributes are thought to help promote good representation. The other type is agency representation, in which two individuals are formally bound together, sometimes with a contract, so that the representative is in some way accountable to those he or she is representing. There is an incentive to provide good representation here because there is the possibility of being punished or somehow held accountable for failing to speak properly for their constituents. They could be fired, or not be re-elected.

The social composition of Congress is divided into several categories. The religious affiliations of members are overwhelmingly Protestant. Catholics comprise the second largest category, with Jews as a much smaller third category. In the past twenty years minority representation has increased to include representatives who are African American, Latino, and Asian American. The legal profession is dominant, with business and industry and public service also being significant. A composite of a typical member of Congress would be a middle-aged male lawyer whose father was of the professional or managerial class; a native-born "white," or, if he cannot avoid being an immigrant, a product of northwestern or central Europe, or Canada.

Representatives are agents for the people, similar to the way a lawyer is an agent for his or her client. At the very least, representatives are expected to be constantly seeking to discover the interests of their constituency and speaking for those interests in Congress. Communication is constant between constituents and congressional offices. Over one-quarter of a representative's time and two-thirds of the time of his or her staff members is devoted to constituency service (called "case work").

There are several factors that determine who gets into office. First, of course, is who decides to run and how ambitious they are, because candidacy must be decided early. Another factor is having enough money to fund a credible campaign. The right connections to interest groups, politicians, and national party organizations are important. Incumbents generally have a better chance than their challengers because of a history of service to their constituents. Every ten years, state legislatures redraw congressional districts to reflect population changes, and this redistricting can create open seats and pit incumbents of the same party against one another, ensuring that one of them will lose. Redistricting can also give an advantage to one party by clustering voters with some ideological or sociological characteristics in a single district, or by separating such voters into several districts.

The direct benefits that congressional members provide for their constituents are called "direct patronage," and the most important opportunity for it is called "pork-barrel legislation." This is a type of legislation that specifies both the projects or other authorizations and a location within a particular district. These bills are seen as important for re-election. The most important rule for pork-barreling is that any member of Congress whose district receives a project as part of a bill must support all other projects on the bill. A limited amount of other direct patronage also exists. One form is to intervene with federal administrative agencies on behalf of constituents. A related form is getting an appointment to one of the military academies for the child of a constituent. A private bill, a different form of patronage, is a proposal to grant some kind of relief, special privilege, or exemption to a specific person named in the bill. About 75 percent of all private bills are concerned with immigration issues.

The presiding officer of the Senate is called the president of the Senate, and that position is held by the vice president of the United States. The Senate also has a president pro-tempore, a temporary president to serve in the absence of the U.S. vice president. The role of the president pro-tempore is mainly ceremonial.

Every two years, members of each party gather to elect their House leaders. This gathering is called the "conference." The candidate of the majority party becomes Speaker of the House, the House's presiding officer. The House majority also elects a majority leader, and the minority elects a minority leader. Both parties elect whips (managers) to line up party members and relay voting information to the leaders. Next in line of importance for each party is its Committee on Committees, which assigns new legislators to committees and deals with requests of incumbent members for transfer from one committee to another. Party leaders may also seek to establish a legislative agenda.

The committee system is central to the operation of Congress. Congress relies on committees and subcommittees to sort through alternatives and write legislation. Standing committees exist from congress to congress. Their jurisdiction is defined by subject matter, and except for the House Rules Committee, all standing committees receive proposals for legislation and process them into bills. Select committees are not permanent and do not have the power to report legislation. They hold hearings and serve as focal points for the issues they are charged with considering. Joint committees involve members from both the House and Senate and are permanent but do not have the power to report legislation. Conference committees are temporary, formed to work out the differences between the House and Senate versions of the final bill. In all of these committees, the hierarchy is usually based on seniority, determined by years of continued service on a particular committee.

The whip system is primarily a communications network. Between twelve and twenty assistant and regional whips (managers) are selected to take polls of all the members in order to learn their intentions on specific bills, and to convey leadership messages to other members. An agreement between two or more members of Congress who have nothing in common except the need for support on their bills is called logrolling. The agreement states basically, "you support my bill and I'll support yours." Good logrolling does not appear to be hampered by ideological concerns.

Every congressional member employees many staff members who bear the primary responsibility for formulating and drafting proposals, organizing hearings, dealing with administrative agencies, and negotiating with lobbyists. Roughly three thousand committee staffers are employed by Congress. Their jobs are permanent, regardless of who is in office. They are responsible for organizing and administering the committee's work, including research, scheduling, organizing hearings, and drafting legislation.

Staff agencies are designed to provide the legislative branch with resources and expertise independent of the executive branch. The agencies enhance Congress's capacity to oversee administrative agencies and to evaluate presidential programs and proposals.

The caucuses, also known as legislative service organizations, exist as an informal organizational structure in Congress. They consist of groups of senators or representatives who share certain opinions, interests, or social characteristics.

How a bill becomes a law depends on both the institutional structure of Congress and the rules of congressional procedures. First a bill is sent to an appropriate committee which usually refers it to a subcommittee for deliberation. A full committee may accept the recommendations of the subcommittee, or it may hold its own hearings and prepare its own amendments. 95 percent of the roughly eight thousand bills introduced in a typical congressional session die in committee. Once a bill has passed the committee in the House, the Rules Committee determines the time allotted for debate by giving it a rule. A bill's supporters usually prefer a closed rule, which severely limits floor debate and amendment, while its opponents prefer an open rule, which permits potentially damaging floor debate and makes it easier to add amendments that may cripple the bill or weaken its chances for passage. When it comes to debate on a bill, the Speaker of the House and the president of the Senate have the power of recognition. The time allotted for debate is controlled by the bill's sponsor and by its leading opponent. In the Senate, the leadership has much less control over floor debate; in fact, the Senate allows unlimited debate. Once given the floor, a senator can speak as long as he or she wishes, and senators have used this right to prevent legislation that they opposed. This tactic is called a filibuster. The votes of three-fifths of the Senate are needed to end a filibuster. This procedure is called cloture.

The final step, if a bill has come this far, is to send it to the president for approval. If the president chooses to sign the bill, the bill becomes law. If the president chooses to veto, it must be returned to Congress (to the chamber it originated in) within ten days with a list of objections to the bill. However, a veto may be overridden by a two-thirds vote in Congress.

There are several factors that determine what kind of legislation Congress ultimately produces. Constituents may affect congressional policy choices because members of Congress realize that policy choices they make can affect their chances for re-election. Interest groups are able to influence constituents and are influential in setting a legislative agenda. Party discipline in Congress is an important factor in determining legislation. Party leaders have a great deal of influence over the behavior of their party members. A party vote is when 90 percent of the members of one party take one position and 90 percent of the members of the other party take the opposing position.

Powerful interest groups can influence Congress if particular policies are important to them, but on other issues, Congress may be less attentive to narrow interest groups and more willing to consider what they see as the general interest.

Congress also has the power of oversight, which is the effort to oversee or supervise how legislation is carried out by the executive branch. The Senate has a special power called "advice and consent," which means it has the power to approve or reject presidential job appointments and treaties. Congress can also limit the president's ability to conduct foreign policy through an executive agreement by refusing to appropriate the funds needed to implement an agreement.

Throughout the nineteenth century Congress was the dominant institution, and the most powerful figures in American government were the Speaker of the House and the leaders of the Senate, not the president. The House of Representatives was the most accessible institution, and Congress was the most representative governmental institution. By the middle of the twentieth century, certainly by the 1960s, the executive had become the dominant branch of American government. Congress continued to be influential in the area of foreign policy, but the focus of decision making was now clearly in the executive branch, and the presidency was seen as far more accessible than Congress.

Today there is a resurgence of congressional power. Congress has become more influenced by special-interest groups. However, the decentralization and fragmentation of congressional power has made decision making more prone to "gridlock," and Congress has lost popularity with the American public.

REVIEW QUESTIONS

1. Consider the constitutional powers of Congress. Which are most important? Why?
2. How do the House and Senate differ in regard to their constituencies, length of terms, their members' relationship to locally entrenched interests, and their electoral politics and procedures?
3. What type of representation is described when representatives have the same ethnic, racial, religious, or educational background as their constituents?
4. What type of representation is described when constituents have the power to hire and fire their representatives? How can this be good representation?
5. Explain what advantages or disadvantages an incumbent has in an election. How can this be limited?
6. Define pork-barrel and private bills. What type of patronage are they an example of?
7. Explain the processes at the beginning of a new Congress.
8. Compare the different types of committees. What factors determine committee assignments?
9. Explain how debate time is controlled in the House and the Senate.
10. What factors influence the decisions a member of Congress makes?
11. What is congressional oversight? Why is it important?
12. The Senate has the power to give advice and consent in what areas?

13. Discuss the roles of hearings, private laws, and debates in Congress. What functions do they serve?
14. What services do members of Congress typically provide their constituents?
15. Compare the Congress of the nineteenth century to our present Congress. Which was more powerful?
16. Explain the term "gridlock." How does it relate to the legislative power of the present Congress? What is it the result of?
17. Why is representation so important to a democracy? The Senate is not a truly representative body; should it be reformed on a population basis in order to conform with the principles of representation? Why or why not?

KEY TERMS

agency representation
appropriations
bicameral
bill
caucus (congressional)
caucus (political)
closed rule
cloture
conference committee
constituency
delegate
executive agreement
filibuster
incumbent
joint committee
line-item veto
logrolling
majority leader
minority leader
open rule
oversight
party vote
patronage
pocket veto
political action committee
pork barrel
private bill
redistricting
roll-call vote
select committee
seniority
sociological representation
Speaker of the House
staff agency
standing committee
term limits
trustee
veto
whip system

FILL-IN-THE-BLANK QUIZ

Use the key terms to complete the following sentences.

1. When ninety percent or more of the House Republicans vote against a bill, it is an example of a ____________.

2. A permanent congressional committee is a ____________ committee.
3. The president opposes a bill and refuses to sign it. He is exercising his ____________ power.
4. A committee made up of members of both houses that drafts a compromise bill from the House and Senate versions is a ____________ committee.
5. Unlimited speaking in the Senate is called a ____________ and can only be ended by ____________.
6. The Rules Committee has determined that no amendments can be added to the bill during debate. They have given the bill a(n) ____________.
7. You are a Senator who is facing re-election. You have an advantage over your opponent because you are the ____________.
8. Members can serve unlimited terms in Congress, unlike the president, who is barred by ____________ from seeking more than two terms.
9. If the members of Congress were truly representative of the characteristics of Americans in terms of race, sex, education, and income, we would have ____________ representation.
10. Your aunt is an immigrant who needs to stay in the United States to seek long-term specialized medical treatment unavailable in her native country. The Immigration and Naturalization Service wants to deport her. You call your congressional representative to ask if a ____________ can be introduced in Congress to allow her to stay.
11. Congress adjourned three days after they sent a bill to the president that he opposes. The bill will probably die from a ____________.
12. "You vote for my railroad museum money and I'll vote for your bike path." You are ____________.
13. New amendments can be added to a bill in floor debate in the House if the bill has been given a(n) ____________.
14. The head of the House is called the ____________, and he is always the ____________.
15. The leader of the smaller party in Congress is the ____________.
16. Members of Congress who can be hired and fired by their constituents are providing ____________.
17. A bill that provides money for an agency or program is a(n) ____________ bill.
18. A two-house legislature is ____________.

19. A law is only a ____________ until it is passed by Congress and signed by the president.

20. The president eliminated your appropriation for the railroad museum, although he did not cut the bike path. He has used the ____________.

21. A committee that combines both House and Senate members is a ____________ committee.

22. A temporary committee has been appointed to investigate white-collar crime, although it cannot propose legislation. This is a(n) ____________ committee.

23. The purpose of the decennial census is to count the population in order to more accurately draw the lines of congressional districts, a practice known as ____________.

24. Every two years at the beginning of a new congressional session, the Republicans meet in a ____________, and the Democrats hold a ____________.

25. All of the women in Congress meet for lunch together one day a week to discuss legislation and policies. These women have formed a ____________.

26. Representatives have to constantly struggle between two roles: the ____________, who represents his or her constituents' interests closely, or the ____________, who votes according to what he or she believes is best for the nation.

27. Counting the votes within the party for upcoming legislation is the purpose of the ____________.

28. You are running for re-election to Congress, but your opponent is gaining on you in the polls. "Quick!" you say to the Speaker. "I need $3 million for a special project that will make me popular with the voters." You are trying to dig into the ____________ for some ____________.

29. Congress' responsibility to monitor the bureaucracy is its ____________ power.

30. Money is given to candidates through ____________.

31. The people in your congressional district are your ____________.

32. The Case Act limited the president's ability to complete ____________.

33. The chairman of a committee is usually the person in the committee who belongs to the majority party and who has ____________.

34. Some of the votes in Congress are taken orally and some are ___________.

35. The General Accounting Office is a ___________.

MULTIPLE-CHOICE QUESTIONS

1. According to recent polls, ___________ is the least trusted of America's national institutions.
   a. Congress
   b. the president
   c. the Supreme Court
   d. the bureaucracy

2. The US House of Representatives has ___________ members, and the U.S. Senate has ___________ members.
   a. 100, 100
   b. 329, 50
   c. 435, 100
   d. 50, 50

3. In recent years, the incumbency rate for the House of Representatives has been about ___________ percent, and the similar rate for the Senate has been about ___________ percent.
   a. 95, 86
   b. 50, 63
   c. 75, 50
   d. 25, 36

4. The leader of the majority party in the House of Representatives is the:
   a. President Pro Tempore.
   b. Majority Leader.
   c. Majority Whip.
   d. Speaker of the House.

5. In a typical congressional session, ___________ percent of the roughly ___________ bills introduced die in committee.
   a. 50, 1,000
   b. 50, 5,000
   c. 75 , 7,500
   d. 95, 8,000

6. A presidential veto can be overridden by:
   a. a two-thirds vote in both houses of Congress.
   b. a majority vote in both houses of Congress.
   c. a three-fourths vote in the Senate.
   d. a majority vote in the House of Representatives.

7. The president's ability to bypass the Senate and make foreign policy directly through the use of "executive agreements" was limited by Congress in 1972 with the passage of the:
   a. War Powers Act.
   b. Congressional Budget and Impoundment Act.
   c. Hatch Act.
   d. Case Act.

8. A *two-house* legislature is called a ___________ legislature.
   a. dual
   b. bicameral
   c. parliament
   d. democratic

9. This type of representation takes place when representatives have the same racial, ethnic, religious, or educational backgrounds as their constituents.
   a. sociological
   b. delegate
   c. trustee
   d. agency

10. This type of representation occurs when constituents have the power to hire and fire their representatives.
   a. sociological
   b. delegate
   c. trustee
   d. agency

11. This type of legislation specifies a project to be funded or other authorizations, as well as the location of the project within a particular district.
   a. concurrent resolution
   b. private bill
   c. pork barrel
   d. casework resolution

12. A proposal to grant some kind of relief, special privilege, or exemption to the person named in a bill is the definition of:
   a. a private bill.
   b. casework.
   c. oversight.
   d. pork barrel.

13. Real power in the Senate is in the hands of:
   a. the Speaker pro Tempore.
   b. the majority leader.
   c. the minority leader.
   d. the majority and minority leaders.

14. The most important arenas of congressional policy making are:
   a. the floors of the House and Senate.
   b. the halls of Congress where lobbyists roam.
   c. standing committees.
   d. conference committees.

15. These are temporary committees whose members are appointed by the Speaker of the House and the presiding officer of the Senate. They are charged with reaching a compromise on legislation once it has been passed by the House and the Senate.
   a. standing
   b. conference
   c. joint
   d. select
   e. subcommittee

16. Within each committee, hierarchy is based on:
   a. seniority.
   b. age of the congressperson.
   c. party.
   d. demographic characteristics (e.g., gender, race, occupational background).

17. The Congressional Research Service and the General Accounting Office are examples of:
   a. offices in the Executive Office of the president that provide information to Congress.
   b. legislative/executive liaison offices.
   c. congressional staff agencies.
   d. independent agencies

8. Groups of senators or representatives who join together because they share certain opinions, interests, or social characteristics is the definition of:
   a. congressional lobbies.
   b. sociological groups.
   c. congressional caucuses.
   d. voting blocks.

19. The ____________ Committee in the House of Representatives allots the time for House debate and decides to what extent amendments to the bill can be proposed from the floor.
   a. Ways and Means
   b. Rules
   c. Administrative Procedures
   d. Appropriations

20. In the Senate, ____________ can be used to "talk a bill to death" unless three-fifths of the Senate vote for ____________.
   a. unanimous consent, a discharge petition
   b. the voice vote rule, a "gag" order petition
   c. filibuster, cloture
   d. none of the above

21. A vote on which 90 percent or more of the members of one party take one position while at least 90 percent of the members of the other party take the opposing position is called a ____________ vote.
   a. super-majority
   b. partisan
   c. block
   d. party

22. Typically, party unity is higher in ____________ than in ____________.
   a. the Senate, the House
   b. the House, the Senate
   c. conference committees, standing committees
   d. Congress, the bureaucracy

23. During the first century of American government, ____________ was the dominant institution.
   a. Congress
   b. the president
   c. the bureaucracy
   d. the court

24. Originally, members of the U.S. Senate were appointed by state legislatures for six-year terms, were to represent the elite members of society, and were to be more attuned to the interests of:
   a. population.
   b. property.
   c. the states
   d. business.

25. According to the authors of the text, in recent years, the House has exhibited considerably more intense partisanship and ideological division than the Senate. Why?
   a. Because of their narrow constituencies, senators are less inclined to seek compromise than are House members.
   b. Since House members represent more homogeneous districts in which their party is dominant, they are less willing to seek compromise.

c. Since the 1950s, the Republicans have controlled the House, but this has not been the case in the Senate.
d. Leadership is more important in the Senate than in the House, thus senators follow party lines more strictly than do House members.

26. In general, from a "sociological representation" perspective, how representative is the U.S. Congress?
    a. Congress mirrors the social origins of the U.S. population.
    b. Representative only with respect to gender and race.
    c. Representative only with respect to occupational backgrounds.
    d. Not representative at all.

27. In general, from a "representatives as agents" perspective, how representative is the U.S. Congress?
    a. not at all representative
    b. congressional staffs are representative, but not members of Congress
    c. very representative
    d. only symbolically

28. According to the authors of the text, incumbency tends to:
    a. produce change in Congress.
    b. preserve the status quo in Congress.
    c. result in the election of new committee chairpersons.
    d. reduce the importance of seniority in Congress.

29. According to the authors of the text, the most important rule of pork barreling is:
    a. that any member of Congress whose district receives a project as part of a bill must support all the other projects on the bill.
    b. to block any other pork barrel projects in a legislative district sponsored by the other political party.
    c. send the "pork" home no matter what the costs.
    d. ask the party leadership how your "pork" project fits within the overall projects being pursued by other members in Congress.

30. As the authors note, "Over its more than two hundred year history, Congress has established procedures for creating a division of labor, setting an agenda, maintaining order through rules and procedures, and placing limits on debate and discussion." As a consequence:
    a. the work of Congress is relatively routine and noncontroversial.
    b. the committee system in Congress today does not play a pivotal role in the development of public policy; policy is largely the product of the efforts of individual congresspeople.
    c. it is far easier to pass bills that represent incremental change rather than comprehensive reform.
    d. all of the above

31. In the House of Representatives, a bill's supporters generally prefer a(n) ____________ rule, which puts severe limits on floor debate and amendments.
   a. open
   b. restrictive
   c. closed
   d. binding

32. According to the authors of the text, all of the following *except* one are influences from *inside* government that help determine how Congresspeople vote.
   a. party leadership
   b. constituents
   c. the president
   d. congressional colleagues

33. In general, the purpose of the congressional *whip system* is:
   a. communications.
   b. staffing.
   c. to discipline congresspeople who break party unity.
   d. to make committee assignments.

34. "You support me on bill X and I'll support you on another bill of your choice." This statement illustrates the concept of:
   a. casework.
   b. reciprocity.
   c. pork barrelling
   d. logrolling

QUESTIONS FOR DISCUSSION AND THOUGHT

1. Assume you are a member of the state legislature and now must cast the deciding vote on a very controversial issue. If you knew that your personal position was contrary to that held by the majority of the people in your district, would you vote in accord with your beliefs or their interests? If you were able to vote anonymously, would this change your vote?

2. Why does the American public have such a low opinion of Congress? Less than one-quarter approve of the way Congress does its job, although nearly 60 percent approve of the job their member of Congress is doing. How can this contradiction be explained?

3. Do you think that tax cuts for the middle class were given by taking away money from the welfare programs? Or were they unrelated? If we were in a recession, do you think the American public would support substantial cuts in the welfare programs?

4. How representative is Congress? Most legislators are white, upper-middle-class males, although this group is a very small part of our entire population. What impact does this skewed representation have in terms of liberty, equality, and democracy? Can these people really represent women, minorities, poor people? Realistically, could a poor person ever get elected? Would you want a poor person as your representative?

5. If you were to run for Congress, what would be your three most important campaign issues? Why did you select those issues? Whose interests do those issues reflect? What could you do that would make a difference in solving these issues?

THE CITIZEN'S ROLE

Can ordinary students influence Congress? Many students rely on the federal student aid program to allow them to stay in college. Several organizations, such as Rock the Vote, the United States Student Association, and the Higher Education Project of the Public Interest Research Group are circulating a petition called Save Student Aid! The petition is printed below. Circulate the petition to obtain ten signatures from students (American citizens only) and then send the petition to your congressional representative. Alternatively, you may create and mail a petition on a political topic of your own choice, using the petition below as a model.

SAVE STUDENT AID!

The doors to a college education are being closed, and students are being driven into decades of debt because of the failure of state and federal governments to adequately support access to higher education. We demand that the White House and Congress act in a bipartisan manner to eliminate financial barriers to a college education. Specifically, Congress should substantially increase Pell and other need-based grants, reduce the cost of student loans, and provide significant tax relief to low- and middle-income students. A college education is the best investment in America's future. Support student aid and stop the doors of college from closing on America's future.

Print name	Signature	Address (City, State, ZIP)

1. How many people did you have to ask before you got ten signatures?
2. Did the signers read the petition and understand what they were signing?
3. What reasons did people give for not signing the petition? Were you surprised at their reasons?
4. What is the name and mailing address of your local congressional representative?
5. Do you think that petitions like this have an effect on Congress? Explain.

GOVERNMENT IN YOUR LIFE

Congressional Quarterly magazine maintains a web site at http:www.pathfinder.com/CQ that lists all of the votes of Congress over the past several years. Select a member of Congress, a subject (such as energy, defense, or agriculture), and search for his or her votes over the past year on this topic.

1. Record the votes taken by this person.
2. Did you choose an issue that is important in this person's district or state, or was this an issue of personal interest to you?
3. Were you surprised by the pattern of voting? Did you agree with his or her votes?
4. Does this person appear to represent the interests of the constituency?
5. What is agency representation? Is this person a good example of agency representation on this issue? Explain.

ANSWER KEY

Fill-in-the-Blank Quiz

1. party vote
2. standing
3. veto
4. conference
5. filibuster, cloture
6. closed rule
7. incumbent
8. term limits
9. sociological
10. private bill
11. pocket veto
12. logrolling
13. open rule
14. speaker, majority leader
15. minority leader
16. agency representation
17. appropriations
18. bicameral
19. bill
20. line-item veto
21. joint
22. select
23. redistricting
24. conference, caucus (political)

25. caucus (congressional)
26. delegate, trustee
27. whip system
28. pork barrel; patronage
29. oversight
30. political action committees
31. constituency
32. executive agreements
33. seniority
34. roll-call votes
35. staff agency

Multiple-Choice Quiz

1. a
2. c
3. a
4. d
5. d
6. a
7. d
8. b
9. a
10. d
11. c
12. a
13. d
14. c
15. b
16. a
17. c
18. c
19. b
20. c
21. d
22. b
23. a
24. b
25. b
26. d
27. c
28. b
29. a
30. c
31. c
32. b
33. a
34. d

CHAPTER 13 The Presidency

THE CHAPTER IN BRIEF

"The American presidency is the most democratized leader among all modern democracies." The American president today runs a "permanent campaign" in which Americans are constantly observing and evaluating the office-holder through the prism of the media, public opinion polls, and political parties. The president must represent all the people, unlike those in Congress who have more narrow and specific constituencies. This makes the presidency a frustrating job, for no one can please everyone all of the time. For this reason, every president loses popularity over time.

The Founders intended that the legislative branch would be the dominant branch. Hence, Article I of the Constitution is longer and more detailed than Article II. In 1885, Woodrow Wilson wrote *Congressional Government*, which aptly described nineteenth-century American government. In the twentieth century, however, power has shifted to the presidency.

Article II lists several presidential powers: to "take care that the laws be faithfully executed," serve as commander-in-chief of the military forces, grant pardons and reprieves, and "receive ambassadors and other public ministers." Although the constitutional powers seem weak and vague, in fact the presidency today is powerful because Congress has delegated to it substantial authority to operate government on a day-to-day basis. For example, the Constitution states that presidents must receive senatorial approval of treaties, but Congress has delegated the power of executive agreement, which allows presidents to implement international agreements without Senate approval.

Congress tried to take back some of its delegated powers when it passed the War Powers Resolution in 1973, which was intended to force presidents to inform Congress of intended military actions. Presidents still act unilaterally, however, on many occasions. The independent counsel law is another attempt to limit presidential power. On the other hand, Congress extended presidential power even further when they granted a line-item veto power, although that was later overturned by the Supreme Court as a violation of separation of powers. Presidents also claim "executive privilege," or the right to withhold information from Congress on issues critical to national security and survival. Generally, the Supreme Court has approved the expanded powers of the presidency.

In the domestic arena, the president is the head of government. Militarily, as commander in chief, the president has explicit power to protect states against invasion and domestic violence by deploying federal troops, but the Constitution restrains this power by providing that the state legislature or governor must request federal troops. However, this provision is not absolute. Presidents are not obligated to provide troops when requested, and a president may deploy troops without a state's request by declaring a "state of emergency."

The president also has legislative power. The Constitution states that the president must provide Congress with information regarding the "state of the union" and recommend legislation to Congress. This gives the president the power of initiative, that is, the power to initiate decisive action and formulate proposals for important policies. The president can also use the budgeting process as the primary initiator of proposals for legislative action in Congress. The president has the constitutional power to veto, or turn down, acts of Congress and the implied power to impound funds—that is, to refuse to spend money that Congress has appropriated for certain purposes. Congress enacted the line-item veto in 1995, which was later overturned by the Supreme Court.

The president has resources of power within the institution of government as well as those given by the Constitution. Using patronage as a tool of management, the president selects high-level political appointees, picking individuals who will attempt to carry out the president's own agenda and who will allow him to build links to powerful political and economic constituencies. Until the 1970s, appointees were mainly from outside government experience, but since that time, presidents have picked more Washington "insiders."

Another institutional resource for the president is the Cabinet: the traditional but informal designation for the heads of all the major federal government departments. The Cabinet has no constitutional status and is not a collective body. Each Cabinet appointment must be approved by the Senate, but Cabinet members are not responsible to the Senate or to Congress. Cabinet appointments help build party and popular support, but the Cabinet is not a party organ. Cabinet members have their own constituencies and are usually selected by the president because of the support they bring with them. Each Cabinet member heads a department that is a large bureaucracy with a momentum of its own. Cabinet appointees are diverse and many meet each other and the president for the first time after their selection. Presidents rely more heavily on the "inner Cabinet": the National Security Council, which is composed of the president, the vice president, the secretaries of State, Defense, and Treasury, the attorney general, and other officials.

A third resource of the president is the White House staff, which is composed mainly of analysts and advisers. From a small informal group (popularly called the Kitchen Cabinet), the White House staff has grown very large. The biggest variation among presidential management practices lies in organization. Presidents have increasingly preferred the White House staff instead of the Cabinet as their means of managing the gigantic executive branch.

The Executive Office of the President (EOP), sometimes called the "institutional presidency," consists of the permanent agencies that perform defined management tasks for the president, such as the Office of Management and Budget (OMB), the Council of Economic Advisers (CEA), the Council on Environmental Quality (CEQ), and the National Security Council (NSC). The director of the OMB was granted Cabinet status under President Reagan. The OMB director sets terms of discourse for agencies as well as for Congress.

The vice presidency exists for two purposes: to succeed the president in case of death, resignation, or incapacitation, and to preside over the Senate to cast a tie-breaking vote when necessary. The main value of the vice presidency as a political resource for the president is electoral. The emphasis in choosing a running mate is on geographical or ideological balance. The emphasis today is strongly toward an ideological balance. Vice presidents have historically not had a lot of responsibilities, but Vice President Al Gore has enhanced the status of the office with more responsibility than previous vice presidents.

The first lady is generally a symbol of the nation rather than of a partisan perspective or policy position. Hillary Clinton initially played an important political and policy role in her husband's administration. She was politically effective at first because the opposition was reluctant to attack a first lady, but later she was seen more as a politician and became vulnerable to intense media scrutiny. By 1995 she was forced to withdraw to a more traditional role.

The president has various political resources. One resource is elections. A landslide election can give a president a mandate, meaning that the electorate approved the programs offered in the campaign and that Congress ought therefore to go along. President Clinton was hampered in this respect by having been elected by a minority of the popular vote. Another political resource is party. The political party that has the congressional majority determines the presidential "batting average" in Congress, or the percentage of winning roll-call votes in Congress on bills publicly supported by the president. Party has limitations as a resource because if a president pursues a bipartisan strategy to win Congressional support, it is difficult to build party loyalty and party discipline to maximize the support of the president's own party in Congress. Interest groups can also be used as a presidential resource. The classic case in modern times was the New Deal coalition. It was composed of regional interests (such as southern whites), urban industrial residents, and blacks, and organized groups in labor, agriculture, and the financial community. The groups were held together by a judicious use of patronage, in jobs and in policies.

Presidents use public opinion polls to determine opinion and shape policy. The trouble with polls is that they only show what the public wanted yesterday, not what they will want tomorrow. For that reason, many presidents find that they are several steps behind shifts in opinion. Some presidents, therefore, have decided to do what they believe is best and trust or hope that public opinion will shift in their favor.

Mass popularity can be both a resource and a liability. The American people tend to react to presidential *actions* rather than mere speeches or image-making devices. They tend to respond negatively to most domestic issues, and positively to international actions or events associated with the president. This is called the "rallying effect." An example of that is the way President Bush enjoyed very high popularity at the beginning of the Gulf War. There was an unprecedented decline in his popularity after the Gulf War, however, a decline that was related to the absence of international events associated with the president.

The popular base of the presidency is important because it gives the president consent to use all of the powers already vested in the office by the Constitution. The years that the American government was a congressional government, from about 1800 to 1933, are referred to as the "legislative epoch." The presidency was strengthened somewhat in the 1830s when the national convention system of nominating presidential candidates replaced the caucus system. This gave the presidency a base of power, independent of Congress, but it did not immediately transform the presidency into the office we recognize today because the parties disappeared back into the states and Congress once the election was over.

The turning point in the history of American national government came during the administration of Franklin Roosevelt. The president's constitutional obligation to see "that the laws be faithfully executed" became, during Roosevelt's presidency, virtually a responsibility to shape the laws before executing them. The national government began intervening into economic life in ways that had once been reserved to the states. The national government discovered that it, too, had "police power" and could directly regulate individuals. This trend, during the 1930s, tilted the American national structure away from a Congress-centered government toward a president-centered government. Congress has the power to rescind these delegations of power, or it can restrict them with later amendments, committee oversight, or budget cuts. However, for the most part it has not, and presidential government has become an established fact of American life.

REVIEW QUESTIONS

1. What two variables lead the authors to speak of the "dual nature of the presidency," and why is this so?
2. What was the revolution that occurred in the American national government and the presidency in the twentieth century? What forces spurred this change?
3. How is executive power defined in the Constitution?

4. What prompted Congress to pass the War Powers Resolution, and what was the underlying premise?
5. Why do you think President Reagan violated the War Powers Resolution more than once? What were the overall consequences of his actions within the framework of the government?
6. How did President Eisenhower unilaterally use presidential power in 1957 in opposition to the wishes of a state government?
7. Describe the main difference in the ways that Presidents Bush and Clinton organized their staffs. What have been the results for President Clinton?
8. What is the significance of the "inner Cabinet"?
9. Why is the Office of Management and Budget (OMB) the most important agency in the Executive Office of the President (EOP)?
10. What do some of the various EOP agencies do for the president?
11. Explain the difference between "bottom-up" and "top-down" budgeting.
12. Why is the office of vice president considered a constitutional anomaly? What value does the vice presidency have for the president?
13. What is a "mandate" as it refers to a landslide election?
14. What is meant by a "presidential batting average" in Congress? What is the key factor in whether it is high or low?
15. Why would a president pursue a bipartisan strategy in forming legislative requests, and how could that be a liability?
16. What is the authors' consensus about successful presidents and their use of public opinion polls? Why do you think that is?
17. Explain the "democratization of the presidency." What are the consequences, both good and bad, of this transformation?
18. What are some of the consequences of divided government? In what ways does divided government restrict the power of the president?

KEY TERMS

Cabinet
caucus (political)
Commander in Chief
delegated powers
divided government
executive agreements
Executive Office of the President
inherent powers
Kitchen Cabinet
legislative initiative
line-item veto
mandate

National Security Council
New Deal coalition
patronage
permanent campaign
pocket veto
rallying effect
veto
War Powers Resolution
White House staff

FILL-IN-THE-BLANK QUIZ

Use the key terms to complete the following sentences.

1. The group of advisers who work closely with the president on a daily basis are his ___________.
2. Article II of the Constitution lists the ___________ powers of the president; those that are not listed but are inferred are the ___________ powers.
3. Even though the president does not wear a military uniform, he nevertheless possesses military powers in his role as ___________.
4. The president's ability to give out jobs is his ___________ resource.
5. The president's advisers who assist him in determining policy for the defense and safety of the nation are the ___________, which is part of a larger group of advisers known as the ___________.
6. Checks and balances between the president and Congress are shown in the president's refusal to sign a bill, known as a ___________, and in his power to kill any bills passed in the last ten days of a session by not signing them, known as a ___________.
7. Public opinion of a president often goes up after he acts in an international crisis, but this ___________ usually doesn't last very long.
8. Congress tried to give the president more power over appropriations through the ___________, but the Supreme Court overturned it as an unconstitutional delegation of power.
9. Although the president cannot introduce bills in Congress, he nevertheless has a list of bills known as his ___________ that he wants his supporters to introduce and support.
10. Unlike a parliamentary system, the federal government department heads who form the ___________ in a presidential system do not have any collective powers or responsibility.
11. A president who wins with a plurality, not a majority, has difficulty asserting that he has a ___________ to carry out his program.

12. The informal group of advisers around a president are his ___________.

13. Every president in his first term is concerned with re-election, and as a result he runs a ___________.

14. Congress has delegated power to the president to negotiate treaties that do not require senatorial approval, but these are called ___________ instead of treaties.

15. A closed meeting of political advisers to plan strategy is a ___________.

16. A major problem of a presidential system is that it allows the president and Congress to be controlled by different parties, which leads to ___________.

17. Congress tried to restrain the president's power in sending troops abroad by passing the ___________, although presidents don't always abide by the law.

18. Franklin Roosevelt used his patronage power to build the ___________, based on the interests of the financial community, labor, and agriculture.

MULTIPLE-CHOICE QUIZ

1. The powers of the presidency are outlined in ___________ of the U.S. Constitution.
   a. Article I
   b. Article II
   c. Article III
   d. Article IV

2. The ___________ was established by law in 1947 and is composed of the president; the vice president; the secretaries of state, defense, and the treasury; the attorney general; and other officials invited by the president.
   a. Office of Management and Budget
   b. Executive Office of the President
   c. National Security Council
   d. Cabinet

3. The most important agency in the Executive Office of the President is the:
   a. Office of Management and Budget.
   b. National Security Council.
   c. Council of Economic Advisors.
   d. Council of Environmental Quality.

4. In 1995, only eighty-eight bills were enacted during the entire session—the lowest legislative output since:
   a. 1919.
   b. 1933.
   c. 1964.
   d. 1989.

5. One of the first presidents to use the media was ___________, who referred to the presidency as

a "bully pulpit" because its visibility allowed him to preach to the nation and bring popular pressure to bear against his opponents in Congress.
   a. Woodrow Wilson
   b. Theodore Roosevelt
   c. Franklin Roosevelt
   d. Harry Truman

6. In 1885, an obscure political science professor named ___________ entitled his general textbook *Congressional Government* because American government was dominated by Congress.
   a. Theodore Roosevelt
   b. Franklin Roosevelt
   c. Dwight Waldo
   d. Woodrow Wilson

7. According to the authors of the text, which of the following is not an "imperial quality" of the president as head of state?
   a. the military power of Commander in Chief
   b. the judicial power of Chief Justice
   c. the diplomatic power to receive ambassadors
   d. the judicial power to grant reprieves and pardons

8. A ___________ veto can occur when the president is presented a bill during the last ___________ days of a legislative session and ___________ be overridden by a two-thirds vote in both houses of Congress.
   a. regular , 10, cannot
   b. pocket, 10, can
   c. pocket, 10, cannot
   d. regular, 10, can

9. Presidential high-level political appointments are:
   a. a form of patronage.
   b. a presidential management tool.
   c. an institutional resource of presidential power.
   d. all of the above.

10. The "Cabinet," heads of all major federal government departments,
    a. is called for in Article II, Section 3.
    b. is similar to parliamentary systems.
    c. has no constitutional status.
    d. is created by law and must be bipartisan.

11. The White House staff is composed mainly of:
    a. analysts and advisors.
    b. economists.
    c. media specialists.
    d. congressional liaison personnel.

12. According to the authors of the text, the vice president exists primarily:
    a. to succeed the president in case of death, resignation, or incapacitation.
    b. to serve as president of the Senate.
    c. to cast a vote in the Senate in case of a tie vote.
    d. a and b only

13. Historically, first ladies have served what role?
    a. policy advisor to the president
    b. ceremonial functions
    c. prior to the Twenty-fifth Amendment, to assume the duties of the president in case of incapacitation
    d. all of the above

14. Generally speaking, popular support for a president:
    a. increases over time.
    b. increases over time, unless the president is a "lame duck" president.
    c. declines over time.
    d. remains at a fairly consistent level.

15. According to the authors of the text, after FDR:
    a. the presidency was typified by "divided government."
    b. every president has been strong, whether committed to a strong presidency or not.
    c. the "dormant" presidency emerged.
    d. some presidents have been "strong executives" and some presidents have been "caretakers."

16. The constitutional phrase that the president "shall take Care that the Laws be faithfully executed" establishes the president as:
    a. Chief Legislator.
    b. Chief of Party.
    c. Chief Executive.
    d. Commander in Chief.

17. If a president wished to make foreign policy without having to get the two-thirds vote in the Senate needed to ratify a treaty, he or she most likely would:
    a. evoke executive privilege.
    b. make an executive agreement with the head of a foreign nation.
    c. evoke the treaty-making provisions in the War Powers Act of 1973.
    d. make a secret treaty and simply not inform Congress.

18. As the authors note, in passing the War Powers Act of 1973, Congress made an obvious effort to revive the principle that the presidency is an office of:
    a. delegated powers.
    b. reserved powers.
    c. implied powers.
    d. inherent powers.

19. According to the authors of the text, which of the following is not part of the constitutional basis of the domestic presidency?
    a. executive power
    b. legislative power
    c. military power
    d. diplomatic power

20. In January President Clinton delivers his "State of the Union Message." In doing so he is performing his role as:
    a. Chief Legislator.
    b. Chief Executive.
    c. Chief of State
    d. Commander in chief

21. The president vetoes a bill passed by Congress. This is an example of:
    a. the president as Chief Legislator.
    b. checks and balances.
    c. limited government.
    d. all of the above.

22. Which of the following is a "political resource" of the president?
    a. an electoral mandate
    b. a Congress in which the president's party is a majority

c. interest groups
d. the media
e. all of the above

23. The president is a Democrat, and both houses of Congress are controlled by Republicans; this is an example of:
   a. divided government.
   b. stalemate.
   c. limited government.
   d. bicameralism.

24. President Clinton hired David Gergen to shape and influence public opinion. Previously Mr. Gergen had performed the same job for Ronald Reagan. Why was President Clinton criticized?
   a. for hiring someone on a full-time basis to shape and influence public opinion
   b. for hiring a Republican
   c. for hiring a former Reagan employee
   d. for hiring a "crossover" employee who seemed to care more about influencing the public than about the politics he was hired to promote

25. Which of the following was overturned by the Supreme Court as an unconstitutional delegation of power?
   a. the veto
   b. the pocket veto
   c. the adjournment veto
   d. the line-item veto

26. The agenda of bills that a president wants to see enacted is called the president's:
   a. legislative initiative.
   b. legislative calendar.
   c. bills of concern.
   d. presidential docket.

27. The presidential right to withhold information from Congress is called:
   a. executive agreement.
   b. executive authority.
   c. executive privilege.
   d. inherent authority.

QUESTIONS FOR DISCUSSION AND THOUGHT

1. Most Americans did not know that President Franklin Roosevelt was severely crippled from polio and had to use a wheelchair, or that John Kennedy entertained women in the White House. The media censored itself due to respect for the office and the man. Which do you think is better: not knowing very much or knowing a lot about the personal lives of the presidents? Does what goes on in their personal lives affect their ability to govern? Have our most effective presidents also been the most exemplary? Have the most moral been the most effective?

2. Why do you think the American president is often called "the most powerful leader in the world"? If that is true, what special responsibilities does that carry? Should we limit the president's role in world affairs? Should America

be less of a world leader? If America did reduce its role, what country might take its place?

3. Are the responsibilities of "the most powerful leader in the world," the American president, too large a job for one person? Why has the American presidency grown so large? Are there any powers you think should be taken away from the president? Do we overidealize the president? Do you think it is safe for a democracy to put so much faith in a single leader?
4. A federal district judge has ruled the line-item veto to be unconstitutional because it violates separation of powers. Yet the veto can be overridden by a two-thirds vote in each house, just as any other bill is vetoed. Do you agree with the judge that the veto violates separation of powers?
5. If we limit a president to two terms, as required by the Twenty-second Amendment, shouldn't we also limit the terms of the Congress? How about federal judges, who are appointed for life?

THE CITIZEN'S ROLE

The White House web site at http://www.whitehouse.gov contains the text of daily press briefings, weekly Saturday radio broadcasts, and other news. Go to the site and read the text of one of the recent Saturday broadcasts.

1. What was the topic of the speech?
2. Was the speech highly partisan or did it seem to be nonpartisan?
3. Was the speech informative? Did you learn anything from it about the issue(s)?
4. How effective do you think the speech was in terms of affecting public opinion?
5. Why would a president take five minutes every Saturday for a radio broadcast?

GOVERNMENT IN YOUR LIFE

The Starr report on President Clinton's affair with Monica Lewinsky broke an old tradition in Washington—that the personal lives of politicians would remain private unless they affected the business of government. As a result of the Starr report, several other high-ranking politicians, including the chairman of the House Judiciary Committee, which received the report, have felt compelled to admit to having extramarital affairs.

1. In your opinion, does knowing about the private lives of politicians affect your opinion of their ability to perform their office?
2. Which do you prefer: knowing about every private aspect of politicians' lives, or the previous tradition of not reporting about such activities?
3. Do you think the American public makes a distinction between private and public actions of politicians?
4. Is the ability of a politician to be effective damaged by these personal revelations?
5. Would it affect your willingness to run for public office if you know that your private life might be subject to intense public scrutiny?

ANSWER KEY

Fill-in-the-Blank Quiz

1. White House staff
2. delegated, inherent
3. Commander in Chief
4. patronage
5. National Security Council; Executive Office of the President
6. veto, pocket veto
7. rallying effect
8. line-item veto
9. legislative initiative
10. Cabinet
11. mandate
12. Kitchen Cabinet
13. permanent campaign
14. executive agreements
15. caucus (political)
16. divided government
17. War Powers Resolution
18. New Deal coalition

Multiple-Choice Quiz

1. b
2. c
3. a
4. b
5. b
6. d
7. b
8. c
9. d
10. c
11. a
12. d
13. b
14. c
15. b
16. c
17. b
18. a
19. d
20. a
21. d
22. e
23. a
24. d
25. d
26. a
27. c

CHAPTER 14 Bureaucracy in a Democracy

THE CHAPTER IN BRIEF

A bureaucracy is a universal form of organization, and the word itself refers to the offices, tasks, and principles of organization that are employed to run a formal and sustainable organization. A bureaucracy has six primary characteristics. The first is a division of labor, in which workers are specialized. Next is the allocation of functions, which means that each task is assigned. Third, the allocation of responsibility means that each task is a contractual obligation. The fourth is supervision: some workers are assigned to watch over others rather than contribute directly to the creation of the product—this is called a "chain of command." Next is the purchase of full-time employment, in which the organization controls all the time the worker is on the job. Last is identification of career within the organization, where workers come to identify with the organization as a way of life. A bureaucracy could be a large business, an army, or a government.

Since 1950, the ratio of federal service employment to the total workforce has been steady. In 1993, the number of civilian federal employees was a little over three million. Popular sentiments that the federal government has grown too large have contributed to a slight decrease in federal service jobs in the past fifteen years,.

The role of bureaucrats is to communicate. Copies of communication, called a "paper trail," are recorded as a routine means of making sure every responsibility is met, who to blame for a failure, and where routines ought to be improved. Those first two activities add up to a third—implementation—where the objectives of the organization are laid down by the bosses. In a fourth job, interpretation, bureaucrats carry out what they hope is the intention of their superiors. Public bureaucrats, those that work for government agencies, must maintain a much larger paper trail than private bureaucrats because of the constraints the public places on them. They are also much more accessible than private bureaucrats, giving citizens a greater opportunity to participate in the decision-making processes of public agencies. Much of the lower efficiency of public agencies can be attributed to the political, judicial, legal, and publicity restraints we put on public bureaucrats.

In 1883, governments at all levels in the United States attempted to imitate business by passing the Civil Service Act, which established the merit system. This system provides greater job security for public bureaucrats than that found in private organizations. Appointees to public offices must be qualified for the job to which they are appointed. Public bureaucrats also are given a form of tenure and have legal protection from being fired without a show of just cause.

Our civil servants make up the permanent civilian white-collar federal workforce. Sixty-five percent have at least some college education. The infusion of technological skills and requirements in the federal service has expanded far faster and to a greater extent than in the American workforce at large. The federal civil service is now composed of 43 percent women. Of those, 16.8 percent are African American, which gives African Americas a slight overrepresentation compared to the national workforce at large. However, Latinos, Asians, and Native Americans are underrepresented at the present time. The federal bureaucracy continues to be more diverse than the private sector as a result of an active pursuit of affirmative action.

The executive bureaucracy is arranged in a hierarchy of positions and responsibilities. The heads of departments are called secretaries (for example, the secretary of the treasury). Below the secretaries are several top administrators, such as inspectors general and general counsels, who oversee several operating agencies within the department. Of equal status are the assistant secretaries, who manage groups of operating agencies. The third tier is called the "bureau level," where the highest level of actual programs exists. Within the bureaus are divisions, offices, services, and units, which are all part of the hierarchy.

There are at least three ways that bureaucracy might be reduced. The surest way of reducing the size of the bureaucracy is termination, which calls for the elimination of programs. This method, so far, has proven difficult. The second method is devolution, which calls for downsizing the federal bureaucracy by delegating the implementation of programs to state and local governments. That might, however, result in the elimination of some programs in some states and not in others, and there could be large inequalities between the states in the provision of services and benefits to citizens, which is not good in a democracy. The third method is privatization, which means that government services or programs are contracted out to private companies but still government-supervised.

Each expansion of the national government in the twentieth century has been accompanied by a parallel expansion of presidential management authority. This pattern began with President Wilson, whose policy innovations were followed, in 1921, with the Budget and Accounting Act, with which Congress turned over the legislative power of budgeting to the executive branch as a management tool. After President Franklin Roosevelt and his 1937 Committee on Administrative Management, the "managerial presidency" was an established fact. President Carter was preoccupied with administrative reform and reorganization more than any president in this century. He reorganized the civil service with the Civil Service Reform Act of 1978. He also tried to impose a new budgetary process on all executive agencies. President Clinton has engaged in a systematic effort to "reinvent government." His National Performance Review (NPR) has made substantial progress and is quite respectable and impressive, even to Republicans, as it has streamlined certain procedures and has already saved the American people billions of dollars.

In an effort to fill gaps in executive management, over the past thirty years members of the White House staff called "special assistants to the president" have been given more specialized jurisdiction over certain departments and strategic issues. This has increased their access to confidential information and thus increased their power. As the White House grows and the Executive Office of the President grows, the management bureaucracy becomes a management problem. Congress is constitutionally essential to responsible bureaucracy because ultimately the key to bureaucratic responsibility is legislation. Through oversight (the effort by Congress, through hearings, investigations, meetings, and other techniques, to exercise control over the activities of the executive agencies), we understand that there is no ultimate or sure solution to the problem of bureaucracy in a democracy, but a sober awareness of the nature of the problem.

REVIEW QUESTIONS

1. Define bureaucracy. What is essential in a bureaucracy?
2. Why is a paper trail necessary? Why has the time lengthened for bureaucracies to promulgate a rule?
3. Are there lower efficiencies in public agencies than in private organizations? Why?
4. Explain the merit system. What purpose does it serve?
5. Describe the composition of the federal workforce. Is it a mirror of society?
6. Why are the Cabinet heads referred to as "secretaries"? Explain the "bureau level."
7. Define the ways the federal bureaucracy can be reduced.
8. Why was the Budget and Accounting Act an important executive branch innovation?
9. Explain the NPR. What has it been successful at accomplishing?
10. Why have new powers been granted to the White House staff? How can this pose a management problem?

11. Describe the role congressional committees and subcommittees play in "oversight" of executive agencies.
12. Explain the Freedom of Information Act of 1966. How is it a method of "oversight"?
13. Should our government be more bureaucratic? Why or why not?
14. What is the Department of Defense characterized as "military pluralism"?
15. What is a clientele agency? Explain why welfare agencies are not true clientele agencies.
16. Explain the difference between deregulation and privatization.
17. Why do the authors state that there is a "management vacuum" in American government? What agency has attempted to fill the vacuum?
18. How can the executive and legislative branches make the bureaucracy accountable to the people?
19. Does the bureaucracy treat all people equally in our system, or do some groups or people wield excessive amounts of power? What does this say about the nation as a democracy?

KEY TERMS

accountability
administrative adjudication
bureaucracy
clientele agencies
departments
deregulation
devolution
Federal Reserve System (Fed)
fiscal policies
government corporation
implementation
independent agency
iron triangle
means testing
merit system
oversight
paper trail
privatization
redistributive agency
regulatory agencies
revenue agency

FILL-IN-THE-BLANK QUIZ

Use the key terms to complete the following sentences.

1. A stand-alone agency, not connected to any department, is a(n) ____________ agency.
2. The Department of Agriculture was the first ____________ agency.

3. A synonym for "red tape" is a ____________.
4. Congress provides ____________ of the bureaucracy through hearings and investigations.
5. The government programs that control taxing and spending are called ____________, while monetary policy is controlled by the ____________.
6. The Customs Service is a(n) ____________ agency.
7. Rules made by the regulatory agencies have the force of law even though they are not approved by Congress. This is the power of ____________.
8. The Air Force contracts with private companies to perform much of its aircraft maintenance. They are practicing ____________.
9. Amtrak is a(n) ____________ because it performs a service normally provided by the private sector.
10. The obligation to answer to authority is the definition of ____________.
11. If you wanted to work for the federal government after graduation, you would have to have the right job qualifications. This is because the government uses the ____________ for hiring personnel.
12. The Social Security Administration shifts large amounts of money from workers to retired and disabled workers. Therefore, it is a(n) ____________ agency.
13. The Federal Communications Commission and the Food and Drug Administration are examples of ____________ agencies.
14. Anyone who qualifies for Social Security receives it, regardless of personal incomes. In certain agencies, ____________ is applied to determine if you deserve a federal payment.
15. The relationship between a congressional committee, an interest group, and a government agency is called a(n) ____________.
16. The airlines are no longer subject to extensive federal controls because the industry has been ____________.
17. "Rule by desks" is called ____________.
18. State government employment has grown faster than federal employment because of ____________, in which federal programs are passed down to the states for administration.
19. Departments must translate the laws passed by Congress into workable rules and routines, a practice known as ____________.
20. The secretaries of the ____________ serve in the Cabinet.

MULTIPLE-CHOICE QUIZ

1. The federal "merit system" was created under the:
   a. Civil Service Reform Act of 1978.
   b. Civil Service Act of 1883.
   c. Classification Act of 1923.
   d. Classification Act of 1949.

2. The first "clientele agency" was the:
   a. Department of Agriculture.
   b. Department of Transportation.
   c. Department of Labor.
   d. Department of the Interior.

3. About ____________ percent of all civilian federal government workers work in Washington, D.C.
   a. 10
   b. 20
   c. 30
   d. 40

4. By far the most important of the "revenue agencies" is the:
   a. Treasury Department.
   b. Federal Reserve System.
   c. Office of Management and Budget.
   d. Internal Revenue Service.

5. The best known agency in the Justice Department is the:
   a. Federal Bureau of Investigation.
   b. Office for Civil Rights.
   c. Equal Employment Opportunity Commission.
   d. Antitrust Division.

6. Two departments which occupy center stage for maintaining national security are:
   a. the State Department and the Department of War.
   b. the Defense Department and the National Security Council.
   c. The National Security Council and the joint chiefs of staff.
   d. The Defense Department and the State Department.

7. Which of the following is an example of an "independent" regulatory agency?
   a. National Park Service
   b. Social Security Administration
   c. Environmental Protection Agency
   d. all of the above

8. This agency has authority over the interest rates and lending activities of the nation's most important banks.
   a. Federal Reserve System
   b. Office of Management and Budget
   c. Bureau of the Budget
   d. Congressional Budget Office

9. President ____________ was probably more preoccupied with administrative reform and reorganization than any other president in this century.
   a. Richard Nixon
   b. Lyndon Johnson
   c. Jimmy Carter
   d. Ronald Reagan

10. The ____________ was the first major revamping of the federal civil service since its creation in 1883.
    a. Civil Service Reform Act of 1978

b. Pendleton Act of 1964
c. Hatch Act of 1939
d. Government Reorganization Procedures Act of 1976

11. According to the authors, most organizations are ____________ and most of their employees are ____________.
 a. bureaucracies, bureaucrats
 b. matrix organizations, white-collar workers
 c. nonbureaucratic, nonbureaucrats
 d. flat hierarchies, patronage workers

12. According to the authors, which of the following is not a characteristic of bureaucracy?
 a. division of labor
 b. allocation of functions
 c. hiring based on patronage
 d. supervision

13. The word "bureaucracy" means a form of rule by:
 a. the people.
 b. the rich.
 c. offices and desks.
 d. the church.

14. Which of the following statements is true about the size of the federal civilian service?
 a. Since World War II the size of the federal government civilian service has grown steadily.
 b. The major growth in federal government civilian service has occurred since 1980.
 c. Despite rhetoric to the contrary, the federal civilian service has hardly grown at all during the past twenty-five years.
 d. The size of the federal government civilian service has declined precipitously since the 1970s.

15. They are directed by law to foster and promote the interests of a particular group or segment of American society.
 a. iron triangles
 b. regulatory agencies
 c. revenue agencies
 d. clientele agencies

16. A pattern of stable relationships between an agency in the executive branch, a congressional committee or subcommittee, and one or more organized groups of agency clientele is the definition of:
 a. issue networks.
 b. clientele groups.
 c. "picket-fence" legislation.
 d. iron triangles.

17. Taxing and spending policies are called:
 a. monetary policy.
 b. redistribution policies.
 c. fiscal policy.
 d. Fed policies.

18. Applicants for this system must demonstrate that their total annual cash earnings fall below the officially defined poverty level.
 a. welfare
 b. Social Security
 d. social safety net
 d. means-tested program

19. According to the authors, the bureaucracy can be "downsized" in which of the following ways?
 a. devolution

b. termination
c. privatization
d. all of the above

20. According to the authors of the text, the only certain way to reduce the size of the bureaucracy is:
a. devolution.
b. termination.
c. privatization.
d. none of the above

21. Downsizing the federal bureaucracy by delegating the implementation of programs to state and local governments is called:
a. privatization.
b. devolution.
c. termination.
d. downdrafting.

22. The concept of ___________ implies that there is some higher authority by which the actions of the bureaucracy will be guided and judged.
a. responsiveness
b. equity
c. efficiency
d. accountability

23. In essence, bureaucracy is:
a. inefficient.
b. found only in organizations with over 500 employees.
c. a form of organization not found in the private sector.
d. a method to organize and process work.

24. While the bureaucracy tries to maximize several values, bureaucracy as a concept places premier emphasis on:
a. effectiveness.
b. accountability.
c. efficiency.
d. equity.

25. According to the authors, if an organization is not efficient enough, it is probably because:
a. the organization has overbureaucratized.
b. the organization is too large.
c. the organization is too rule-bound.
d. the organization is not bureaucratized enough.

26. According to the authors of the text, why are public bureaucracies powerful?
a. Because by definition all large-scale organizations are powerful.
b. Because legislatures and chief executives, and indeed the people, delegate to the bureaucracy vast power.
c. Because bureaucracies are "pawns" in the hands of powerful executive and legislative actors.
d. all of the above

27. According to the authors, which of the following was the first "information network"?
a. bureaucracy
b. parliaments/congresses
c. churches
d. the Internet

28. According to the authors bureaucrats do four things, and generally these events occur in the following sequence:
a. implementation, maintaining a "paper trail," communication, and interpretation.

b. communication, maintaining a "paper trail," implementation, and interpretation.
c. interpretation, communication, maintaining a "paper trail," and implementation.
d. communication, maintaining a "paper trail," interpretation, and implementation.

29. As the authors of the text note, when bureaucrats "interpret" a law, they are in effect engaged in:
a. subversion.
b. carrying out legislative intent.
c. lawmaking.
d. evaluation.

30. To ensure a "merit system" government employees are hired:
a. based on open, competitive exams.
b. through patronage.
c. by the "spoils system."
d. based on "who they know."

31. With respect to "sociological representation" (a concept learned in the chapter on Congress), the federal bureaucracy is _________ representative than Congress.
a. much more
b. more
c. not as
d. about as

32. Each federal bureau-level agency is usually operating under a(n) ____________, adopted by ____________, that set up the program and gave the agency its authority and jurisdiction.
a. executive order, the president
b. statute, Congress
c. court order, the judiciary
d. consent decree, department-level agencies

33. Which of the following is true with respect to reducing the size of the bureaucracy through the process of termination during the twelve years of the Reagan and Bush administrations?
a. Literally dozens of programs and thousands of federal workers were terminated.
b. While there is little evidence that people were terminated, a large number of programs were terminated.
c. Presidents Reagan and Bush were successful in eliminating the Departments of Education, Commerce, and Labor.
d. Not a single national government agency or program was terminated.

34. Most of what is called "privatization" involves:
a. terminating government programs.
b. deregulation.
c. the provision of government goods and services by private contractors under direct government supervision.
d. all of the above.

QUESTIONS FOR DISCUSSION AND THOUGHT

1. Have you ever considered seeking a career in government? How do you feel about working for government after having read this chapter? What level of government interests you most: federal, state, or local government? What agency would you like to work for?

2. Suppose you were aware of some corruption that was occurring in the government agency in which you work. What would you do? Would you be a whistleblower? What are the possible consequences to you for reporting the corruption? Do you believe yourself to be an honest and ethical person? If you didn't report the corruption, would you still consider yourself to be honest and ethical?

3. Many people complain about government "red tape." Suppose we were to abolish the red tape and just let bureaucrats make their own decisions, using their own judgment. Would you support this change?

4. Suppose the civil service were abolished and all federal jobs were given out through patronage. Would this create a more responsive bureaucracy? What problems do you see with this proposal? Would you support it? Would you support some larger proportion of patronage jobs, say 30 percent?

5. There are laws that seek to limit the ability of presidential appointees to "cash in" on their relationships, usually as lobbyists. Do these restrictions limit the freedom of these individuals in a way that is unfair, or do you think that the laws are appropriate? If you worked at the White House, would you attempt to benefit financially from those connections after leaving your job?

6. As governments downsize, they often contract with private companies to perform what was once considered to be the traditional work of government. What are the advantages and disadvantages of privatizing: jails, public schools, military plane maintenance, state welfare agencies, state employment agencies?

THE CITIZEN'S ROLE

Many students think that government jobs are only for political science majors, but, in fact, government at all levels needs people with highly specialized skills. On the Internet, locate at least one government agency that relates to your college major. The Federal Web Locator at http://www.law.vill.edu/fed-agency/fedwebloc.html is the easiest source for accessing the many federal agencies. Listed below are some examples of agencies that are of particular interest to a few career fields:

Career field	Example agencies or programs
Agriculture	Agriculture Research Service
Architecture	National Center for Preservation Technology and Training
Education	National Center for Education Statistics
Engineering	Construction Engineering Research Laboratories
History	Center of Military History
Medicine	National Institutes of Health
Military	Joint Strike Fighter Information System
Science	Brookhaven National Laboratory
Social work	Administration for Children and Families

1. List the agencies you found that have careers that fit your major interests.
2. Were you surprised to find government jobs for so many different careers? What sort of majors did you think were recruited by the federal government?
3. Was the agency's web site clear and understandable? Did it provide information on how to apply for employment with the agency?
4. Would you consider a career working for the federal government? Explain.
5. Has your impression of the federal bureaucracy changed as a result of this project? For better or worse? Why?

GOVERNMENT IN YOUR LIFE

Politicians today talk a lot about "privatizing" government, which can mean either selling off a government agency to the private sector or simply contracting with a private agency to run the organization. All of the functions listed below have been proposed for privatization or are, in some places, already privatized. Use the table below to express your opinion on what should or should not be privatized.

Should This Function Be Privatized?

Function	Yes	No	Your Reasons
Local jails			
Social Security			
National parks administration			
National Weather Service			
Public schools			
Local trash collection			
Child support payment collection			
Municipal bus transportation			
Municipal hospitals			
Manned mission to Mars			

1. How many functions did you identify for privatization?
2. What was the basis for your opinion? Explain.
3. What are some of the advantages of privatization?
4. What are some of the disadvantages of privatization?
5. Overall, are you satisfied with the job that government is doing, or do you believe that the private market can serve the public interest more effectively?

ANSWER KEY

Fill-in-the-Blank Quiz

1. independent
2. clientele
3. paper trail
4. oversight
5. fiscal policies, Federal Reserve System (Fed)
6. revenue
7. administrative adjudication
8. privatization
9. government corporation

10. accountability
11. merit system
12. redistributive
13. regulatory
14. means testing
15. iron triangle
16. deregulated
17. bureaucracy
18. devolution
19. implementation
20. departments

Multiple-Choice Quiz

1. b
2. a
3. a
4. d
5. a
6. d
7. c
8. a
9. c
10. a
11. a
12. c
13. c
14. c
15. d
16. d
17. c
18. d
19. d
20. b
21. b
22. d
23. d
24. c
25. d
26. b
27. a
28. b
29. c
30. a
31. a
32. b
33. d
34. c

CHAPTER 15 | The Federal Courts

THE CHAPTER IN BRIEF

Originally, a court was where a sovereign ruled. Settling disputes was, for a king, part of government. Judging (or the settling of disputes) was slowly separated from the king and made into a separate institution of government. The basis of authority for judges in the United States is the Constitution and the laws.

Cases that reach the courts are divided into three types: criminal, civil, and public law cases. In criminal cases, the government charges an individual with violating a statute that has been enacted to protect public health, safety, morals, or welfare. The government is always the plaintiff (*The People v. . . .*) and alleges that a criminal violation has been committed by a named defendant.

Civil law cases consist of disputes among individuals or between individuals and the government. The one who brings the complaint is called the "plaintiff," and the one against whom the complaint is brought is called the "defendant." Losers cannot be fined or sent to prison, although they can be required to pay damages for their actions. The two most common types of civil cases are contracts and torts. In a contract case, the plaintiff charges that he has suffered damages because of the defendant's violation of a specific agreement. A tort case involves injury to one person by another person's negligence or malfeasance. In deciding civil cases, the courts apply statutes and legal precedent.

A major form of public law is constitutional law, in which a court will see if certain actions by the government conform to the Constitution as interpreted by the judiciary. A criminal case can become public law if a defendant claims that his or her constitutional rights were violated by the police. A civil case can also become a matter of public law if an individual asserts that the government violated a statute or abused its power under the Constitution. Most Supreme Court cases involve judicial review of the constitutional or statutory basis of the actions of governmental agencies.

Both federal and state court systems are organized in three tiers. The lower tier is composed of the trial courts, both municipal and superior; the middle tier is the appellate, or appeals courts; and at the top is the Supreme Court. Ninety-nine percent of all cases are heard by state courts. In both criminal and civil matters, most cases are settled before they go to trial through negotiated agreements between the parties. Cases are heard in the federal courts if they involve federal statutes, treaties with other nations, or the U.S. Constitution, or where the U.S. government is a party. Individuals found guilty of breaking a state criminal law might appeal their conviction to a federal court by raising a constitutional issue.

Although the federal courts hear only a small fraction of the cases decided every year, it is ultimately the federal courts that dominate the judicial system. The lower federal courts are usually the courts of original jurisdiction; they are responsible for discovering facts and creating a record upon which judgment is based. The lowest federal courts are the district courts, of which there are eighty-nine in the fifty states, plus one in Washington, D.C., one in Puerto Rico, and three territorial courts.

There are twelve judicial circuits and each circuit has a U.S. Court of Appeals, or appellate court. Approximately 10 percent of all lower court and agency cases are accepted for review by the federal appeals courts and by the Supreme Court in its capacity as an appellate court. All appellate court decisions are final, unless the appeal is taken to the Supreme Court. Three or more judges hear appealed cases, sitting together *en banc.* The most frequent and best-known action of circuit justices is that of reviewing requests for stays of execution when the full Supreme Court is unable to do so, as during summer recess.

The Supreme Court is America's highest court. It has the power to review any lower court decision where a substantial issue of public law is involved. The Supreme Court consists of a chief justice and eight associate justices. Each justice, including the chief justice, casts one vote. In addition to the judges, three other agencies or groups play an important role in shaping the flow of cases through the Supreme Court. These are the solicitor general, the Federal Bureau of Investigation (FBI), and the Court's law clerks.

The solicitor general is third in status in the Justice Department, below the attorney general and the deputy attorney general. The solicitor general controls the flow of cases into the Supreme Court by reviewing them before they reach the Court. Although others can regulate the flow of cases, the solicitor general has the greatest control, with no supervision by any higher authority. The solicitor general has the power to enter a case with a "friend of the court" brief, even when the federal government is not a direct litigant, and can also shape arguments used before the Court.

The FBI is an important influence on the flow of cases through the appellate judiciary. Its data are the most vital source of material for cases in the areas of national security and organized crime. It also links the Justice Department closely to cases being brought by state and local government officials.

The third group is composed of the law clerks. Each Supreme Court justice is assigned four clerks. The clerks are almost always honors graduates of the country's most prestigious law schools, and the position indicates that the individual is likely to reach the very top of the legal profession. The work of the clerks is a closely guarded secret, but it is probable that justices rely heavily on their clerks for advice.

Federal judges are appointed by the president and are generally selected from among the more prominent or politically active members of the legal profession. A senator from a state in which a U.S. District Court vacancy has occurred, if that senator is from the president's party, suggests candidates to the president in an informal nominating procedure. Presidents generally endeavor to appoint judges whose partisan and ideological views are similar to the president's own. Once the president has formally nominated an individual, he or she must be considered by the Senate Judiciary Committee and confirmed by a majority vote in the Senate. Federal Appeals Court nominations follow much the same pattern, but candidates are generally suggested to the president by the Justice Department or by important members of the administration. Through Supreme Court appointments, presidents attempt to create either a conservative Court or a liberal Court, depending on their own political philosophies.

The power of judicial review makes the Supreme Court a major lawmaking body as well as a judicial agency. Though the Constitution does not specifically give the Supreme Court the power of judicial review of congressional enactments, disputes over the intentions of the framers were settled in 1803, when the case of *Marbury v. Madison* established the power of the Court to review acts of Congress.

The Supreme Court also exercises judicial review of state actions. The supremacy clause of Article VI declares the Constitution and all laws made under its authority to be the "supreme law of the land." The Judiciary Act of 1789 conferred on the Supreme Court the power to reverse state constitutions and laws whenever they conflict with the U.S. Constitution, federal laws, or treaties. Many Supreme Court rulings set precedents that were henceforth obeyed in all states. When a police officer reads an arrested person his rights, he is doing it because of a 1966 case, *Miranda v. Arizona.*

The original jurisdiction of the Supreme Court includes cases between the United States and one of the fifty states; cases between two or more states, such as disputes over land, water, or old debts; cases involving foreign ambassadors or other ministers; and cases brought by one state against citizens of another state or against a foreign country.

Decisions handed down by a lower court can reach the Supreme Court in one of two ways. The first is a writ of *certiorari,* which is granted whenever four of the nine justices agree to review a case and only where there are special and important reasons. These reasons include the following: where a state has made a decision that conflicts with previous Supreme Court decisions, where a state court has come up with an entirely new federal question, where one court of appeals has rendered a decision in conflict with another, where there are other inconsistent rulings between two or more courts or states, or (rarely) where a single court of appeals has sanctioned too great a departure by a lower court from normal judicial proceedings. The second is a writ of *habeas corpus,* which is a fundamental safeguard of individual rights applying to prisoners already convicted in state courts.

The courts have developed specific rules that govern which cases within their jurisdiction they will and will not hear. These rules of access fall under three major categories. The first is that the case must be an actual controversy, not a hypothetical one, with two truly adversarial parties. The second is standing, meaning that parties to a case must show that they have a substantial stake in the outcome of the case. The requirement for standing is to show injury to oneself—personal, economic, or aesthetic. Each member of a class action suit must show specific injury. The third criterion is mootness—cases that are brought too early or too late to be relevant are disqualified. Putting aside the formal criteria, the Supreme Court is also likely to accept cases where there have been conflicting decisions by circuit courts, cases presenting important civil rights or civil liberties questions, and cases where the federal government is the appellant. Ultimately, the question of which cases to accept can come down to the preferences and priorities of the justices.

Interest groups in recent years have been lobbying for access to the Supreme Court, and they use several types of strategies to do so. Lawyers representing interest groups have to choose the proper client and proper case, so that the issues in question are the most dramatically and appropriately portrayed. They also have to pick the right jurisdiction or district in which to bring the case, and sometimes even wait for the appropriate political climate. Group litigants have to plan when to use and when to avoid publicity. Groups such as the NAACP and the ACLU often encourage private parties to bring suit and then join the suit as friends of the court.

Once the Supreme Court accepts a case, attorneys on both sides must prepare briefs, which are written documents filled with case precedents in which attorneys explain why the Court should find in favor of their client. Attorneys ask sympathetic interest groups for their support as *amici curiae* (friends of the court). Once the case is in court, each attorney has a half-hour to present his or her case in an oral argument, in which the attorney may be interrupted many times by the justices asking pointed questions. Arguing a case in the Supreme Court is a singular honor for an attorney. After both sides are presented, the Court discusses the case in secret conference. The chief justice presides, and the others follow in order of seniority. They reach a decision on the basis of a majority vote, but if the Court is divided, compromise decisions may be reached.

After a decision is made, the writing of the opinion is assigned to one of the majority members. If the chief justice is a majority member, he or she makes the assignment, but if the chief justice is on the losing side, the assignment is made by the most senior justice in the majority. The assignment of the opinion is important because every opinion of the Supreme Court sets a major precedent for future cases throughout the judicial system.

Justices who disagree with the Court may choose to publicize the character of their disagreement in the form of a dissenting opinion, which is the most dependable way for an individual justice to exercise a direct and clear influence on the Court. It encourages lawyers to keep bringing similar cases in, and thus influences the flow of cases through the Court.

Supreme Court decisions are explained in terms of law and precedent; that is, each decision is justified by references to statutes and to previous case decisions. Throughout history, the Court has shaped and reshaped the law based on shifts in judicial philosophy. These shifts result from changes in the Court's composition over time. One element of judicial philosophy is the issue of activism versus restraint. Advocates of judicial restraint believe that courts should interpret the Constitution according to the intentions of its framers and defer to Congress. This is called "strict constructionism." Judicial activists, on the other hand, believe that the Court should go beyond the words of the Constitution or statute to consider broader societal implications of their decisions. The second element of judicial philosophy is political ideology. Liberal judges traditionally have been activists, willing to use the law to achieve social and political change. Conservative judges have been associated with restraint and strict constructionism; they are usually opposed to the use of the courts to bring about social change. Some conservatives, however, have become activists in order to undo the results achieved by liberal jurists over the past three decades.

In the past fifty years there has been a striking transformation of the role and power of the Supreme Court. Traditionally, the power of the federal courts was subject to five limitations. First, access to the courts was limited to individuals who could show that they were particularly affected by the government's behavior in some area, which diminished the judiciary's capacity to forge links with important political and social forces. Second, the courts acted only to offer relief or assistance to individuals and not to broad social classes, which inhibited alliances between the courts and important social forces. Third, the courts lacked their own enforcement powers. If executive or state agencies were unwilling to assist the courts, their judicial enactments could go unheeded. Fourth, the president and Congress can shape the composition of the federal courts and ultimately, perhaps, the character of judicial decisions. Fifth, Congress has the power to change both the size and the jurisdiction of the Supreme Court and other federal courts.

Since World War II there have been two judicial revolutions. The first and most obvious was a revolution in judicial policy. The Supreme Court was at the forefront of a series of sweeping changes in the role of the U.S. government and in the character of American society. At the same time, a second, less visible revolution was beginning: a series of changes in judicial procedures that expanded the power of the courts. First, the federal courts liberalized the concept of standing. Second, the federal courts began accepting class action cases in addition to individuals. Third, the federal courts began to apply "structural remedies," that is, retaining jurisdiction of cases until the court's mandate had actually been implemented to its satisfaction. These three judicial mechanisms expanded national judicial power in the 1960s and 1970s. The courts today have an active role in the democratic political process.

REVIEW QUESTIONS

1. Explain the difference between contract cases and tort cases. Under what category of law are they found?
2. How do courts decide civil cases?
3. What specific types of cases are heard in the federal courts? How do individuals convicted of breaking state laws get their cases heard in federal courts?
4. How does the chief justice lead the Supreme Court?
5. How does the solicitor general control the flow of cases through the Supreme Court?
6. What is the role of the FBI in federal cases?
7. Who, generally, are the law clerks of the federal courts, and what do they do? Are their tasks important to the running of the courts?
8. What do presidents consider when they appoint judges to the federal courts, and especially to the Supreme Court? How can their appointments ultimately shape national policy?
9. What Supreme Court case established the power of judicial review?
10. What do the cases of *Gideon v. Wainwright, Escobedo v. Illinois,* and *Miranda v. Arizona* have in common? The legal precedents established in these cases grant certain protections to what group of people?
11. What are the criteria for "standing" in a court case, particularly in a class action case?
12. What litigation strategies might an interest group use to pursue its goal through the federal courts? How does the case of *Plyler v. Doe* in Texas illustrate this?
13. What are attorneys' briefs? What are briefs called that are filed by interest groups?
14. Explain the procedure for oral argument by attorneys and what follows in Court.
15. How can a dissenting opinion ultimately influence the Court even more than an opinion that decides a case?
16. Explain judicial activism and judicial restraint, and how they are related to political ideology.
17. How has the role of the federal courts changed since World War II?

18. Why is it important in a democracy that the judicial branch be separated from the executive and legislative branches?

19. "Equality before the law" is a basic principle of the American democratic system. Do you think this really exists?

KEY TERMS

amicus curiae
appellate court
briefs
Chief Justice
civil law
class action suit
criminal law
defendant
dissenting opinion
due process of law
judicial activism
judicial restraint
judicial review
jurisdiction
Miranda rule
mootness
opinion
oral arguments
original jurisdiction
per curiam
plaintiff
plea bargains
precedent
public law
senatorial courtesy
solicitor general
standing
stare decisis
supremacy clause
Supreme Court
trial court
Uniform Commercial Code
writ of *certiorari*
writ of *habeas corpus*

FILL-IN-THE-BLANK QUIZ

Use the key terms to complete the following sentences.

1. The requirement that persons under arrest be informed of their rights is known as the ___________.
2. Administrative law and constitutional law are forms of ___________ law.
3. The written explanation of the Supreme Court's decision is called a(n) ___________; judges who disagree may write a(n___________.
4. A court that hears appeals from lower courts is a(n___________.
5. The federal courts are superior over the state courts because of the ___________ of the Constitution.
6. Cases are decided on the basis of law and ___________, also known as ___________.

7. Most states have adopted the ____________ for contract law because it reduces confusion between states.

8. Interest groups often file ____________ briefs to indicate support for one side in a case.

9. You believe that a law recently passed by Congress is unconstitutional, but you are unable to sue to challenge it because you have not been damaged by the law. You do not have ____________.

10. The person who argues cases in the Supreme Court that involve the federal government is the ____________.

11. The Supreme Court issues two kinds of writs: one which orders a review of a decision from a lower court, called a writ of ____________. and the other which orders the release of a person being unconstitutionally retained, a writ of ____________.

12. The person who brings a complaint is the ____________; the person against whom the complaint is brought is the ____________.

13. Lawyers summarize their arguments in ____________.

14. When an appellate court decides not to review the decision of a lower court, it is issuing a(n) ____________ ruling.

15. Attorneys who appear before the Supreme Court have only thirty minutes in which to make their ____________.

16. Federal district courts are ____________ courts, or courts of ____________ jurisdiction.

17. The highest court in the United States, the ____________, can review the actions of the other branches of government, a practice known as ____________.

18. You are a college student who files suit against the administration because you object to the criteria used for determining grades. Five years later, when the court examines the case, it is rejected because you have already graduated. The grounds for rejection are ____________.

19. Generally, conservative judges believe in judicial ____________, while liberal judges support judicial ____________.

20. Someone who is arrested under ____________ law for violating the safety of society may want to plead guilty in return for a lesser sentence, a practice known as ____________.

21. When he agrees with the majority, the ____________ writes the Supreme Court decision.

22. A court case that is settled by determining liability instead of guilt and often involves monetary payments is a case in ____________.

23. The power of a court to hear a particular kind of case is its ____________.

24. When nominating a federal judge, the president will consult with senators of his own party from that state, a practice known as ____________.

25. You bought a microwave for your dorm room that was defective and caused you to burn your popcorn. You want to join with others who bought the same model to file a ____________.

26. Every citizen has the right of ____________, which means protection from arbitrary acts of government.

MULTIPLE-CHOICE QUIZ

1. Every year nearly ____________ million cases are tried in American courts and one American in every ____________ is directly involved in litigation.
   a. one , 1,000
   b. ten, 100
   c. twenty-five, nine
   d. fifty, two

2. More than ____________ percent of all court cases in the United States are heard in ____________ courts.
   a. 50, federal
   b. 99, federal
   c. 99, state
   d. 50, state

3. In total, how many federal district courts exist in the United States?
   a. 50, one in each state
   b. 94
   c. 100
   d. 250

4. The country is divided into ____________ judicial circuits, each of which has a U.S. Court of Appeals.
   a. 12
   b. 50
   c. 94
   d. 112

5. The U.S. Supreme Court is comprised of one Chief Justice and ____________ associate justices.
   a. five
   b. eight
   c. nine
   d. fifteen

6. In 1803 in the case of ____________, the Supreme Court established the principle of judicial review.
   a. *McCulloch v. Maryland*
   b. *Brown v. Board of Education*
   c. *Gibbons v. Ogden*
   d. *Marbury v. Madison*

7. Cases of ____________ law are those in which the government charges an individual with violating a statute that has been enacted to protect the public health, safety, morals, or welfare.
   a. criminal

b. civil
c. public
d. all of the above

8. The party that brings charges into a court of law is the:
   a. defendant.
   b. district attorney.
   c. plaintiff.
   d. litigant.

9. The doctrine of *stare decisis:*
   a. means "send the records of a case up."
   b. applies only to criminal law.
   c. is applicable only to the U.S. Supreme Court.
   d. means "let the decision stand."

10. In which of the following state courts are juries used?
    a. trial courts
    b. appellate courts
    c. Supreme Court
    d. court of last resort

11. In both criminal and civil matters, most cases are settled before trial through negotiated agreements between the parties. In criminal cases these agreements are called:
    a. consent decrees.
    b. joint settlements.
    c. plea bargains.
    d. pardon and parole decisions.

12. Which of the following is not a case in which the federal courts would have jurisdiction?
    a. a case in which the U.S. government is a party
    b. a case involving a treaty with another nation
    c. a case involving burglary of a house
    d. a case involving federal laws

13. The ____________ is the third-ranking official in the Justice Department but is the top government lawyer in virtually all cases before the appellate courts where the government is a party.
    a. Attorney General
    b. Deputy Attorney General
    c. head of the Federal Bureau of Investigation
    d. Solicitor General

14. The authority and the obligation to review any lower court decision where a substantial issue of public law is involved is the definition of:
    a. writ of review.
    b. judicial review.
    c. standing.
    d. due process.

15. The courts do not have the power to render advisory opinions to legislatures or agencies about the constitutionality of proposed laws or regulations. This is the definition of the court access requirement called:
    a. mootness.
    b. standing.
    c. cases and controversies.
    d. all of the above.

16. Parties in a case must show ____________; that is, they must show that they have a substantial stake in the outcome of a case.
    a. mootness
    b. standing
    c. cases and controversies
    d. all of the above

17. Most cases reach the Supreme Court through:
    a. writs of *mandamus.*

b. writs of *certiorari.*
c. writs of appeal.
d. none of the above

18. The three steps in the Supreme Court's procedures, in order, are:
    a. preparing briefs, writing opinions, giving oral argument.
    b. writing opinions, preparing briefs, giving oral argument.
    c. preparing briefs, giving oral argument, writing opinions.
    d. writing opinions, giving oral arguments, preparing briefs.

19. Justices who disagree with the majority decision of the Court may choose to publicize the character of their disagreement in the form of:
    a. a concurring opinion.
    b. a dissenting opinion.
    c. a nonconsensus opinion.
    d. a disagreeing opinion.

20. The Founders called the Supreme Court the:
    a. "most powerful branch" of American government.
    b. "least dangerous branch" of American government.
    c. "most dangerous branch" of American government.
    d. "most important branch among equals."

21. Which of the following concepts is the least related to the other concepts?
    a. precedent
    b. *stare decisis*
    c. let the decision stand
    d. judicial policy making

22. For the most part, original jurisdiction courts in the federal judiciary:
    a. are federal district courts.
    b. are the U.S. Supreme Court.
    c. are federal appellate courts.
    d. All of the above courts have original jurisdiction.

23. Which of the following factors affect how federal district court judges are chosen?
    a. legal experience and good character
    b. ideological views similar to the president
    c. senatorial courtesy
    d. all of the above

24. The power of the Supreme Court to review state legislation or other state action and to determine its constitutionality is neither granted by the Constitution nor inherent in the federal system. Rather the authority is derived from:
    a. the Supremacy Clause.
    b. the Judiciary Act of 1789.
    c. the due process and equal protecting clauses of the Fourteenth Amendment.
    d. all of the above

25. Why did Congress confer on federal courts the authority to issue writs of *habeas corpus*?
    a. distrust of Southern courts after the Civil War
    b. to ensure the Tenth Amendment guarantee of due process of law
    c. to ensure the Fourth Amendment guarantee of the equal protection of the laws

d. to give federal courts the power of judicial review over state judicial decisions

26. A member of the U.S. Supreme Court believes that she should interpret the Constitution according to the stated intentions of its framers and defer to the views of Congress when interpreting federal statutes. This person is an advocate of:
   a. judicial restraint.
   b. judicial activism.
   c. "loose constructionism."
   d. all of the above.

27. Which of the following is a limitation on federal courts?
   a. limits on the character of the relief they can offer
   b. appointment by the president
   c. confirmation by the Senate
   d. Congress sets the size and jurisdiction of the Supreme Court.
   e. all of the above

QUESTIONS FOR DISCUSSION AND THOUGHT

1. Do we have "equal justice under the law" as the Constitution promises? Draw up a list of arguments on both sides of the issue. What are the main impediments to equal justice, in your opinion? What does this say about the United States as a democracy? About our ability to provide equality before the law?

2. How much privacy do you think you have? Are you aware of all the daily intrusions into your private life? Do you ever call an 800-number? Use a credit card at a grocery store? Order from a catalog? Use the Internet? Use E-mail? Give out your Social Security number? Subscribe to a magazine? Every one of these examples provides important personal information about you to telemarketers, marketing companies, private investigators, even government agencies. What steps can you take to ensure your privacy?

3. Have you ever been called for jury duty? Did you serve? What were the ages and occupations of those you served with? What was your reaction to what you observed? Do you think everyone should have to serve?

4. Ninety-nine percent of all felonies are settled by plea bargains, whereby the suspect pleads guilty in promise of receiving a lower sentence. Obviously, this means that the suspect gives up some of his constitutional rights. What rights are these? Are plea bargains a good idea?

5. How can judges control a courtroom procedure in order to guarantee a fair trial? Think about some of the recent trials which have received a lot of publicity. Is it ever possible to completely control all the variables in order to protect the right of a fair trial?

6. Suppose the federal courts did not have the power of judicial review. Instead, all acts of Congress and the president would be considered constitutional. How would this change our system? Would you favor such a change?

THE CITIZEN'S ROLE

The American jury system for federal courts was borrowed from the British in 1789. At that time, British trials required a unanimous verdict. In the 1960s, however, the British laws were changed to allow verdicts of ten to two, although judges are supposed to try to get unanimous verdicts. Another difference is that the British attorneys cannot pick their juries, a process we call *voir dire.* A third contrast is that British judges are allowed to give more guidance to jurors; they can comment on the case and on the evidence. Select one of the three British reforms and complete the table below, listing the advantages and disadvantages of changing American law.

Advantages	Disadvantages

1. Which side has the stronger arguments, in your opinion?
2. Of these three reforms, which one do you like the most? The least? Why?
3. Which of these reforms would be most effective in reducing inequality in the judicial system? Why?
4. Do you think Americans would tolerate any changes to the existing judicial system? If so, what changes?
5. Does the American system of justice provide both justice and fairness? Explain.

GOVERNMENT IN YOUR LIFE

Who are the people on the Supreme Court? To learn more about them, go the web site for "The Oyez Project," at http://oyez.nwu.edu and select three Supreme Court justices. Complete the table below.

Information	Justice:	Justice:	Justice
Date appointed			
Appointed by			
Age at appointment			
Political party			
Confirmation vote			
Conservative/liberal			

1. What are the political philosophies of these justices? Is there a relationship between political party and judicial philosophy? Did you encounter any exceptions?
2. Were the confirmation votes nearly unanimous? If presidents select nominees with a particular political view, why do you think most justices win confirmation easily? Do Americans expect these justices to be neutral or partisan? Why is this an important issue?
3. Do you think that it is important that there is a diversity in terms of race, religion, gender, etc. on the Supreme Court? Does this Court represent diversity, in your opinion? Explain.
4. Federal judges serve for life; if the average Supreme Court justice retires at age seventy-five, how old will you be when each of these justices retires? Does this help you understand why the confirmation process is so important?
5. What consequences do you see, good and bad, for someone to serve for such a long time on the Court? Would you favor fixed terms? Explain.

ANSWER KEY

Fill-in-the-Blank Quiz

1. *Miranda* rule
2. public
3. opinion, dissenting opinion
4. appellate court
5. supremacy clause
6. precedent, *stare decisis*
7. Uniform Commercial Code
8. *amicus curiae*
9. standing
10. solicitor general
11. *certiorari, habeas corpus*
12. plaintiff, defendant
13. briefs
14. *per curiam*
15. oral arguments
16. trial, original
17. Supreme Court, judicial review
18. mootness
19. restraint, activism
20. criminal, plea bargaining
21. Chief Justice
22. civil law
23. jurisdiction
24. senatorial courtesy
25. class action suit
26. due process of law

Multiple-Choice Quiz

1. c
2. c
3. b
4. a
5. b
6. d
7. a
8. c
9. d
10. a
11. c
12. c
13. d
14. b
15. c
16. b
17. b
18. c
19. b
20. b
21. d
22. a
23. d
24. d
25. a
26. a
27. e

CHAPTER 16 Government and the Economy

THE CHAPTER IN BRIEF

The maintenance of public order is essential to economic stability. Everyone agrees on the goal of economic growth, but the public policies designed to achieve this goal are open to debate. In a government where freedom and control are balanced, control has to be their first priority in order to protect freedom. We generally call government control "public policy." A public policy is defined as an officially expressed intention backed by a sanction, which can be a reward or a punishment. Other names for a public policy are law, rule, statute, edict, regulation, or order. Examples of public policies are increasing interest rates, restricting imports, or raising or cutting taxes. All public policies are coercive.

Techniques of control are the tools of policy makers, and they can be grouped into three categories: promotional, regulatory, and redistributive techniques. Promotional techniques are a form of encouragement. Subsidies, for example, are government grants of cash or other valuable commodities, such as land. Most subsidies come from taxation, and their effect must be measured in terms of what people would be doing if a particular subsidy had not been available. Contracts aid private corporations and encourage corporations to improve themselves. Contracts build up whole sectors of the economy, and encourage certain goals such as equal employment opportunity. Privatization is a type of contract wherein a government program is transferred to a private company to provide the service under a contract with the government, paid for by the government, and supervised by a government agency. Besides subsidies and contracts, there is a third promotional technique—licensing. A license, or permit, is a privilege granted by a government to do something that it otherwise considers to be illegal. Some examples are driving a car, practicing medicine, keeping an exotic animal as a pet, operating a business, and fishing. There are many other activities that are allowed only by license.

The second type of technique of control is regulatory, or the direct government control of conduct. Police regulation controls conduct that is immoral or potentially harmful. Convictions result in fines or public service for violating civil laws, and criminal penalties can involve imprisonment, heavy fines, and the loss of certain civil rights or civil liberties. Administrative regulation tries to minimize injury or inconvenience. It relies on courts to issue orders enforcing rules made by agencies, regulating important economic activity such as public utilities. It protects companies from destructive or predatory competition. The threat of losing a valuable subsidy, license, or contract can be used by government to improve compliance with the goals of regulation. A contract or its denial can be used as a reward or punishment to gain obedience in a regulatory program. For example, the government can prohibit discrimination by firms receiving government contracts. Taxation can be regulatory. In many instances, the primary purpose of a tax is not to raise revenue but to discourage or eliminate an activity altogether by making it too expensive for most people. Regulatory taxation is more efficient than other forms of regulation, requiring less bureaucracy and less supervision. A widely used type of regulation is expropriation, or the seizing of private property for public use. This is the power of eminent domain, inherent in any government. There are safeguards against abuse, in that no property can be taken without due process, and fair market value must be offered for the land. Another form of expropriation is forcing individuals to work for a public purpose, as in the draft for the armed forces, court orders for strikers to return to work, or sentences for convicted felons to do community service.

The third type of technique of control is redistributive, also called macroeconomic techniques, which control people by manipulating the entire economy rather than by regulating people directly. Fiscal techniques are the government's taxing and spending powers. Personal and corporate income taxes are the most prominent examples, and the source of most government revenue. President Clinton's commitment to a middle-class tax cut is an example of a fiscal policy designed to increase consumption. Monetary techniques manipulate the economy through the supply or availability of money. The Federal Reserve Board can increase the interest rate it charges member banks, as an attempt to curb inflation. It can increase or decrease the reserve requirement, which sets the actual proportion of deposited money that a bank must keep on demand as it makes all the rest of its deposits available as new loans. It can also use open market operations—the buying and selling of Treasury securities to absorb excess dollars or to release more dollars into the economy. Member banks can also borrow from each other (the "federal funds market"). The most important redistributive technique is the use of the "spending power" as fiscal policy; this is a combination of subsidies and contracts.

One of the main goals of the national government is making and maintaining a market economy. In some ways the states were a hindrance to a national market because of their various laws. In *Gibbons v. Ogden* (1824), a decision was handed down that prohibits individual states from passing laws that could interrupt or burden the free flow of commerce among the states. In the nineteenth century the national government was almost exclusively a promoter of markets. It built national roads and canals, installed national tariff policies, and heavily subsidized the railroads with land grants, cash, and credit. Traditional promotional techniques were expanded in the twentieth century, and new ones were invented. Most of the current promotional activity is done through categorical grants.

Some companies grew so large that they could eliminate competitors and impose conditions on consumers. They had what was called "market power." Small businesses, laborers, farmers, and consumers wanted protective regulation. The Interstate Commerce Act of 1887 created the Interstate Commerce Commission (ICC) to regulate the railroads. The Sherman Antitrust Act (1889) extended regulatory power over all monopolies. These were strengthened in 1914 with the enactment of the Federal Trade Act (which created the Federal Trade Commission, or FTC) and the Clayton Act. In 1912 the Federal Reserve System was established to regulate the banking system. Comprehensive national regulation began in the 1930s to deal with specific sectors of American industry. All of these programs were backed by both parties. Until about 1960, the federal government regulations were applied industry-wide, such as in the railroad or airline industries. In the 1960s and 1970s, though, a major change took place in the regulatory environment. New agencies such as the Occupational Safety and Health Administration and the Environmental Protection Agency were created which regulated all industries across the entire economy.

Today's conservatives oppose government regulation of the economy. The deregulation movement began under Presidents Ford and Carter. President Reagan proposed termination of the ICC and cut regulatory agency budgets by 20 percent. Reagan appointed people who were not in sympathy with regulatory missions of specific agencies, and he used his power of "presidential oversight." Presidents Bush and Clinton favored deregulation as a principle, but were not as successful as Reagan had been at reducing federal regulations.

There are many reasons that the government gets into regulatory policies. These reasons include public opinion, politics, morality, efficiency, convenience, and equity. With all of these reasons for regulating, it is unlikely that any president will significantly reduce the level of government regulation for long. As a general rule, conservatives are moved by moral reasons to favor regulation; liberals are moved by instrumental reasons, such as reduction of risk or injury, or to gain equity; but both favor regulation some of the time.

Government and capitalism depend on each other. Most U.S. regulatory policies have been distinctly capitalistic; that is, they have aimed at promoting investment and ownership by individuals and corporations in the private sector. Monetary policies manipulate the growth of the entire economy through the supply or availability of money to the banks. Congress established the Federal Reserve System in 1913 to integrate private banks into a single system. The federal government provides insurance to foster credit and encourage private capital investment. Another promoter of investment is the federal insurance of home mortgages through the Federal Housing Administration (FHA) and the Veterans Administration (VA).

Taxation is a part of capitalism, and all taxes discriminate. The most important choice Congress ever made about taxation was the decision to raise revenue by taxing personal and corporate incomes—the income tax. Congress chose to make the income tax progressive, or graduated, with the heaviest burden carried by those most able to pay. A tax is progressive if the rate of taxation goes up with each higher-income bracket. A tax is regressive if people in lower income brackets pay a higher proportion of their income toward the tax than people in higher-income brackets. Examples are sales taxes and the Social Security tax. A second objective of the graduated income tax is to reduce the disparities of wealth between the lowest and the highest income brackets. This is called a policy of redistribution, using the income tax to offset regressive taxes in order to redistribute wealth and to encourage a capitalist income.

Government spending is another technique for influencing the economy and redistributing wealth. It can supplement private spending and heat up the economy. On the downside, it might merely inflate the economy. Much of the federal budget is already mandated, and therefore inflexible.

The welfare state, seen as a fiscal policy, contributes to the stability of the economy by cutting down on the harshest extremes of fluctuations in the business cycle.

Public policies will continue to reflect the interests of those with influence. Moral and ethical principles are involved, as each policy decision affects the balance between citizens' liberties and government's power. Freedom depends upon control.

REVIEW QUESTIONS

1. How are beneficial public policies such as various promotional techniques coercive toward the American people? Are government "giveaways" such as land and cash grants coercive? How?
2. Why is privatization of government programs not really a restoration of programs to the private sector? What is it instead?
3. When the government allows a single company to become a legal monopoly, how do administrative regulations protect consumers?
4. Other than raising revenue, another purpose of a tax is to discourage or eliminate an activity by making it too expensive for most people. Is regulatory taxation efficient in such matters as gasoline consumption, or alcohol or tobacco use? How is it more efficient for the government than other methods, such as rationing or prohibition?

5. How is the military draft akin to a public works departmental takeover of private land for the building of a highway? What is the general term for the government power that encompasses both?
6. Do redistributive techniques regulate people directly? If not, what do they manipulate or alter in order to affect the economy?
7. What techniques does the Federal Reserve Board use to control the economy? At what time in history was the Federal Reserve System established?
8. What is the primary difference between the regulatory policies of the 1930s and those of the 1970s?
9. Describe President Reagan's actions toward deregulation. What were the results?
10. How are morality and convenience related to government regulations? Does public opinion play a role in the formation of public policies?
11. How do monetary techniques manipulate the growth of the entire economy?
12. Explain the difference between progressive taxes and regressive taxes.
13. Give some examples of mandated expenditures in the annual federal budget. Why are they called uncontrollable?
14. On a cycle when the economy is declining, how can raising welfare payments actually help the economy?
15. In regard to government policies, how can freedom depend upon control at the same time that freedom is threatened by control?
16. Why did people turn to the national government for protective regulation in the late nineteenth century, when the states already had regulatory policies in effect?
17. Capitalism is based on the right of the individual to operate freely in the economy, even though that may create substantial inequality. How can we reconcile both values: liberty and equality?
18. Is capitalism consistent with democracy? What values of democracy are enhanced by capitalism? What values are diminished by capitalism?

KEY TERMS

administrative regulation
categorical grants
civil penalties
contracting power
criminal penalties
deregulation

discount rate
eminent domain
expropriation
Federal Reserve Board
Federal Reserve System (Fed)
fiscal policy
inflation
license
monetary policy
monopoly
open market operations
police power
policy of redistribution
progressive taxation
public policy
regressive taxation
regulation
regulatory tax
reserve requirement
subsidies
uncontrollables

FILL-IN-THE-BLANK QUIZ

Use the key terms to complete the following sentences.

1. Banks loan out most of their money to customers but they must keep some money on hand to meet depositors' demands, a rule known as the ___________.
2. The Federal Reserve Board controls ___________ policy, while Congress and the president determine ___________ policy.
3. The government uses its ___________ to impose conditions on companies that wish to sell to the government.
4. When the government purchased your house in order to build a highway, it was using its power of ___________, also known as ___________.
5. The more income you make, the higher your tax rate. This is a ___________ tax.
6. The Social Security tax is ___________ because income over $68,400 is not taxed.
7. The government regulates competition in order to prevent ___________, in which one firm controls the industry.
8. The authority of the state to regulate for the health and safety of its citizens is its ___________ power.
9. When Robin Hood took from the rich to give to the poor, he was practicing a policy of ___________.
10. Monetary policy is controlled by the ___________, made up of seven members.
11. President Carter eliminated most of the federal controls on the airlines, a practice known as ___________.

12. Rules made by regulatory agencies have the force of an act of Congress. This power is called ___________.

13. Violating the Clean Air Act may cost a company thousands of dollars in fines in ___________.

14. The American West was settled by homesteaders who received ___________ of free land from the federal government.

15. ___________ is not neutral; it reflects the choices and morals of a nation.

16. The Federal Reserve Board sells government securities in its ___________ in order to control the amount of money in circulation.

17. Nursing students worry about passing the state examinations that allow them to receive a ___________ to practice.

18. The amount of money in circulation can be expanded or retracted by the interest rate, also known as the ___________, that the Fed charges its member banks.

19. Congress can have little effect on the federal budget because of the ___________, or financial commitments that cannot be altered, such as Social Security.

20. When government places rules on the conduct of citizens, it is imposing ___________.

21. The twelve "bankers' banks" are called the ___________.

22. A ___________ of $5 on a package of cigarettes would seriously discourage their consumption by teenagers.

23. When the federal government gives states money to build parks, it is giving ___________.

24. The officers of a company who violate the Sherman Antitrust Law can be sent to prison for a maximum of three years. This act carries both civil and ___________.

MULTIPLE-CHOICE QUIZ

1. The chairperson of the Federal Reserve Board is:
   a. Leon Panetta.
   b. Alice Rivlan.
   c. David Stockton.
   d. Alan Greenspan.

2. According to the authors, there was no significant increase in the development of national policies until:
   a. 1866.
   b. 1919.

c. 1933.
d. 1960.

3. In ____________, the Supreme Court told the states in no uncertain terms that they could not pass laws that would tend to interrupt or otherwise burden the free flow of commerce among the states.
a. *Marbury v. Madison*
b. *Engle v. Vitale*
c. *Gibbons v. Ogden*
d. *Barron v. Baltimore*

4. The ____________ of 1889 was aimed at regulating monopolistic practices.
a. Sherman Antitrust Act
b. Interstate Commerce Act
c. Federal Trade Act
d. Clayton Act

5. According to the authors of the text, the deregulation movement began with:
a. Presidents Ford and Carter.
b. Presidents Kennedy and Johnson.
c. Presidents Reagan and Bush.
d. President Clinton.

6. According to the authors of the text, in 1990, approximately what percentage of the total federal budget was comprised of so-called uncontrollables?
a. 30 percent
b. 50 percent
c. 60 percent
d. 75 percent

7. A consistent increase in the general level of prices is called:
a. price stabilization.
b. macroeconomic policy.
c. microeconomic theory.
d. inflation.
e. economy of scale.

8. ____________ can be defined simply as an officially expressed purpose or intention backed by a sanction, which can be a reward or a punishment.
a. Politics
b. Public policy
c. Fiscal policy
d. Monetary policy

9. ____________ are simply government grants of cash or other valuable commodities.
a. Subsidies
b. Regulations
c. Regulatory taxation
d. all of the above

10. A ____________ is a privilege granted by a government to do something that it considers to be illegal.
a. license
b. pardon
c. contract
d. regulation

11. ____________ usually refer to imprisonment but can also involve heavy fines and the loss of certain civil rights and liberties, such as the right to vote or the freedom of speech.
a. Criminal penalties
b. Civil penalties
c. Regulatory penalties
d. Administrative penalties

12. Which of the following is an example of "regulatory taxation"?
a. taxes on the rich
b. taxes on the poor

c. taxes on alcohol
d. taxes on utilities

13. Seizing private property for public use is called:
a. expropriation.
b. regulatory taxation.
c. extra-procurement.
d. all of the above.
e. only a and b.

14. Fiscal techniques of control concern:
a. government microeconomic policies.
b. government taxing and spending powers.
c. the Federal Reserve System.
d. all of the above.

15. The interest rate the Federal Reserve System charges member banks is called:
a. the commercial interest rate.
b. "best rate" quote.
c. the discount rate.
d. the "market leverage" rate.

16. The buying and selling of Treasury securities to absorb excess dollars or to release more dollars into the economy is called:
a. fiscal policy.
b. the discount rate.
c. the reserve requirement.
d. open market operations.

17. In general, when the Federal Reserve Board raises interest rates:
a. the economy slows down.
b. it does so to slow inflation.
c. borrowing for investment and consumption is discouraged.
d. all of the above

18. According to the authors of the text, in Chapter 16, the purpose of government is:
a. to manage conflict.
b. to deliver goods and services.
c. to tax.
d. to make public policies.

19. Techniques of control available to policy makers are:
a. promotional.
b. regulatory.
c. redistributive.
d. all of the above

20. Why have government "subsidies" as a control technique been favored by politicians?
a. Subsidies are treated as "benefits."
b. They can be used to "buy off" the opposition.
c. Those that receive the benefits do not perceive the controls inherent in them.
d. Once created, the threat of removal of benefits is a significant technique of control.
e. all of the above

21. Contracting as a control technique in policy making was of great significance for the Reagan and Bush administrations because of their commitment to:
a. redistribution of income and wealth.
b. privatization.
c. labor unions.
d. regulation.

22. According to the authors of the text, which of the following is not a form of regulation?
a. police regulation

b. administrative regulation
c. regulatory taxation
d. privatization

23. In essence, when government through administrative regulation grants a monopoly to a private sector company or to a public sector enterprise, it:
   a. is ensuring competition.
   b. has eliminated competition.
   c. has privatized the service.
   d. is creating an economy of scale.

24. When private corporations are required to be "equal opportunity employers" or not receive government contracts, the government is:
   a. creating an unfunded mandate.
   b. using reward and punishment to secure private sector obedience.
   c. distributing grants-in-aid.
   d. practicing so-called "coercive federalism."

25. With respect to federalism and public policy, most public policies in American history have been adopted by:
   a. the national government.
   b. city governments.
   c. state legislatures.
   d. county governments.

26. According to the authors of the text, a great proportion of the promotional activities of the national government are now done indirectly through:
   a. advertising.
   b. public relations firms.
   c. the Commerce Department.
   d. categorical grants-in-aid.

27. Which of the following is a reason why the national government gets into, out of, and back into regulatory policies?
   a. responding to public opinion
   b. "paying off" a debt to an interest group
   c. efficiency
   d. all of the above

28. According to the authors, all taxes:
   a. are fair.
   b. are progressive.
   c. discriminate.
   d. are evil.

29. Although the primary purpose of the graduated income tax is to raise revenue, an important second objective is to collect revenue in such a way as to reduce the disparities of wealth between the lowest and the highest income brackets. We call this:
   a. a policy of redistribution.
   b. microeconomic theory.
   c. pareto optimality.
   d. economic pluralism.

QUESTIONS FOR DISCUSSION AND THOUGHT

1. Does the president have the necessary tools to manage the economy? Should there be someone in control of the economy? If our system is so decentralized, how much influence can government policies have in directing the economy? How much influence does public opinion have on economic policy?
2. Steve Forbes campaigned for the presidency on a "flat tax" platform, which would eliminate a progressive income tax and establish instead a flat rate of 17 percent on all earned income; unearned income (dividends and interest payments) would not be taxed. Do you agree with this idea? What groups in our society would benefit most from this proposal? Is this another form of welfare—for the rich?
3. The American economy has been undergoing some major shifts away from high-paying manufacturing jobs, lifetime employment, and guaranteed pension plans. Have you thought about how these trends will affect your working life? How can you best prepare yourself to live in an uncertain economy?
4. The Republican party wants to cut taxes on the middle class, even if it means reducing or even abolishing some federal programs. Do you support a tax cut if it means some services would be cut? What services or agencies do you think should be abolished?
5. Recently many people have argued that we should "privatize" much of government; that is, turn over to the private sector such traditional governmental programs as running prisons, Social Security, public broadcasting, and even public schools. Do you think this is a good idea? What programs might you propose be privatized? What disadvantages do you see in privatization?

THE CITIZEN'S ROLE

To understand how your county's economy correlates with others in your state, select an urban and a rural county in your state for comparison. Then complete the table below, using the U.S. Census Bureau at http://www.census.gov/datamap/www/index for a start. There are also links to other sites that might be easier to use; for example, your state department of economic development or commerce may post figures as well. Try to find the latest year's statistics.

Measure (include year)	Urban county	Rural county
Population		
Percent high school graduates		
Percent college graduates		
Percent unemployed		
Per capita personal income		
Per capita retail sales		
Per capita federal funds and grants		

1. Does the urban or rural county have the stronger economy?
2. What relationship do you see between level of education, per capita income, and retail sales?
3. Compare the difference between the per capita incomes by dividing the larger amount into the smaller amount. Subtract the result from 100 and you will have the percentage difference in per capita income. For example: $17,424 divided by $18,860 is 92.4 percent or, rounded down to 92 and subtracted from 100, gives a difference of eight percent.
4. Now compare the difference between the per capita federal funds and grants, using the same formula. What is the relationship between per capita income and per capita federal funds and grants? Explain.
5. What economic issues do you think would be important in each county? Explain.

GOVERNMENT IN YOUR LIFE

Government enters into the field of regulation or providing services directly when the public believes that the competitive, free market has failed. Many Americans have argued for years that health care in the United States, based on a system of privately held health insurance and public assistance for the indigent, is a good example of market failure. The statistics show that the United States spent 13.6

percent its gross domestic product on health care in 1992, compared to the next highest developed nation (Canada, at 10.3 percent). The lowest was Denmark, with 6.5 percent. Yet the infant mortality rates for the same three nations show 8.9 deaths per 1,000 live births in the United States, 6.8 in Canada, and 7.3 in Denmark. All of the western democratic nations except the United States either have a national health insurance system or mandate national health coverage by employers and private insurers.

In 1995, President Clinton proposed a system of national health care which was rejected by Congress, and today Americans with health insurance are most often in health maintenance organizations (HMO), many of which have been accused of making high profits while lowering the quality of medical care. About 35 million Americans, however, have no health coverage at all, even through Medicare or Medicaid.

1. Is health care in the United States an example of market failure? Explain.
2. Would you prefer a national health system or a universal health insurance program? Why?
3. The federal government already runs two large health care systems, one for the elderly through Medicare, and another for the members of the military and their families. In your opinion, how successful are these programs?
4. Most European nations' health systems cover nursing home care, dental services, eyeglasses, and prescription drugs. Americans must usually purchase additional insurance for these services, if it is available at all. Would you favor an American health insurance system with minimum coverage or one that was as extensive as in Europe? How should we pay for this system?
5. List at least three interests that you think would gain by having national health insurance, and three that would lose. What did you learn about government and economic power?

ANSWER KEY

Fill-in-the-Blank Quiz

1. reserve requirement
2. monetary, fiscal
3. contracting power
4. expropriation, eminent domain
5. progressive
6. regressive
7. monopoly
8. police
9. redistribution
10. Federal Reserve Board
11. deregulation
12. administrative regulation
13. civil penalties
14. subsidies
15. Public policy
16. open market operations

17. license
18. discount rate
19. uncontrollables
20. regulation
21. Federal Reserve System (Fed)
22. regulatory tax
23. categorical grants
24. criminal penalties

Multiple-Choice Quiz

1. d
2. c
3. c
4. a
5. a
6. d
7. d
8. b
9. a
10. a
11. a
12. c
13. a
14. b
15. c
16. d
17. d
18. d
19. d
20. e
21. b
22. d
23. b
24. b
25. c
26. d
27. d
28. c
29. a

CHAPTER 17 Social Policy

THE CHAPTER IN BRIEF

Americans value equality of opportunity. However, there is always going to be a struggle between economic liberty and economic equality. There has always been a welfare system in the United States to answer the problem of poverty, but until 1935 it was private, a system of voluntary philanthropy through churches, communities, and generous rich people. There was a tradition of distinguishing between two classes of poverty. The deserving poor were widows, orphans, and others rendered dependent by some misfortune. The undeserving poor were able-bodied persons unwilling to work, transients new to the community, and others of whom, for various reasons, the community did not approve. Much of the private charity was in cash, called "outdoor relief." Worker's compensation laws were enacted in a few states, but they did not involve public expenditures. The movement that led to the modern welfare state was the establishment of mothers' pensions, in place in forty states by 1926. It was the forerunner of Aid to Families with Dependent Children (AFDC) and Temporary Assistance to Needy Families (TANF). In most states, a mother was deemed unfit if her children were illegitimate, and was therefore denied assistance. The criteria of moral unfitness proved to be racially discriminatory toward African Americans in the South and ethnic minorities in the North. When the Great Depression hit and millions of people were instantly unemployed without any resources to fall back on, poverty and dependency were accepted as inherent in the economic system, and a public welfare system was not far away.

The Social Security Act of 1935 provided for two separate categories of welfare, contributory and noncontributory. Contributory programs were financed by payroll taxation of employers and employees. Old-age insurance was the original contributory program. Survivors' coverage was added in 1939. A disability provision was added in 1956. Unemployment compensation was the second important part of the original contributory system. A payroll tax was imposed on employers to finance this program.

Noncontributory programs are also known as public assistance, or welfare. The most important categories were old-age assistance, to which aid to the blind and permanently disabled were later added, and Aid to Dependent Children (ADC), which was gradually transformed into what we call welfare today. Important additions were made after 1935, such as Medicare, which is a contributory program, and Medicaid, which is noncontributory.

The welfare state matured in the years between 1965 and 1995. The Medicare program expanded health benefits to the elderly, which provided additional incentives for the aging population to retire on Social Security. In 1974, Congress established the principle of "indexing," whereby benefits paid out under contributory programs would be modified annually by cost of living adjustments (COLAs) based on changes in the official Consumer Price Index. Noncontributory programs underwent a similar transformation. In 1974, Supplemental Security Income (SSI) set the first national standard on benefits. The AFDC program expanded in the 1970s for several reasons, the most complex of which is called "entitlement." In 1970, in the case of *Goldberg v. Kelly,* the Supreme Court held that financial aid benefits under AFDC could not be denied without proper notice, a hearing, and presentation of evidence. This provided that once the eligibility for AFDC was established, and as long as the program was on the books, the benefit could not be denied without due process.

With the billions being spent on welfare programs every year, welfare reform was high on the Republican agenda in the 1980s. With the cooperation of the Democrats, they proceeded immediately to cut the "rate of increase" of all of the major programs. However, despite Republican railing against them, no public assistance programs were terminated; the AFDC program, however, was turned into a block grant program, TANF. Social Security has remained extremely popular. The Earned Income Tax Credit (EITC), by which working households with children can file through their income tax returns for an income supplement if their annual income falls below about $20,000, aids the working poor. Clinton campaigned to "end welfare as we know it." The 1995 Republican Contract with America contained the Personal Responsibility Act, which dealt with welfare. It proposed to "reduce illegitimacy, control welfare spending, and reduce welfare dependence." The Republicans' plan was far more radical than anything Clinton had in mind. The final bill did, in fact, substantially change the existing welfare system. AFDC was eliminated, and TANF was created in its place as a block grant. Time limits were placed on welfare benefits, states were required to meet work participation rates, teenage mothers were required to live at home or with acceptable adults and to attend school, and states could terminate cash payments to women who have additional children while on welfare. The bill also forced states to become more aggressive in enforcing child support payments and significantly reduced benefits to immigrants.

The elderly (those over sixty-five) are a large and powerful group in this country, and are the beneficiaries of the two strongest and most generous social policies: Social Security and Medicare. These are universal programs, available to everyone over sixty-five, whether they are poor or not.

The middle-class benefits from social policies also. Medical care and pensions for the elderly relieve many middle-class, middle-aged people of the burden of caring for elderly relatives. In addition, the middle class benefits from medical insurance and pensions offered by their employers, which are subsidized by the federal government, as well as the tax exemption on mortgage-interest payments. All these benefits are called tax expenditures.

The working poor receive only limited assistance from government social programs. They are typically employed in jobs that do not provide pensions or health care. Often they are renters because they can't afford to buy homes. For these reasons they cannot benefit from the "shadow welfare state" that subsidizes the social benefits enjoyed by middle-class Americans. They cannot get assistance through programs such as Medicaid and TANF, which are largely restricted to the nonworking poor. Two main programs assist the working poor: the Earned Income Tax Credit and food stamps. They have no organized political support to protect them from proposed cuts in these programs.

Parents who are caring for children are the only nonworking able-bodied poor people that receive federal assistance. TANF is the main source of cash assistance. They also may receive Medicaid and food stamps. There is no federal program to assist able-bodied adults that are not caring for children. However, many states provide small amounts of cash to these individuals through programs called "general assistance." In the past decade, states have begun to abolish or greatly reduce their general assistance programs in an effort to promote work.

The groups in this country who are disproportionately poor are minorities, women, and children. Minorities are more likely to become unemployed and remain unemployed for longer stretches than white Americans, and African Americans typically have experienced unemployment rates twice as high as other Americans. Minorities are less likely to have jobs that give them access to the "shadow welfare state." In the past several decades, policy analysts began to talk about the "feminization of poverty." By this they meant that women were more likely to be poor than men. Women still typically earn less than men. The rate of child poverty in 1992 was 21.1 percent, nearly 6 percent higher than that of the population as a whole.

Two types of federal policies helpful for people trying to break out of poverty are education policies and health policies. The policy of universal compulsory public education is an important force in the distribution of opportunity. The most important national education policies have been created since World War II: the G. I. Bill of Rights of 1944, the National Defense Education Act (NDEA) of 1958, the Elementary and Secondary Education Act of 1965 (ESEA), and various youth and adult vocational training acts since 1958. Since the G. I. Bill was aimed at college education, the national government did not really enter the field of elementary education until after 1957. NDEA was aimed specifically at math and science; the United States was embarrassed that the Soviets had beaten us into space. Clinton's most concrete achievement in education policy was the Improving America's Schools Act of 1994, also known as Goals 2000. It set uniform national standards for educational achievement and committed $400 million in federal funds to help establish these standards.

The government has sponsored several employment and training programs since the New Deal, but these have fared poorly in terms of expenditures, stability, and results. The first of these, the Civilian Conservation Corps, put young men to work on environmental projects in rural areas. The Works Progress Administration (WPA) employed many different kinds of workers. Programs devised in the 1960s aimed to train and retrain poor workers rather than provide them with public employment. Many different training programs were rolled into a single block grant in 1973, the Comprehensive Employment and Training Act (CETA). It was abolished in 1981. In 1982, Congress created the Job Training Partnership Act (JTPA), which retrains adult workers and provides funding for summer jobs for youth.

Health care policies until recent decades were concerned only with public health. Billions of dollars have been spent on research, public health education, and regulations. Only recently have policies been introduced for limiting the rising costs of the American health care system and providing universal health insurance coverage for all Americans. Clinton's universal health care plan fell flat.

Housing policies originated with the Wagner-Steagall National Housing Act in 1937. There have been many policies since then that have helped reduce substandard housing and reduce overcrowding. Public housing and subsidized rents have assisted many families.

The American values of liberty, equality, and democracy are in conflict with the welfare state. Different ideologies hold different views about social policies. The libertarian view holds that government social policy interferes with society too much and, in the process, has created more problems than it has solved. "New paternalists" want to use the power of the government to enforce certain standards of behavior among beneficiaries of government social programs. Measures are also backed by many liberals to require work in exchange for welfare benefits, and to compel absent parents (usually fathers) to make child support payments. Conservatives believe that the main problems are not economic in origin, but instead stem from individual differences. Liberals believe that the root of many social problems is economic and argue that the aim of social policy should be to provide equality of opportunity. Political debates about social policy connect most closely with the public when they consider which mix of policies represents the appropriate balance among the ideals of liberty, equality, and democracy, rather than when they ask the public to choose among them.

REVIEW QUESTIONS

1. What is the belief in equality of opportunity?
2. Explain the differences between the "deserving poor" and the "undeserving poor."
3. Explain the differences between the two separate categories of welfare provided by the Social Security Act of 1935.
4. Explain the principle of "indexing."
5. Summarize the story of "entitlement."
6. Which groups receive the most adequate coverage from our social policies?
7. Which groups receive the fewest benefits?
8. Explain what universal programs are.
9. Explain what the "shadow welfare state" is.
10. What is the most unpopular spending program? The most popular?
11. What groups are economically less well off than the rest of the population?
12. Explain the "feminization of poverty."
13. Name some important challenges confronting policy makers today.
14. Explain the different political views of social policy.
15. What sort of equality did the Founders have in mind? Do you think they wanted equality of results?
16. According to conservatives, what causes poverty?
17. Compare the views of the new paternalists with the libertarians.
18. According to liberals, what causes poverty?
19. How is democracy damaged by extreme differences between the rich and the poor?

KEY TERMS

Aid to Families with Dependent Children (AFDC)
contributory program
cost of living adjustments (COLAs)
entitlement
equality of opportunity
food stamps
Goldberg v. Kelly
indexing
in-kind benefits
libertarian
means testing

Medicaid
Medicare
new paternalism
noncontributory program
shadow welfare state
Social Security
Supplemental Security Income (SSI)
tax expenditures
Temporary Assistance to Needy Families

FILL-IN-THE-BLANK QUIZ

Use the key terms to complete the following sentences.

1. The major federal program to assist families in need, the ____________ program, was replaced in 1996 by the ____________ program.
2. Two programs that have made substantial reductions in poverty among the elderly are ____________ and ____________.
3. Conservatives of the ____________ wing believe that government social policies should be used to enforce moral behavior of recipients.
4. Conservatives of the ____________ wing believe that government welfare programs should be eliminated because they foster dependency and interfere with individual freedom.
5. Since ____________, states have not been able to terminate a person's welfare benefits without due process.
6. Two federal health programs are quite different because Medicare is a ____________ program while Medicaid is a ____________ program.
7. Only one federal welfare program for the poor gives cash; the other programs provide ____________.
8. Workers who receive pension and health insurance benefits from their employers are participating in the ____________.
9. The blind and disabled qualify for a federal pension through the ____________ program.
10. People cannot receive food stamps until they can prove that they are needy. This requirement is called ____________.
11. A benefit that everyone receives regardless of income or other characteristics is a(n) ____________.
12. Social Security benefits are revised for inflation automatically through annual ____________ which are based on a(n) ____________ formula.
13. Medical services for the poor are provided through the ____________ program.

14. An employer who provides health insurance is given a federal tax deduction which is called a ____________.

15. Americans believe that everyone should have ____________, but they generally do not support equal results.

16. An in-kind benefit that is not restricted to single parents is ____________.

MULTIPLE-CHOICE QUIZ

1. In 1994, the Republican Party, as part of its ____________, vowed to scale back growth of the welfare system.
   a. "Devolution Revolution"
   b. "Contract with America"
   c. "Broom Brigade"
   d. "Republican Revolution"

2. In 1993, about ____________ percent of the U.S. population, 39 million people, lived in what the government defines as poverty.
   a. 5
   b. 14
   c. 24
   d. 33

3. In order to pay for Social Security and Medicare the government automatically withholds ____________ percent of the first $68,400 of earnings for Social Security and ____________ percent of all earnings for Medicare.
   a. 5, 5
   b. 6.2 , 1.45
   c. 9.9, 3.9
   d. 9.9, 5.8

4. In terms of reducing poverty among the elderly, Social Security has been very successful. In 1959, the poverty rate for the elderly was 35 percent; in 1992, the rate had dropped to:
   a. about 30 percent.
   b. about 20 percent.
   c. about 13 percent.
   d. about 7 percent.

5. The rate of child poverty in America is ____________ of the population as a whole.
   a. 10 percent
   b. 15 percent
   c. 22 percent
   d. 29 percent

6. Health care policy is an important topic to many Americans and public officials since almost ____________ lack health insurance.
   a. 100 thousand
   b. 10 million
   c. 40 million
   d. 100 million

7. The freedom to use whatever talents and wealth one has to reach one's fullest potential is the definition of:
   a. liberty.
   b. freedom.
   c. democracy.
   d. equality of opportunity.

8. Which of the following are examples of "contributory welfare" programs?
   a. Social Security and Medicare
   b. Medicare and AFDC
   c. food stamps and AFDC
   d. Social Security and Medicaid

9. Which of the following is true about Social Security?
   a. It mildly redistributes wealth from higher- to lower-income people.
   b. It quite significantly redistributes wealth from younger workers to older retirees.
   c. In essence it is a "forced savings" account.
   d. all of the above

10. The most important "noncontributory" social welfare program is:
    a. Social Security.
    b. TANF.
    c. food stamps.
    d. Supplemental Security Income.

11. A procedure that requires applicants to show a financial need for assistance is the definition of:
    a. means testing.
    b. determining eligibility.
    c. poverty.
    d. "red tape."

12. A program that provides extended medical services to all low-income persons who have already established eligibility through means testing under TANF is:
    a. Medicare.
    b. Medicaid.
    c. Medihealth.
    d. Medihelp.

13. This 1974 program augments benefits for the aged, blind, and disabled.
    a. Supplemental Security Income
    b. Medicaid
    c. food stamps
    d. Medicare

14. Noncash goods and services that would otherwise have to be paid for in cash by the beneficiary is the definition of:
    a. grants-in-aid.
    b. Medicare.
    c. Social Security.
    d. in-kind benefits.

15. This court case established the concept of social programs as "entitlements."
    a. *Brown v. Board of Education*
    b. *Roe v. Wade*
    c. *Griswold v. Connecticut*
    d. *Goldberg v. Kelly*

16. According to the authors of the text, when we study social policies from a group perspective, we can see that the elderly and the middle class receive the ____________ benefits from the government's social policies and that children and the working poor receive the ____________ benefits.
    a. most, fewest
    b. fewest, most
    c. positive, negative
    d. active, passive

17. An example of a "tax expenditure" is:
    a. Social Security.

b. the ability to deduct mortgage-interest payments from federal taxable income.
c. education spending.
d. all of the above

18. These two government programs assist the working poor.
a. Social Security and AFDC
b. Social Security and Medicaid
c. Earned Income Tax Credit and food stamps
d. Food Stamps and TANF

19. The primary source of cash assistance for the nonworking poor is:
a. Social Security.
b. Supplemental Security Income.
c. TANF.
d. food stamps.

20. According to the authors, as much as we admire it, the ideal of equality of opportunity raises questions and poses problems such as:
a. overcoming prejudice.
b. past inequalities.
c. equality of opportunity inevitably means inequality of results or outcomes.
d. all of the above.

21. With respect to government public welfare assistance, by 1933 the question was:
a. whether there was to be a public welfare system.
b. whether we should keep the Social Security program.
c. how generous or restrictive the system was going to be.
d. whether to convert to socialism.

22. According to the authors, if the welfare state were truly a state, its founding would be:
a. the Declaration of Independence of 1776.
b. the adoption of the U.S. Constitution in 1789.
c. the Emancipation Proclamation of 1863.
d. the Social Security Act of 1935.

23. In the 1970 case of *Goldberg v. Kelly,* the Supreme Court held that the financial benefits of AFDC could not be revoked without due process—i.e., a hearing at which evidence is presented. This ruling:
a. said that the beneficiary had a "right" to government benefits.
b. inaugurated the concept of the "entitlement" program.
c. is based on the Court's interpretation of the "due process clause" of the Fourteenth Amendment.
d. all of the above

24. How does the middle class benefit from social policies?
a. Medicare and pensions for the elderly help the middle class by relieving them of the burden of caring for elderly relatives.
b. They benefit from the "shadow welfare state."
c. They benefit from so-called "tax expenditures."
d. all of the above

25. The concept "feminization of poverty" means and/or implies which of the following?
a. women are more likely to be poor than men.

b. single mothers are more than twice as likely to fall below the poverty line than the average American.
c. single mothers often have children and are in the secondary labor market, so it does not "pay" to work.
d. all of the above

26. According to the authors of the text, the most important single force in the distribution and redistribution of opportunity in America is:
a. family status.
b. income.
c. education.
d. gender.

27. According to the authors of the text, since the 1930s, government-sponsored employment and training systems have:
a. been very successful.
b. been dismal failures.
c. fared poorly in terms of expenditures, stability, and results.
d. been highly supported by the American population in general.

28. With respect to the welfare state and American values, two different conservative perspectives can be distinguished. The ____________ view holds that government social policy interferes with society too much and, in the process, has created more problems than it has solved.
a. libertarian
b. neoconservative
c. new right
d. new paternalist

QUESTIONS FOR DISCUSSION AND THOUGHT

1. What is an "entitlement"? How can people claim to be "entitled" to something like food stamps? Congress has turned some entitlement programs into block grants. What would happen if your state received a block grant and then went into a recession? Do you think Congress would give your state more money to deal with the increased numbers of people who would be applying for welfare programs? What might happen if Congress refused to appropriate any more funds?

2. Former House Speaker Newt Gingrich said, "It doesn't say anywhere in the Declaration of Independence . . . that anyone is entitled to anything except the right to pursue happiness." Do you agree? Do children deserve any special consideration?

3. Generally, liberals believe that people are poor because of circumstances beyond their control (economics, health, society, family background), while conservatives believe people are poor because of their own individual failures (laziness, lack of character). What do you believe? What steps would you propose to reduce poverty, based on what you think causes it?

4. Should Social Security be privatized? Would you support a partial privatization? How would you go about investing your private share for your retirement?
5. We often say that education is the key to improving one's chances in life, but is our educational system really equal? Compare, for example, schools in different states where you or your friends have lived. Then compare schools in the suburbs with schools in the inner cities. Why is there such a variation? Only about one-third of all high school math and science teachers majored in math or science in college. Where do you think those one-third teach? Who is teaching math and science in the other schools? What does that say about equal educational opportunities? Would you support a "voucher" system that would allow students to go to any school they wanted to?

THE CITIZEN'S ROLE

In 1999, 23 percent of the federal budget will go for Social Security, with Medicare taking another 12 percent, for a total of 35 percent of the budget. Medicaid will be 6 percent, means-tested entitlements 6 percent, and all other entitlements 6 percent, or 18 percent for all entitlements outside of Social Security and Medicare. Many people are concerned about the future of Social Security, because the projected demand on its resources will be strained over the next fifty years. Currently, Social Security runs a credit balance, although from its beginnings until the 1960s it ran a deficit and depended on general revenues for extra funds.

Many proposals have been put forth to both increase individual return and to allow the fund to operate without going into debt. Several of these suggestions are given below. Make a list of the "winners" and "losers" for each.

Proposal	Winners	Losers
Raise retirement age to 70		
Means testing to eliminate payments to the wealthy		
Increase the length of the computation period for earnings from thirty-five to thirty-eight years		
Partial privatization		
Total privatization		

1. How would the working class fare under these plans?
2. How would the upper class fare?
3. Which of these plans creates the best cost-benefit analysis, in your opinion?
4. Explain the difference between an entitlement program and a pension program. What is the purpose of Social Security?
5. Do you believe Social Security should be changed? Explain.

GOVERNMENT IN YOUR LIFE

The value of an education can be seen by the statistics compiled by the U.S. Department of Education. Look at the figures for 1995:

Annual earnings	Men	Women	Percent Difference
Some high school	$22,185	$15,825	
High school graduate	29,510	20,463	
Some college, no degree	33,883	23,997	
Associates degree	35,201	27,311	
Bachelors degree	45,266	32,051	
Masters degree	55,216	40,263	
Professional degree	79,667	50,000	
Doctorate	65,336	48,141	

1. Compute the percentage of salary difference between a man and a woman at each level of education. Divide the larger number into the smaller number and subtract the answer from 100. Alternatively, subtract the smaller number from the larger number and divide the difference by the larger number.
2. At which level is the difference the greatest? The least? How can you explain this?

3. Why does a woman with a masters degree make less than a man with a bachelors degree?

4. Compute the following differences:

   Men high school graduates and men college graduates: ____________ percent

   Women high school graduates and women college graduates: ____________ percent

   Men with bachelors degrees and men with masters degrees: ____________ percent

   Women with bachelors degrees and women with masters degrees: ____________ percent

   What generalization can you draw from this data?

5. Does a college education pay? Multiply the average earnings of a high school man and a high school woman (separately) by 47 (the years between ages 18 and 65); then multiply a college graduate's earnings by 43. Subtract from the college graduate's earnings four years of high school level earnings (lost income) and the projected costs of your four-year education. What is the difference? How much income is lost by women compared to men? Should you stay in school? Should you pursue an advanced degree?

ANSWER KEY

Fill-in-the-Blank Quiz

1. Aid to Families with Dependent Children, Temporary Assistance to Needy Families
2. Social Security, Medicare
3. new paternalism
4. libertarian
5. *Goldberg v. Kelly*
6. contributory, noncontributory
7. in-kind benefits
8. shadow welfare state
9. Supplemental Security Income (SSI)
10. means testing
11. entitlement
12. cost of living adjustments (COLAs), indexing
13. Medicaid
14. tax expenditure
15. equality of opportunity
16. food stamps

Multiple-Choice Quiz

1. b
2. b
3. b
4. c
5. c
6. c
7. d
8. a
9. d
10. b
11. a

12. b
13. a
14. d
15. d
16. a
17. b
18. c
19. c
20. d
21. c
22. d
23. d
24. d
25. d
26. c
27. c
28. a

CHAPTER 18 Foreign Policy and Democracy

THE CHAPTER IN BRIEF

Americans have had a basic distrust of foreign policy ever since George Washington warned the American people against making political connections and permanent alliances with foreign countries. Of course the United State was forced from time to time to pursue its national interests in the world, and sometimes that led to fighting a war. The United States eventually emerged as a world power as a result of its foreign entanglements, but Americans still maintain their basic fear and distrust of foreign policy. The reason for that distrust today is the secrecy under which foreign policy decisions are made. In order to gain the support of the public, whose opinions are extremely influential over foreign policy, U.S. officials have resorted to deceit and lies, to the public and the media, such as those that were exposed in the *Pentagon Papers* about the real reasons the United States entered the Vietnam War. Foreign policy decisions are more crucial than domestic policy decisions. A mistake in the former could lead to disaster or war, while a mistake in the latter is more likely just to cost money. Foreign policy issues are complex.

The players in the game of foreign policy making are those who actually make policy and those who shape it. The president is the primary maker of policy, even though many foreign policy decisions are made without the president's knowledge. That is because all such decisions must be implemented in the president's name and have the president's implicit approval.

The key players of policy making in the bureaucracy are the secretary of state, the secretary of defense, the secretary of the treasury, the joint chiefs of staff (JCOS), especially the chair of the JCOS, and the directors of the Central Intelligence Agency (CIA) and the National Security Council (NSC), whose purpose is to integrate the positions of the other key players to confirm or reinforce decisions the president wants to make in foreign or military policy. Another important player is the secretary of commerce, whose role in promoting world trade is increasingly important due to economic globalization, or the world market. There are others, referred to as key staffers, including two or three specialized national security advisers in the White House, the staff of the NSC, and other career bureaucrats in the Departments of State and Defense, whose influence varies according to their specialty and to the foreign policy issue at hand.

Three segments of Congress play a role in making foreign policy. The Senate has to review and approve international treaties. The House of Representatives is essential for the financing of foreign policies. The third congressional player is the relevant foreign policy and military policy standing committees. In the Senate these are the Foreign Relations Committee and the Armed Services Committee. Congress as a whole is involved because of the president's increasing use of executive agreements, which have the force of treaties unless revoked by action of both chambers of Congress.

The shapers of foreign policy are nonofficial and are individuals and groups of people with great influence. The most important nonofficial player, by type, is the interest group, or at least the groups to whom one or more foreign policy issues are of long-standing and vital relevance. The type of group with the reputation for the most influence is the economic interest group, exemplified by single-issue groups such as tobacco interests and the computer hardware and software industries. Another type is the ethnic/national interest group, such as American Jews and Irish Americans, who have helped shape policies dealing with Israel and Ireland. Human rights interest groups such as Amnesty International have altered the practices of many regimes in the world through exposés of human rights deprivations. A related type of group is the ecology or environmental group, which relies more on demonstrations than on the typical strategies of influence in Washington.

Besides interest groups, the media also shape foreign policy, with most of their influence based on the speed and scale with which political communications can be spread. Public opinion polling is another aspect—a feedback medium—that allows policy makers to understand policy shapers very quickly. Another aspect of media influence is known as "media bias," a negative attitude toward public policies and government officials given to the public by television news, and a liberal bias on the part of working journalists.

So who really makes American foreign policy? It is best to evaluate actors and factors as they *interact* with the president. Each case arises under different conditions and with different time constraints. Under conditions of crisis, when time is of the essence, the influence of the president is at its strongest. Access to the decision is at its narrowest, limited to the "foreign policy establishment." As time becomes less of a problem, however, the arena of participation expands, becoming more pluralistic, like domestic policy making. Because the international system is anarchic, and there are many powerful nation-states, severe limits are put on the choices the United States can make.

The traditional system of foreign policy ended with World War I. The European "balance of power" had collapsed, as well as the powers themselves. The war had laid waste to their economies, their empires, and their political systems. The United States was one of the great powers. The United States was soon to shed its traditional domestic system of federalism. Strangely, there was no discernible change in America's approach to foreign policy for almost thirty years, illustrating the strength of the traditional system. The end of World War II brought pressure for a new tradition that came into direct conflict with the old. The new values became apparent during the cold war. Instead of unilateralism, the United States pursued multilateralism, entering into treaties with other nations. The most notable was the North Atlantic Treaty Organization (NATO), which aided the United States in dealing with the Soviet Union by means of containment and deterrence. The wars fought in Korea and Vietnam were an effort to contain Soviet power and prevent the spread of communism. The United States developed a gigantic nuclear arsenal to deter the Soviet Union from attacking the free world.

The instruments of foreign policy are the tools and techniques used by the United States to achieve its goals. The first is diplomacy, which is the representation of a government to foreign governments for the purpose of promoting its national values or interests by peaceful means. However, a traditional distrust of diplomacy still exists in the modern presidential system. Presidents frequently name their own ambassadorial appointees for political reasons, turning to military or civilian personnel outside the State Department to take on special diplomatic roles as direct personal representatives of the president. Despite the professionalization of the American foreign service, career ambassadors are continually displaced by these appointees.

The United Nations was founded in 1945 as an instrument of foreign policy, and for its first decade was a direct servant of American interests abroad. The United States created the United Nations for the purpose of power without diplomacy. The Gulf War victory was really a victory for the United Nations. Somalia was the first conflict in which UN troops were brought in for strictly humanitarian purposes. This conflict, however, did not threaten American national interests as did the conflict in the Gulf, and American troops were withdrawn without any resolution to the conflict. For similar reasons, the United States was reluctant to endanger American troops in the former Yugoslavia, and the United Nations was replaced in the area with a NATO-led force of sixty thousand troops, twenty thousand of which were Americans.

Another important instrument of foreign policy is the international monetary structure. The International Bank for Reconstruction and Development (World Bank) was set up to finance long-term capital. More important today is the International Monetary Fund (IMF), which was set up to provide for the short-term flow of money. It helped needy member countries overcome temporary trade deficits and stabilize foreign currencies. Lately, it has been instrumental in bringing debtor nations into the global capitalist economy.

Economic aid became an integral part of foreign policy right after World War II. The Marshall Plan, formally known as the European Recovery Plan (ERP), was a commitment to help rebuild and defend all countries the world over, wherever the leadership wished to develop democratic systems or to ward off communism. Between 1952 and 1961, U.S. aid shifted toward the developing world. Critics have argued that foreign economic aid is aid for the political and economic elites of a nation and does not reach the people it is meant to help. This may be true, but the United States cannot force a country's leaders to distribute food or other aid. It may also be true that needy people in these desperate countries would be worse off if aid were discontinued. The lines of international communication must be kept open, and foreign aid facilitates diplomacy. Another criticism of U.S. foreign aid policy is that it has not been tied closely enough to U.S. diplomacy within the State Department. For example, the Departments of Defense and Agriculture have, in effect, each conducted their own foreign policy for years.

Collective security as an instrument consists of mutual defense alliances. The first was the Rio Treaty (1947), which created the Organization of American States (OAS). This was the model treaty, anticipating all succeeding collective security treaties by providing that an armed attack against any of its members "shall be considered as an attack against all the American States," including also the United States. The North Atlantic Treaty Organization (NATO) was established in 1949, and ANZUS, a treaty tying Australia and New Zealand to the United States, was created in 1951. In 1954, the Southeast Asia Treaty Organization (SEATO) was created. In addition to these multilateral treaties, the United States has also entered into a number of bilateral treaties—treaties between two countries. The United States has most often been a consumer of security. NATO and the United States are now trying to broaden membership in the alliance without antagonizing Russia. NATO and similar organizations in the future are going to be less like military alliances and more like economic associations to advance technology, reduce trade barriers, and protect the world environment. Another form of collective security involves nations forming temporary coalitions under UN sponsorship to check a particularly aggressive nation.

The final instrument of foreign policy is military deterrence, which consists of constant mobilization and preparedness: the development and maintenance of military strength as a means of discouraging attacks. The current "arms race" is not for quantitative but for technologically qualitative superiority. The Gulf War enhanced the credibility of using military technology as the primary deterrent in the world. The United States today leads the world as a military weapons exporter. This is part of the current world arms race, but it also helps maintain a balance of power in the world to deter countries from attacking one another.

The president's primary foreign policy problem is choosing an overall role for the country in foreign affairs. The Napoleonic role takes its name from post-revolutionary France under Napoleon. The French felt that their new democratic system would not be safe until adopted universally. If protecting their democracy meant intervention into the internal affairs of neighboring countries, and if it meant warlike reactions, so be it. The United States adopted this role in 1917 when President Wilson supported Congress's declaration of war with the statement that "the world must be made safe for democracy." The United States played the Napoleonic role recently in the Philippines, Panama, Nicaragua, and Haiti.

The Holy Alliance role emerged out of Napoleon's defeat and the agreement by the leaders of Great Britain, Russia, Austria, and Prussia to preserve the social order against all revolution, at whatever cost. This role made use of political suppression, espionage, sabotage, and outright military intervention to keep existing governments in power, regardless of their ideologies.

The balance-of-power role is an effort by the major powers to prevent any great power or combination of great and lesser powers from imposing conditions on others. This role accepts the political system of each country, asking no questions except whether the country will join an alliance and will use its resources to ensure that each country will respect the borders and interests of all the others.

The economic expansionist role, also called the capitalist role, also regards the political system or ideology of a country as irrelevant. Its only question is whether a country has anything to buy or sell and whether its entrepreneurs, corporations, and government agencies will honor their contracts.

What roles has America played in recent years? After World War II, the emphasis was on making the world safe for democracy. The distribution of world power was "bipolar," divided by the "iron curtain" between the communist world and the free world. The American foreign policy goal at that time was "prodemocracy," a Napoleonic role dominated by the Marshall Plan. During the 1950s and 1960s, America shifted toward a Holy Alliance role, with "containment" as the primary foreign policy criterion. The reason for our involvement in Korea and in Vietnam was to "contain" communism and keep its influence from spreading. A multipolar world emerged in the 1970s, and the United States experimented with all four of the previously identified roles, depending on which was appropriate to a specific region. For example, the United States played a balance-of-power role in the Middle East. The recent collapse of the Soviet Union and the Warsaw Pact brought "Balkanization" to eastern Europe, the emergence of several new nation-states after years of suppression of their peoples.

The end of the cold war unleashed the globalization of markets, or the globalization of capitalism. This is enormously productive, but the free market can disrupt nationhood. This struggle between capitalism and nationhood produces internal bipolarity, wherein each country is struggling to make its own policy choices to preserve its cultural uniqueness while competing effectively in the global marketplace. Approval of the North American Free Trade Agreement (NAFTA) is a good example of this struggle within the United States.

The global market is here to stay, and American values have changed enough to incorporate it, despite the obvious price we will have to pay by sacrificing some part of an isolated community and family tradition. Many features of the cold war era remain because they turned out to be good adjustments to the modern era. International economic aid continues into this decade, although appropriations for foreign aid have been shrinking. NATO and other collective security arrangements continue. Containment is used to prevent civil wars from spreading beyond borders. The value of making the world safe for democracy has been updated to "making the world safe for democracy and markets." It requires that we act more directly upon the domestic institutions of other countries so that there will be more trade outlets as well as more-stable and less-warlike regimes.

Despite the absence of the Soviet Union today, the Holy Alliance role for the United States seems to be more prominent than ever. Its purpose today is to keep regimes in power, but only as long as they maintain general stability, keep their nationalities contained within their own borders, and encourage their economies to attain some level of participation in the global market. Another indication of our post–cold war attitude is evidenced in the new arms race and our involvement in the international market in military products (weapons). The primary incentive in the international sale of arms is to keep our own defense industry alive and prosperous in the face of domestic defense-budget cuts. In fact, the United States is the world's biggest producer and exporter of advanced weaponry. Countries buy weaponry to use as deterrents against one another. The value of weapons importation can be seen in the regular use the United States and the United Nations make of restrictions and embargoes on weapons against "misbehaving" countries. The downside to the sale of weapons is that most despotic regimes view a big military presence as an essential means of controlling their own populations. Thus, America finds itself supporting distasteful regimes because it likes world stability more than it dislikes undemocratic regimes.

Making foreign policy in a democracy requires finding the institution that best serves as the "vital middle" between the American people and foreign policy. Foreign policy making in the United States will remain for the president's domain, but public deliberation and debate is Congress's domain, and influencing them both is the people's domain.

REVIEW QUESTIONS

1. Since our government is a government of the people, do you feel that Americans have a right to feel betrayed in instances such as the Vietnam War, in which U.S. officials lied to the public in order to manipulate public opinion, or do you feel that secrecy by government officials in matters of foreign policy and U.S. security should be accepted and justified as part of the freedom and protection we enjoy as Americans?

2. Do you think the president should be allowed to claim deniability in cases of failed or controversial decisions, or that he or she should be held fully accountable as the head of government?

3. What is the main role of the House of Representatives in the making of foreign policy? What is its secondary role in concert with the Senate?

4. What part of Congress, besides the Senate and the House, is a major player in foreign policy making?
5. Who are the most important shapers of foreign policy, and what type is most influential?
6. What is the main reason that the media are so influential in the shaping of foreign policy?
7. Under what conditions is the president's influence the strongest in making foreign policy?
8. The United States and the Soviet Union used to be the major superpowers of the world based on their military power and nuclear arsenal. Now other superpowers, such as Japan, are emerging without any significant military power at all. What is the basis of Japan's power, and how does that power work?
9. Differentiate between isolationism and unilateralism. Which was the American position toward the rest of the world up until the middle of this century?
10. Why was there no change in America's approach to foreign policy between World Wars I and II?
11. What was the major reason the United States fought wars in Korea and Vietnam?
12. For what purpose did the United States help create the United Nations?
13. How is the International Monetary Fund important to the capitalist world economy?
14. What was the goal of the Marshall Plan? How has that goal expanded?
15. What is a collective security agreement? Give some examples.
16. How has the United States played the Holy Alliance role in recent years?
17. What are some of the arguments against the free market, such as those against NAFTA? Despite these arguments, do you think NAFTA and similar trade agreements are in America's best interest? In the best interest of the rest of the world?
18. What is the primary incentive for the United States to produce and export advanced military weaponry to other countries? In which foreign policy role does this place the United States?
19. Why is Congress so important in foreign policy today?
20. Should foreign policy in a democracy emphasize human rights?

21. In Chapter 1, you learned that there are very few democracies in the world today. Should the United States assume the Napoleonic role to advance the causes of liberty, equality, and democracy?

KEY TERMS

balance-of-power role
bilateral treaties
cold war
containment
deterrence
diplomacy
economic expansionist role
executive agreements
Holy Alliance role
International Monetary Fund (IMF)
Marshall Plan
multilateral treaties
multilateralism
Napoleonic role
nation-state
North Atlantic Treaty Organization (NATO)
unilateralism
United Nations

FILL-IN-THE-BLANK QUIZ

Use the key terms to complete the following sentences.

1. The president does not have to get Senate approval for to international compacts that are called ____________.
2. The foreign policy role that tries to maintain existing power relationships, even if it means intervening in another nation's affairs, is the ____________ role.
3. Treaties made between two countries are ____________, while those made with more than two are ____________.
4. The United States aided the recovery of Western Europe after World War II through the ____________.
5. International money exchange is facilitated by the ____________.
6. When the United States tried to make the world "safe for democracy" in World War I, it was pursuing the ____________ role of foreign policy.
7. During the Cold War, American policy toward the Soviet Union had two goals: ____________ and ____________.
8. People who share a common cultural experience and common political authority are members of a ____________.
9. When the United States joins with other nations to act against a common enemy, it is engaging in ____________.

10. The foreign policy strategy that uses alliances to counterbalance the power of other nations or alliances is the ___________ role.
11. War is generally considered to be the failure of ___________.
12. The organization of nations formed after World War II to seek multinational solutions to world problems is the ___________.
13. In the nineteenth century, the United States did not follow a policy of isolationism but of ___________.
14. The fall of the Berlin Wall in 1989 signaled the end of the ___________.
15. The capitalist role of foreign policy is also known as the ___________ role.
16. In 1948, the Western nations formed the ___________ to be a defensive organization against the threat from the Soviet Union.

MULTIPLE-CHOICE QUIZ

1. In his farewell address to the nation, ___________ warned the American people, "to have . . . as little political connection as possible" with foreign nations and to "steer clear of permanent alliances."
   a. George Washington
   b. Thomas Jefferson
   c. Theodore Roosevelt
   d. Ronald Reagan
2. Of all demographic, racial, and religious groups in America, which group has the reputation for the greatest influence on foreign policy?
   a. African Americans
   b. Asians
   c. Jews
   d. Catholics
3. The so-called "traditional era" of U.S. foreign policy came to an end with:
   a. the Civil War.
   b. World War I.
   c. World War II.
   d. the collapse of the United Soviet Socialist Republics.
4. The first effort to create a modern foreign service in the United States was made through the:
   a. Rogers Act of 1924.
   b. League of Nations of 1919.
   c. Foreign Service Act of 1946.
   d. Foreign Legion Act of 1789.
5. ___________ was the first country in which UN troops entered for strictly humanitarian reasons.
   a. Korea
   b. Vietnam
   c. Somalia
   d. Bosnia
6. The primary purpose of this agency is to iron out the

differences among the key players in foreign policy and to integrate their positions in order to confirm or reinforce a decision the president wants to make in foreign policy or military police.

a. National Security Council
b. joint chiefs of staff
c. State Department
d. Defense Department

7. For most of American history, the ____________ was the only important congressional foreign-policy player because of its constitutional role in reviewing and approving treaties.
 a. Ways and Means Committee
 b. Foreign Relations Committee
 c. Senate
 d. House of Representatives

8. ____________ have the force of treaties but do not require prior approval by the Senate.
 a. Executive orders
 b. Executive mandates
 c. Executive treaties
 d. Executive agreements

9. When a nation has sufficient self-consciousness to organize itself into a political entity, it is generally referred to as:
 a. sovereign.
 b. a nation-state.
 c. multicultural.
 d. independent.

10. ____________ can be defined as respect by other nations for the claim by a government that it has conquered its territory and is sole authority over its population.
 a. Sovereignty
 b. A nation-state
 c. Nationalism
 d. Multiculturalism

11. ____________ means to try to cut off contacts with the outside, to be a self-sufficient fortress.
 a. Bipolar
 b. Detente
 c. Isolationism
 d. Multilateralism

12. Which of the following terms is associated with post-World War II American foreign policy?
 a. cold war
 b. multiculturalism
 c. isolationism

13. ____________ is the representation of a government to other foreign governments.
 a. Diplomacy
 b. Nationalism
 c. Detente
 d. Collective security

14. The ____________ was established to finance long-term capital, whereas the ____________ was set up to provide for the short-term flow of money.
 a. United Nations, World Bank
 b. International Monetary Fund, United Nations Bank
 c. World Bank, International Monetary Fund
 d. World Bank, Federal Reserve Bank

15. The ____________ was essential for the rebuilding of war-torn Europe.
 a. United Nations
 b. European Common Market
 c. League of Nations
 d. Marshall Plan

16. ____________ is defined as the development and maintenance of military strength as a means of discouraging attack.
    a. Deterrence
    b. Detente
    c. Multilateralism
    d. Collective security

17. With respect to the four types of roles nation-states play in foreign affairs, when the United States ousted Philippine dictator Ferdinand Marcos, Panamanian leader Manuel Noriega, the Sandinista government of Nicaragua, and the military rulers of Haiti, we were playing the ____________ role.
    a. Napoleonic
    b. Holy Alliance
    c. balance-of-power
    d. economic expansionist

18. With respect to the four types of roles nation-states play in foreign affairs, containment is a clear case of playing the ____________ role.
    a. Napoleonic
    b. Holy Alliance
    c. balance-of-power
    d. economic expansionist

19. The *Pentagon Papers* revealed that:
    a. the Chinese were supplying arms to the North Vietnamese.
    b. President Nixon ordered the break-in of the Democratic Headquarters at the Watergate.
    c. U.S. officials had lied through the media to the American public about the country's entry into the Vietnam War.
    d. all of the above

20. As in domestic policy, foreign-policy making takes place in a highly ____________ arena.
    a. elitist.
    b. secretive
    c. hyperpluralistic
    d. pluralistic

21. Who shapes foreign policy? According to the authors, far and away the most important category of nonofficial foreign-policy player is:
    a. interest groups.
    b. the media.
    c. public opinion.
    d. political consultants.

22. According to the authors of the text, the most important element of the policy influence of the media on foreign policy is:
    a. the ability to frame issues.
    b. the ability to report the news.
    c. the speed and scale with which the media can spread political communication.
    d. all of the above.

23. Reliance on television as a source of news gives people negative attitudes toward government and public officials. This phenomenon is called:
    a. "videomalaise."
    b. "the Rush Limbaugh effect."
    c. "countercyclical spin."
    d. conservatism.

24. Which of the following statements is true about who really makes American foreign policy?
    a. Except for the president, the influence of players and shapers varies from case to case.

b. It is best to evaluate other actors and factors as they interact with the president.
c. Each foreign policy issue arises under different conditions and with vastly different time constraints.
d. Foreign policy experts will usually disagree about the level of influence any player or type of player has on policy making.

25. During most of the nineteenth century, American foreign policy was to a large extent:
a. very active.
b. defined not by the president but by Congress.
c. inactive; there was no foreign policy.
d. anti-Communist in orientation.

26. According to the authors of the text, any evaluation of the United Nations must take into account the purpose for which the United States sought to create it, which was to:
a. resolve international crises.
b. create an international police force.
c. eventually serve as a unified world government.
d. achieve power without diplomacy.

QUESTIONS FOR DISCUSSION AND THOUGHT

1. If you had to choose between having a strong economy and a weak military or having a weak economy and a strong military, which would you choose?

2. This textbook has emphasized the themes of democracy, equality, and liberty. Do you think you have a better understanding of those terms today than when you started this course? Do you think the United States has a moral responsibility to spread democracy throughout the world? If so, how should it be done? How could we export our strengths (freedom) without exporting some of our negatives, like low voter turnout?

3. In recent years, the American armed forces have been called upon to perform duties that are more humanitarian than militaristic, such as hurricane and flood relief, relieving starvation in Somalia, and restoring democratic government in Haiti. Should we continue to come to the aid of the miserable, or should that be left to private relief agencies such as the Red Cross?

4. We have seen many cruel political leaders in other countries, such as Hitler, Idi Amin, the Duvaliers in Haiti. Should the United States attempt to remove these vicious rulers? If so, how would you go about doing that? Should we use assassination as a tool of foreign policy?

5. In his autobiography, Robert McNamara, Secretary of Defense under Presidents Kennedy and Johnson, revealed that he had serious reservations about the war in Vietnam even while he was involved in prosecuting it. His defense was that voicing his disapproval would have been an act of disloyalty to the president and would have given "aid and comfort to the enemy." What would you have done if you had been McNamara?

THE CITIZEN'S ROLE

We The People has highlighted the themes of liberty, equality, and democracy in the American political system. Now it is time to look at the rest of the world. Go to the web site for Amnesty International (www.amnesty.org); select two nations, one a developed nation and the other from the Third World, and read the latest reports on human rights violations in both countries.

1. How did these two countries compare? Where did you expect to find the greatest number of abuses? Were your suspicions confirmed?
2. In what ways are human liberties violated around the world? Were you surprised at these violations of human rights? Explain.
3. Do you think that public information campaigns such as those carried out by Amnesty International have any effect on political leaders? Explain.
4. Do you think that American foreign policy ought to promote human rights around the world? Explain.
5. How well, in your opinion, does the United States exemplify the values of liberty, equality, and democracy? What are our strengths? Our weaknesses? How do we compare with the rest of the world?

GOVERNMENT IN YOUR LIFE

The textbook points out that American foreign policy today is working to "make the world safe for democracy and markets." The following countries have been identified as "emerging markets," or new commercial opportunities for American trade: China, Hong Kong, Taiwan, India, South Korea, Mexico, Brazil, Argentina, South Africa, Poland, Turkey, and the Association of Southeast Asian Nations (Brunei, Indonesia, Malaysia, Singapore, Thailand, the Philippines, and Vietnam). Select one of these countries and complete the chart below.

Name of country	
Population	
Per capita income	
Percent literacy	
Major exports	
Major imports	
Human rights record (see Amnesty International)	

1. Why do you think this country was selected as an emerging market?
2. Per capita income in the United States is about $23,000. How does this country compare?
3. Are the major exports of this country important to the United States?
4. Should American foreign policy be aimed today at "making the world safe for democracy and markets"? Explain.
5. What is this nation's record on human rights? How do you feel about the United States doing business with countries that have poor records on human rights? Which is more important to you: economic development or human rights? Can we promote both? If so, how?

ANSWER KEY

Fill-in-the-Blank Quiz

1. executive agreements
2. Holy Alliance
3. bilateral, multilateral
4. Marshall Plan
5. International Monetary Fund (IMF)
6. Napoleonic
7. containment, deterrence
8. nation-state
9. multilateralism
10. balance-of-power
11. diplomacy
12. United Nations
13. unilateralism
14. cold war
15. economic expansionist
16. North Atlantic Treaty Organization (NATO)

Multiple-Choice Quiz

1. a
2. c
3. b
4. a
5. c
6. a
7. c
8. d
9. b
10. a
11. c
12. a
13. a
14. c
15. d
16. a
17. a
18. b
19. c
20. d
21. a
22. c
23. a
24. d
25. c
26. d

APPENDIX Additional Resources

Chapter 1: American Political Culture

BECOMING POLITICAL EXERCISES

1. Interview someone who has served in the military. How does he or she feel about the experience? If a man, was he drafted? Does this person think everyone should have to serve some sort of national service?
2. Take an informal survey of at least twelve people. Ask them where they can find the phrase "all men are created equal." What did you learn from this survey?
3. Interview someone who has lived in another country. Have him or her compare that country with the United States in terms of government structure, political issues, and public attitudes toward the government.
4. Research the life of Thomas Jefferson, using at least three references, and write a 500-word report.
5. Interview someone who has served in the Peace Corps, Teach for America, or a similar volunteer organization. Conduct an interview to learn about the program and the rewards and difficulties of giving a year or two to volunteer service.

FOR FURTHER READING

Level I Articles

1. Fallows, James. The Difference One Man Can Make. *Washington Monthly,* May 1982. One determined person can change the system.
2. Fein, Bruce. The Stain of Watergate. *The World and I,* December 1994. Traces today's public cynicism to Watergate.
3. Gray, Peter. The Lie Society. *Washington Monthly,* May 1992. How dishonest officials subvert democracy.
4. Kaus, Mickey. An American Melting Plot. *Washington Monthly,* July–August 1992. Makes a distinction between social equality and economic equality.
5. Keisling, Phil. Make National Service Mandatory for All. *Washington Monthly,* January–February 1994.
6. Smith, Sam. How NOT to Repair America. *Utne Reader,* September–October 1997. Both positive and negative thinking about how to improve America.

Level II Articles

1. Dahl, Robert. Justifying Democracy. *Society,* January–February 1998. Democracy allows us all to pursue our own goals.
2. *The Declaration of Independence.* (See the Appendix in the text.) Basic statement of American liberal political thought.
3. Etzioni, Amitai. Teledemocracy. *Atlantic Monthly,* October 1992. The pros and cons of electronic town meetings.
4. Kaplan, Robert D. Was Democracy Just a Moment? *Atlantic Monthly,* December 1997. We may not be marching inexorably toward world-wide democracy.
5. Morone, James. The Struggle for American Culture. *PS: Political Science & Politics,* September 1996. The American culture is a "perpetual work in progress."
6. Olson, Mancur. Dictatorship, Democracy, and Development. *American Political Science Review,* September 1993. A scholarly and jargon-free discussion of autocracy and the transition to democracy, conditions required for transition, and the economic effects.
7. *The Magna Carta.* Fundamental document of Western political theory.

8. Norris, Pippa. Does Television Erode Social Capital? *PS: Political Science & Politics,* September 1996. Argues that Putnam's thesis (below) about the negative side of television is wrong.

9. Putnam, Robert. The Strange Disappearance of Civic America. *American Prospect,* Winter 1996. The "bowling alone" theory which claims that America's "social capital" is rapidly disappearing.

10. Schudson, Michael. What If Civic Life Didn't Die? *American Prospect,* March–April 1996. Another response to Putnam's "bowling alone" theory.

VIDEO RESOURCES

1. *Animal Farm.* A classic satire about farm animals who turn their government into a dictatorship. DCA, 1955.
2. *Brazil.* R. A dark, humorous look at a dystopian future. Terry Gilliam, 1985.
3. *Schindler's List.* R. The story of one man's courage in the face of a despotic government. Amblin Entertainment, 1993.
4. *The Mosquito Coast.* PG. A man moves his family to Central America, planning to create his vision of a better society. Warner Bros., 1986.
5. *The Nasty Girl.* PG-13. The true story of a young German woman who discovers that her neighbors supported the Nazi government. Reveals how easily we can fall into accepting tyranny. Sentana, 1990.
6. *To Heal a Nation.* The true story of one man's effort to make a difference by establishing a memorial for Vietnam veterans. Turner Entertainment, 1988.

Chapter 2: The American Political Community

BECOMING POLITICAL EXERCISES

1. Research and write a 500-word report on how the U.S. government responded to one of the following immigration groups: Cubans in the late 1950s, Vietnamese in the 1970s, or Haitians in the 1990s.
2. Analyze the athletic programs at your school for men and women and compare the number of programs and the budgets for each sport. How far has your school gone towards equal opportunity for men and women?
3. Trace the history of California's Proposition 187 through the courts, using the Internet. What were the legal issues involved? Do you think the issue of providing benefits to immigrants has been settled to the public's satisfaction?
4. How many women and minorities serve on the police, fire, and sheriff forces in your community? Is this an adequate number, in your opinion? What barriers do women and minorities face in the selection process?
5. Search the web pages of groups motivated by concerns outlined in this chapter—for example, the NAACP, National Organization of Women, the Christian Coalition, the Anti-Defamation League, the groups arrayed around the abortion issue, immigration concern groups, etc. What can you learn from these groups? Has this helped you develop your own opinions on these issues?

FOR FURTHER READING

Level I Articles

1. Bordewich, Fergus. How to Succeed in Business: Follow the Choctaws' Lead. *Smithsonian,* March 1996. Economic development comes to the Choctaws of Mississipppi.
2. Carnoy, Martin and Rothstein, Richard. Are Black Diplomas Worth Less? *American Prospect,* January–February 1997. Analyzes the persistent gap between wages of blacks and whites.
3. Chinni, Dante. Today's Landed Gentry. *Washington Monthly,* October 1996. How the property tax system for financing public schools creates inequality.

4. Karnow, Stanley. In Orange County's Little Saigon, Vietnamese Try to Bridge Two Worlds. *Smithsonian,* August 1992. Children of immigrants face special problems trying to be both Vietnamese and American.

5. Paradise Lost? *American Heritage,* February/March 1998. Interview with Michael Elliott, who believes that Americans have elevated the 1950s to mythical status, and that our current political issues are the norm, not the exception.

6. Schrag, Peter. When Preferences Disappear. *American Prospect,* January–February 1997. Race preferences are disappearing, but it is unclear what will replace them.

7. Stanfield, Rochelle. Blending of America. *National Journal,* September 13, 1997. Intermarriage is changing the face of America.

8. Stanfield, Rochelle. Multiple Choice. *National Journal,* November 22, 1997. In the 2000 census, Americans will be able to check more than one box on race, although the complications from this are enormous.

9. Talbot, Margaret. Baghdad on the Plains. *New Republic,* August 11 & 18, 1997. Cultural conflicts break out when Iraqi refugees are resettled in Nebraska.

Level II Articles

1. Aleinikof, T. Alexander. A Multicultural Nationalism? *American Prospect,* January–February 1998. Immigrants to America both become part of America and change it as well.

2. Elshtain, Jean Bethke. Exporting Feminism. *Journal of International Affairs,* Winter 1995. Discusses differences between the concerns of feminists in the Western world and those in developing countries.

3. McConnell, Scott. Americans No More? *National Review,* December 31, 1997. Thoughtful discussion of the problems Hispanic immigrants face today compared to immigrants in the past.

4. Passel, Jeffrey and Fix, Michael. Myths About Immigrants. *Foreign Policy,* Summer 1994. Dispassionate analysis of the numbers and characteristics of recent immigrants.

5. Schwarz, Benjamin. The Diversity Myth: America's Leading Export. *The Atlantic Monthly,* May 1995. Critique of the American myth of harmony and reconciliation.

6. Skerry, Peter. Many American Dilemmas: The Statistical Politics of Counting by Race and Ethnicity. *Brookings Review,* Summer 1996. Our changing views of ethnicity create political problems.

7. Verba, Sidney et al. The Big Tilt: Participatory Inequality in America. *American Prospect,* May–June 1997. Examines the class basis of political participation.

8. Wolff, Edward N. How the Pie is Sliced. *National Times,* December/January 1996. Clear statistical evidence that the economic class differences in America are increasing.

VIDEO RESOURCES

1. *Daughters of the Dust.* A Gullah family living on an island off the coast of Georgia contemplates moving to the mainland to join mainstream American society at the turn of the century. Geechee Girl Productions, 1992.

2. *Dim Sum: A Little Bit of Heart.* PG. A mother–daughter relationship depicts the clash between Asian and American ways of life. CIM, 1985.

3. *El Norte.* R. A Guatemalan brother and sister struggle to come to America. Independent Productions, 1983.

4. *Farewell to Manzanar.* A TV movie based on the true story of a Japanese American family that suffered injustice during the World War II internment. 1976.

5. *My Family.* R. Story of three generations of a Latino family who came to the United States in the 1920s. American Playhouse, 1995.

6. *The Color Purple.* PG-13. Sexism and racism are depicted in a moving story of a southern black woman. Guber, Peters, 1985.

7. *Thunderheart.* R. An FBI agent, assigned to work a case on an Indian reservation, comes to appreciate his own Indian heritage. TriBeCa Productions, 1992.

Chapter 3: The Founding and the Constitution

BECOMING POLITICAL EXERCISES

1. Research and write a 500-word report on the contributions of women or African Americans to the American Revolution.
2. Locate a library source that describes the disagreements between Alexander Hamilton and Thomas Jefferson. If you had been there at the time, whom would you have supported? Why?
3. If you had been alive in 1787, would you have supported or opposed ratification? Create a pamphlet in the style of the Federalist and Anti federalist writers, either supporting or opposing ratification. Be sure to include text explaining your position.
4. John Adams and Samuel Adams were cousins, but of completely different political temperaments. Compare the two Adamses in terms of their political attitudes and careers. Write a 500 word report.
5. Make an illustrated map of North America, showing the areas controlled by the English, French, and Spanish just prior to the Revolution. Who owned your state? How did it become part of the Union?
6. In 1789, the year that George Washington became president, a revolution occurred in France that destroyed the monarchy and established a republic. Research and write a 500-word report on the French Revolution: its leaders, its actions, and the results.

FOR FURTHER READING

Level I Articles

1. Brookhiser, Richard. A Man on Horseback. *Atlantic Monthly,* January 1996. Good discussion of George Washington's personal character.
2. Foote, Timothy. What If, Back in 1788, We Hadn't Ratified Mr. Madison's Constitution? *Smithsonian,* June 1988.
3. Hall, Alice. James Madison, Architect of the Constitution. *National Geographic,* September 1987. Excellent portrayal of an important man often overlooked by the general public.
4. Kernan, Michael. In 1789, a Farmer Went to New York to Become President. *Smithsonian,* June 1989. Colorful description of George Washington's first days as president.

5. McDonald, Forrest. To Secure These Blessings of Liberty: The Making of the Constitution. *The World and I,* September 1987.
6. Wernick, Robert. The Godfather of the American Constitution. *Smithsonian,* September 1989. Montesquieu's influence on the Founders.

Level II Articles

1. Arkes, Hadley. The Founders and the "Superintending Principle." *The World and I,* September 1987. Connects monotheism and natural law to the Constitution.
2. *The Federalist Papers,* Number Ten. Classic statement of "factions" as part of human nature.
3. Johnson, Paul. The Organic and Moral Elements in the American Constitution. *The World and I,* September 1987. Relates the Constitution to British common law and the British unwritten constitution.
4. Kammen, Michael. Chapter 1: The Problem of Constitutionalism in American Culture. In *A Machine That Would Go of Itself.* 1986. New York: Random House. Asserts that Americans idolize the Constitution even when they are regrettably ignorant of its features.
5. Wood, Gordon. Chapter 13: Equality. In *The Radicalism of the American Revolution.* 1992. New York: Alfred A. Knopf. Challenges the conventional idea that the American Revolution was "sober and conservative" while the French Revolution was anarchic.

VIDEO RESOURCES

1. *1776.* G. The Broadway musical about the signing of the Declaration of Independence. Columbia, 1972.
2. *April Morning.* A TV movie about a young boy caught up in the American Revolution. Robert Halmi, Inc., 1988.
3. *Blind Ambition.* A TV movie about the downfall of President Nixon, the only American president to resign from that office. 1982.
4. *Johnny Tremain and the Sons of Liberty.* A young boy gets caught up in planning the Boston Tea Party and other revolutionary acts. Walt Disney Productions, 1957.
5. *Revolution.* PG. A father and son fight together in the American Revolution. Warner Home Video, 1985.

CHAPTER 4: FEDERALISM

BECOMING POLITICAL EXERCISES

1. Memorize the states and their capitols. States and capitols must be spelled correctly.
2. Research and write a 500-word report on one of the following Federalist conflicts: Canada and Quebec, the West Indies Federation (1957), Spain and the Autonomous Community issue, or the Federal Union of India (1950).
3. Research and write a 500-word report on the American militia movements of the 1990s. What are their complaints against the federal government? Do they really understand the Constitution and the federal system, or are they simply anti-government in general?
4. Investigate cooperative federalism by researching the funding of a state or local program. For example, call your city's transportation department or parks and recreation office or a county welfare office to ask them how much of their money comes from each level of government and what responsibilities they have when they receive these funds.
5. Create a crossword puzzle or wordfind (with definitions rather than listing the words) using at least ten terms from this chapter. Make a copy for each person in your group.
6. Select a federal agency that interests you, and then go on-line to find information about its history, mission, structure, and powers.
7. Research and write a 500-word report on the European Community. Is the EC moving toward establishing a federal system? What problems do you see in creating a European federation? What advantages?

FOR FURTHER READING

Level I Articles

1. Cook, Gareth. Devolution Chic. *Washington Monthly,* April 1995. The possible negative effects of sending power back to the states.
2. Donahue, John D. The Disunited States. *Atlantic Monthly,* May 1997. Devolution doesn't make economic sense.
3. Manning, Richard. How to Fight Wildfires? Trust the Guy in the Green Shirt. *Governing,* February 1989. Cooperative federalism in firefighting.

4. Perlman, Ellen. The Gorilla that Swallows State Laws. *Governing,* August 1994. The federal government and the states battle preemption.

Level II Articles

1. Commager, Henry Steele. Tocqueville's Mistake: A Defense of Strong Central Government. *Harper's Monthly,* August 1984. Argues that big government protects liberty better than the states.
2. Derthick, Martha. The Enduring Features of American Federalism. *Brookings Review,* Summer 1989. Good analysis of the place of states in the federal system.
3. Donahue, John D. The Devil in Devolution. *American Prospect,* May–June 1997. State borders are becoming more permeable, making more problems national in scope, not local.
4. Elazar, Daniel. Opening the Third Century of American Federalism: Issues and Prospects. *Annals of the American Academy of Political and Social Science,* May 1990. How changing socioeconomic conditions are changing our conceptions of federalism.
5. Garrity, John. *Quarrels That Have Shaped the Constitution.* 1987. New York: Harper & Row. Select one of the following chapters:

   The Case of the Missing Commissions (*Marbury v. Madison*)

   The Bank Cases (*McCulloch v. Maryland* and *Osborn v. Bank of the United States*)

   The Steamboat Case (*Gibbons v. Ogden*)
6. Kincaid, John. From Cooperative to Coercive Federalism. *Annals of the American Academy of Political and Social Science,* May 1990. Argues that the federal government is relying less on cooperation and more on coercion to get its way.
7. Peterson, Paul. Who Should Do What? *Brookings Review,* Spring 1995. Explores the difficulty of trying to decide which level of government should carry out redistribution programs.

VIDEO RESOURCES

1. *All the King's Men.* A fictionalized story of Huey Long, the outrageous populist governor of Louisiana in the 1930s. Columbia, 1949.
2. *Damn Citizen.* The biography of courageous war hero who, when he was appointed superintendent of the state police, fought crime and corruption in Louisiana. Universal, 1958.

3. *Gideon's Trumpet.* The story of Gideon v. Wainwright; it shows the difference between state protections of liberty and the federal Bill of Rights. World Vision, 1980.

4. *Gone to Texas.* Of special interest to Texans, this is a TV movie about Sam Houston and the Texas War of Independence. World Vision, 1986.

5. *Inherit the Wind.* The "Scopes monkey trial" that pitted Tennessee state law against the First Amendment. United Artists, 1960.

Chapter 5: Civil Liberties

BECOMING POLITICAL EXERCISES

1. Interview someone who participated in a political demonstration, such as a Vietnam march, a civil rights action, or an abortion protest. How did they happen to get involved? How did they feel about their participation? Would they do it again?
2. Interview a law enforcement official to learn about how they must conduct their jobs in order to avoid abusing the rights of those whom they apprehend. Do they think we go too far in protecting the rights of the accused?
3. Prepare a survey questionnaire using the statements about political equality found in Table 1.2 of the textbook. Ask ten people if they agree or disagree with these statements. Prepare a chart summarizing your results.
4. Research and create a chart showing the number of deaths by handguns in the United States, England, Japan, Germany, Sweden, Australia, and Canada in recent years.
5. Locate the Gallup polls for the last twenty years that ask the public about their opinions on either abortion or capital punishment. Make a graph showing support over time. What is the direction of movement?

FOR FURTHER READING

Level I Articles

1. Boston, Rob. The Religious Right Hits Libraries. *Education Digest,* April 1996. Establishing "family friendly" libraries leads to censoring libraries.
2. Boylan, James. Punishing the Press: The Public Passes Some Tough Judgments on Libel, Fairness, and "Fraud." *Columbia Journalism Review,* March–April 1997. The public doesn't like some of the tactics of journalists.
3. Crabtree, Susan. "Where Do I Go to Get My Reputation Back?" *Insight on the News,* February 19, 1996. How grand juries favor the prosecutors.
4. Davis, Rod. I'm a Nazi Until Death. *Texas Monthly,* February 1989. Young Skinheads in Dallas.

5. Frankel, Marvin. School Without a Prayer. *New Leader,* December 19, 1994–Jan. 16, 1995. How "moment of silence" laws can be used against religious minorities.
6. Kramnick, Isaac and Moore, R. Laurence. Is God a Republican? Why Politics Is Dangerous for Religion. *American Prospect,* September–October 1996. Politics and religion have always mixed in American society, but are religious leaders giving up their prophetic role when they affiliate too closely with a single party?
7. Sugarmann, Josh. The NRA Is Right: But We Still Need to Ban Handguns. *Washington Monthly,* June 1987. Provocative article which focuses on gun control as a way of reducing suicides and accidental deaths.
8. Zobel, Hiller. The Undying Problem of the Death Penalty. *American Heritage,* December 1997. Brief history of the death penalty in America.

Level II Articles

1. Burr, Chandler. The AIDS Exception: Privacy vs. Public Health. *Atlantic Monthly,* June 1997. Conflict between the right to privacy and the public's need for information to control an epidemic.
2. Gershman, Bennett. Abuse of Power in the Prosecutor's Office. *The World and I,* June 1991. How prosecutors can control and manipulate the legal process.
3. Kaminer, Wendy. Feminists Against the First Amendment. *Atlantic Monthly,* November 1992. Discusses the conflict between gender equality and freedom of the press, especially pornography.
4. Loconte, Joe. Lead Us Not into Temptation: A Christian Case Against School Prayer. *Policy Review,* Winter 1995. Not every conservative Christian believes in school prayer.
5. McCloskey, James. The Death Penalty: A Personal View. *Criminal Justice Ethics,* Summer–Fall 1996. Innocent people are executed in America because no one in the criminal justice system wants to take responsibility for reversing or commuting a sentence.
6. McConnell, Michael. Freedom from Religion? *American Enterprise,* January–February 1993. Argues that the courts have gone too far in excluding religion from public life.
7. Murphy, Paul. The Case of the Miscreant Purveyor of Scandal [Near v. Minnesota]. In Garrity, John. *Quarrels That Have Shaped the Constitution.* 1987. New York: Harper & Row.

8. Platt, Charles. "Americans Are Not as Free as We Think We Are." *Wired,* April 1996. State and local governments are shutting down electronic bulletin boards.

9. Wright, James. Second Thoughts about Gun Control. *Public Interest,* Spring 1988. Questions the conventional wisdom about gun control.

VIDEO RESOURCES

1. *Cry Freedom.* PG-13. An outstanding depiction of anti-apartheid activist Stephen Biko in South Africa. Universal, 1987.
2. *Dead Man Walking.* PG. This movie is based on the true story of nun who helps a death-row inmate deal with his impending execution. [Note: There are several movies with this name.] Polygram, 1996.
3. *Evil in Clear River.* A TV movie based on the true story of a Canadian mother who discovers her son's teacher is teaching anti-Semitism and fights the small-town establishment to get him removed from his teaching position and his job as the town mayor. 1988.
4. *Guilty by Suspicion.* PG-13. A film director who was never a communist finds himself on Senator McCarthy's blacklist. Warner Brothers, 1987.
5. *Promised a Miracle.* PG. Based on a true story of religious parents who are charged with involuntary manslaughter after refusing medical treatment for their dying son, this movie treats both sides fairly. Republic, 1988.
6. *Roe v. Wade.* A TV movie about the landmark abortion case. Paramount, 1989.
7. *School Ties.* PG-13. Anti-Semitism among students at an elite prep school. Jaffe-Lansing, 1992.
8. *Skokie.* PG. The true story of neo-fascist groups who wanted to march in a Jewish suburb. 1981.
9. *Thornwell.* The true story of an African American soldier accused of spying who later learned through the Freedom of Information Act that he had been given LSD by the Army. 1981.

Chapter 6: Civil Rights

BECOMING POLITICAL EXERCISES

1. Interview someone who grew up during the time of "Jim Crow" laws and segregated schools. What were some of the ways segregation was enforced? How did this person feel about Dr. Martin Luther King, Jr. and his peaceful resistance movement?
2. The civil rights movement of the 1960s was symbolized by the anthem, "We shall overcome." What other music did the movement use? Locate examples and bring them to class. What was the value of music to the movement?
3. Research the life of one of the following persons and write a brief biography: W.E.B. DuBois, Booker T. Washington, Rosa Parks, Andrew Young, or Martin Luther King, Jr.
4. Carefully read a newspaper to see if it has adopted gender-neutral language. Do you detect any examples of sexist language? Write a 500-word report on your findings.
5. Locate some of the speeches or writings of Dr. Martin Luther King, Jr., such as the "I Have a Dream" speech. Read the speech out loud and then write a 500-word report on your reactions to this speech.

FOR FURTHER READING

Level I Articles

1. GouldEllen, Ingrid. Welcome Neighbors? *Brookings Review,* Winter 1997. Creating stable racially mixed neighborhoods.
2. Kirsanow, Peter. I Have an (American) Dream. *The World and I,* March 1995. Describes the growth of the black middle class and its increasing conservatism.
3. Leuchtenburg, William. The Conversion of Harry Truman. *American Heritage,* November 1991. How a southern president changed his mind about civil rights.
4. Lynch, Michael. Racial Preferences Are Dead. *Reason,* February 1998. Interview with Ward Connerly, the black man who took on affirmative action in California.

5. Lynch, Michael and Post, Katherine. What Glass Ceiling? *Public Interest,* Summer 1996. The wage gap is not discrimination, but different employment patterns.
6. McLaurin, Melton. The Day I Learned I Was a Racist. *Washington Monthly,* November 1987. A touching article about a young boy's moment of truth.
7. Medley, Keith. The Sad Story of How "Separate But Equal" Was Born. *Smithsonian,* October 1993. The story of Homer Plessy of Plessy v. Ferguson fame.
8. Schrag, Peter. When Preferences Disappear. *American Prospect,* January–February 1997. Affirmative action is disappearing, but this may open the door to some new and better approaches.
9. Stanfield, Rochelle. Affirmative Inaction. *National Journal,* July 12, 1997. Balanced view of problems and strengths of affirmative action.
10. Worth, Robert. Beyond Racial Preferences. *Washington Monthly,* March 1998. New approaches are needed that go beyond affirmative action.

Level II Articles

1. Blauner, Bob. Talking Past Each Other. *The American Prospect,* Summer 1992. Whites view racism as color consciousness, blacks as a system of power.
2. Bordewich, Fergus. Revolution in Indian Country. *American Heritage,* July/August 1996. Indian tribes are asserting new rights.
3. Fish, Stanley. Reverse Racism, or How the Pot Got to Call the Kettle Black. *Atlantic Monthly,* November 1993. Justification for minorities to claim special privileges.
4. Hacker, Andrew. The Myths of Racial Division. *Atlantic Monthly,* March 23, 1992. Analyzes the rise of the black middle class and notes that it differs little from the white middle class.
5. Kennedy, Randall. My Race Problem—And Ours. *Atlantic Monthly,* May 1997. A black man challenges the idea of racial pride.
6. Lind, Michael. The End of the Rainbow. *Mother Jones,* September–October 1997. The rainbow coalition is split by issues such as immigration and affirmative action.
7. Sinsheimer, Joseph. The Freedom Vote of 1963: New Strategies of Racial Protest in Mississippi. *Journal of Southern History,* May 1989. A good look at the summer of 1963 and the strategy of SNCC in Mississippi.

8. Skerry, Peter. The Strange Politics of Affirmative Action. *Wilson Quarterly,* Winter 1997. "Affirmative action babies" are free riders who refuse to acknowledge the efforts of others.
9. Stanfield, Rochelle. The Split Society. *National Journal,* April 2, 1994. Segregation is no longer an important public policy issue, even though racist incidents are increasing.
10. Starr, Paul. Civil Reconstruction: What to Do Without Affirmation Action. *American Prospect,* Winter 1992. Explores alternatives to affirmative action, such as a National Endowment for Black America and pro-family social policies.
11. Traub, James. Separate But Equal. *The Atlantic Monthly,* September 1991. The time for school desegregation may have passed.

VIDEO RESOURCES

1. *A Soldier's Story.* PG-13. A lawyer investigates a murder on an army base in Louisiana in 1944 and learns about racial tensions firsthand. Columbia, 1984.
2. *Crisis at Central High.* A TV movie about the integration of Central High School in Little Rock in 1957. Lightning, 1980.
3. *Gandhi.* PG-13. The life of the pacifist Mohandas Gandhi, who formulated the passive-resistance philosophy used in the American civil rights movement. International Film, 1982.
4. *Get On the Bus.* R. Follows several black men as they ride to the Million Man March in Washington, D.C. 15 Black Men/40 Acres & A Mule Filmworks, 1996.
5. *Long Walk Home.* PG13. A black maid walks nine miles to her job in Montgomery, Alabama in order to observe the bus boycott led by Dr. Martin Luther King, Jr. New Visions Pictures, 1989.
6. *Malcolm X.* PG13. Life of the controversial black leader. 40 Acres & A Mule Filmworks, 1992.
7. *Miss Evers' Boys.* PG. The Story of the infamous "Tuskegee Study of Untreated Blacks With Syphilis." Anasazi Productions, 1997.
8. *Mississippi Burning.* R. Fact-based story of three civil rights workers who disappeared in Mississippi and were later found dead by the FBI. Frederick Zollo, 1988.

9. *Philadelphia.* PG13. Tom Hanks is an AIDS-infected attorney who fights for his job. TriStar, 1993.
10. *Separate But Equal.* PG13. A TV drama about the struggle to desegregate public schools. Republic, 1991.
11. *The Autobiography of Miss Jane Pittman.* A TV movie traces the life of a black woman from the Civil War to the civil rights movement. 1974.
12. *When Billy Broke His Head . . . And Other Tales of Wonder.* A documentary of how we mistreat and misunderstand the disabled. 1995.

Chapter 7: Public Opinion

BECOMING POLITICAL EXERCISES

1. Have a discussion with someone who is not of your generation (your parents, for example) and ask them about their own political beliefs. How did they acquire them, what are their beliefs, and have they ever changed their political party? Then compare their process of political socialization with yours.
2. How much do college students know about politics? Put together a brief questionnaire asking students questions such as who are the vice president and the lieutenant governor, what is in the First Amendment, etc. Summarize the findings in a table.
3. Select a topic such as the Equal Rights Amendment, the Balanced Budget Amendment, or abortion, and trace public opinion on it from as far back as you can find records to the present, using the Gallup polls or other public opinion polls. Construct several graphs to show the direction of opinions. Has public opinion shifted over time? If so, how?
4. Select a current issue in politics, such as the flat tax, and read one article on the subject in the *National Review* and a second article on the same subject in *The New Republic* or *The Nation*. Compare the two viewpoints.
5. Write a 500-word essay describing your own political socialization. Discuss the importance of your family, teachers, peers, and religion in developing your own attitudes.

FOR FURTHER READING

Level I Articles

1. Clausen, Christopher. The Libertarian Heresy. *New Leader,* Februrary 10, 1997. Critique of libertarian philosophy.
2. Democracy and Technology. *The Economist,* June 17, 1995. New technology changes the way political information is exchanged. Is this always good?
3. Greider, William. Why I Don't Believe What He Believes. *Rolling Stone,* July 13–27, 1995. A liberal's response to P. J. O'Rourke's article (listed below).
4. Keisling, Phil. Repoll Man. *Washington Monthly,* September 1992. Polls aren't always right, and their errors can be costly.

5. O'Rourke, P. J. Why I Believe What I Believe. *Rolling Stone,* July 13–27, 1995. A libertarian states his beliefs.
6. Starobin, Paul. Bullier Pulpits. *National Journal,* January 13, 1996. The Religious Left begins to speak out.
7. Starobin, Paul. Civil War. *National Journal,* July 26, 1997. Conservatives are creating tensions in the Republican party.
8. Witham, Larry. The Real Face of the Christian Right. *The World and I,* October 1994. Describes three levels of membership in the Christian Right.

Level II Articles

1. Boynton, Robert. The New Intellectuals. *Atlantic Monthly,* March 1995. The rise of African American intellectuals such as Cornel West, Stephen Carter, and Toni Morrison, who transcend racial politics in their thinking.
2. Dallek, Matthew. Liberalism Overthrown. *American Heritage,* October 1996. Liberalism's slow death began in 1966.
3. Greenberg, Stanley. Private Heroism and Public Purpose. *American Prospect,* September–October 1996. Political opinions of the working class.
4. Judis, John. Crosses To Bear. *The New Republic,* September 12, 1994. The Religious Right is changing its public face while struggling to maintain its religious principles.
5. Starr, Paul. Restoration Fever. *American Prospect,* March–April 1996. Doubts about a conservative restoration
6. Yankelovich, Daniel. How Public Opinion Really Works. *Fortune,* October 5, 1992. Public opinion actually goes through seven stages, from awareness to mature and moral judgment.

VIDEO RESOURCES

1. *Blood in the Face.* A documentary that shows that the Nazis, KKK, and Aryan Nation are alive and well today. Right Thinking, 1991.
2. *Kent State.* A TV movie about the National Guard's killing of four college students during an anti-Vietnam demonstration. MCA/Universal, 1981.
3. *Reds.* PG-13. The life story of American Communist John Reed, who went to live in Russia and became disillusioned with the harsh realities of communist society. Paramount, 1981.
4. *The Way We Were.* PG-13. Political opinions expressed in the past come back to haunt a marriage. Rastar, 1973.

Chapter 8: The Media

BECOMING POLITICAL EXERCISES

1. Compare the way a major news story is treated in two different newspapers. Analyze the length of each story, any special slant given to it, sources used, and the way in which the story is treated editorially.
2. Compare the way two television stations cover the same story. Analyze the length of each story, any special slant given to it, sources and visuals used.
3. Compare the way a newspaper and a television station cover the same story. Analyze the length of each story, any special slant given to it, and sources and visuals used.
4. Collect at least five cigarette ads from the print media and analyze them according to their appeal and effectiveness. What age group do they seem to be going for? Are these ads realistic portrayals of smoking? What images are aimed at children? At teenagers? The American Heart Association reports that most people start smoking between ages 12 and 17 and most begin because of advertising from magazines, billboards, sports arena ads, and merchandise offers. What does this tell you about the power of the media to influence our behavior?
5. Many news organizations, newspapers, and magazines have web sites; some include summaries of news stories or on-line copies of print information. Visit some of these, and classify them by their overt political orientation—left, right, or ostensibly "neutral." Then look at the stories that have been chosen and how those stories have been presented. Do they betray liberal or conservative biases? Try looking at some "nonpolitical" areas, such as business news. What biases can be found? What does this say about the supposed neutrality or liberal bias of the news?
6. While national journalists, especially print reporters, tend to have grown up in middle- to upper-class families and have gone to elite schools, the reporters on the local news in your town probably reflect a different background. In recent years, we have seen journalists well-trained in technical aspects of video and print, but less knowledgeable about the very subjects they are covering. If your school offers a program in journalism or mass communications, analyze the degree requirements to see if you believe the students are adequately trained to report on political, economic, and legal issues. What sort of training do you think reporters should have?

FOR FURTHER READING

Level I Articles

1. Andrews, Peter. The Press. *American Heritage,* October 1994. Lengthy but entertaining article recounting the development of the free press.

2. Davidson, John. Menace to Society. *Rolling Stone,* February 22, 1996. Saturday morning cartoons may be the most dangerous media violence, ahead of boxing matches and the evening news.

3. Fitzwater, Marlin. The Wild West Wing. *Washington Monthly,* October 1994. An hour in the life of a presidential press secretary.

4. Georges, Christopher. Confessions of an Investigative Reporter. *Washington Monthly,* March 1992. Most investigative reporters are only reporting on government investigations.

5. Hanson, Christopher. Lost in Never-Never Land. *Columbia Journalism Review,* May–June 1996. Analyzes the "horse race" aspect of the 1996 Republican presidential primaries.

6. Harwood, Richard. Are Journalists "e-l-i-t-i-s-t"? *American Journalism Review,* June 1995. Most journalists are ordinary people, not media superstars.

7. Hodges, Glenn. When Good Guys Lie. *Washington Monthly,* January/February 1997. How misleading statistics are purveyed through the media to support policy agendas.

8. Mahtesian, Charles. The Endless Struggle Over Open Meetings. *Governing,* December 1997. The struggle in Texas over toughening the state's open meetings law.

9. Shepard, Alicia C. Celebrity Journalists. *Columbia Journalism Review,* September 1997. When journalists become entertainers, their credibility declines.

10. Stark, Steven. Local News: The Biggest Scandal on TV. *Washington Monthly,* June 1997. Crime and disasters make up most of local news.

11. Starobin, Paul. An Ear for Gossip. *National Journal,* October 4, 1997. We love to read the gossip about our politicians.

12. Tron, Barrie. Staging Media Events: What We Learned from the Contract with America. *Campaigns & Elections,* February/March 1996. Inside look at how media events are planned and staged.

Level II Articles

1. Fallows, James. Why Americans Hate the Media. *The Atlantic Monthly,* February 1996. Why? Because the media ask stupid questions, don't do their research, and are arrogant.
2. Graber, Doris. The "New" Media and Politics: What Does the Future Hold? *PS: Political Science & Politics,* March 1996. The Internet changes the way news is delivered by empowering the media users.
3. Kaid, Lynda, et al. Television News and Presidential Campaigns: the Legitimization of Televised Political Advertising. *Social Science Quarterly,* June 1993. A review of the characteristics of news coverage of political advertising.
4. Starobin, Paul. The Conceptual Scoop. *Columbia Journalism Review,* January/February 1996. Journalists don't like to hit the beat anymore; they prefer to think about it instead.
5. Stossel, Scott. The Man Who Counts the Killings. *Atlantic Monthly,* May 1997. A long but fascinating look at the relationship between violence on television and violence in our culture.

VIDEO RESOURCES

1. *Absence of Malice.* PG-13. A reporter implicates a politician in a murder case and then struggles with the ethics of journalistic privilege. Columbia, 1981.
2. *Attack on Fear.* A TV movie about two real-life journalists who won a Pulitzer Prize when they investigated the Synanon drug-rehabilitation center, even though their lives were threatened. 1984.
3. *Broadcast News.* R. A romantic comedy set in a frenetic television newsroom. Good depiction of how TV newsrooms work. Fox, 1987.
4. *Brother's Keeper.* A documentary about a man accused of murdering his brother; it provides an insightful look at the power of the media. Creative Thinking, 1992.
5. *The Killing Fields.* R. This is based on the true story of an American reporter who struggles to rescue his Cambodian interpreter during the Khmer Rouge coup. Enigma, Goldcrest, 1984.
6. *Missing.* PG. An American journalist disappears in South America and his family can't get the truth from the U.S. government. Based on a true story. Polygram, 1982.

7. *Network.* R. A satire about an insane newscaster who wins the ratings wars. MGM, 1976.

8. *News at Eleven.* A TV movie about the pressures to report a sex scandal. Turner Entertainment, 1986.

9. *Under Fire.* R. A political thriller about a reporter who gets involved in the war between the Sandinista revolutionaries and the Somoza government of Nicaragua. Lion's Gate, 1983.

CHAPTER 9: POLITICAL PARTIES

BECOMING POLITICAL EXERCISES

1. Interview someone who is active in politics. Find out why and how they got interested in politics, what it has cost them in personal terms, and what satisfactions they have received from being a political activist.
2. Research and write a 500-word report on the costs of running for public office. How much did each of the following candidates spend in the 1996 presidential campaign: Bob Dole, Pat Buchanan, Steve Forbes, Lamar Alexander, Alan Keyes, Bill Clinton? Where did their money come from—big contributors, PACs, personal money?
3. Create a crossword puzzle or wordfind (using clues, not the words themselves) using at least ten terms from this chapter. Bring a copy for each person in your group and record their scores in your report.
4. How can you become active in politics? Contact the county office of your party to learn about how one gets to the county convention or participates in a caucus in your state.
5. Visit the web site of a political party to see what they are saying about some of the current political issues. Besides the Republicans and Democrats, many smaller parties, such as the Libertarians, Committees of Correspondence, and the Reform Party also have sites. What do the parties have to say about the issues of the day: the state of the family, gay rights, affirmative action, health care, reproductive rights? Would the party be characterized as extreme left or right, moderately left or right, or somewhere else on the spectrum? If a third party, is it closer in spirit to the Republicans or Democrats? Why would it be a separate party and not a coalition within one of the big parties?

FOR FURTHER READING

Level I Articles

1. Barone, Michael. Beneath the Two-Party System. *National Review,* December 11, 1995. Identifies seven different groups of voters, such as Dowagers, Ethnic Conservatives, and Liberal Activists.
2. Fallows, James. A Democrat Who Admits It. *Atlantic Monthly,* November 1997. Dick Gephardt is an old-time Democrat going against the conservative tide.

3. Forer, Lois. Patron saints. *Washington Monthly,* July/August 1991. A defense of political machines.
4. Maharidge, Dale. The Sleeping Giant Awakes. *Mother Jones,* January/February 1998. The rise of the Latino voters.
5. Meacham, Jon. What the Religious Right Can Teach the New Democrats. *Washington Monthly,* April 1993. Conservative Christians have been caricatured in the press, but they are providing an important service by raising moral issues liberals don't like to confront.
6. Murdock, Deroy. Blacks and the GOP. *The World and I,* March 1995. Black Americans are voting for Republicans, even electing two of their own to Congress.
7. Prospects for a Third Party: Top Pros Speak Out. *Campaigns & Elections,* September 1995. Three experts make predictions about the prospects of a third party rising in the next decade.
8. Victor, Kirk. Duking It Out in Dixie. *National Journal,* December 13, 1997. Democrats want to "take back the South."
9. Wernick, Robert. The Know-Nothings Knew How to Win . . . For a While. *Smithsonian,* November 1996. Fears about immigration are not new; the United States once had an entire political party based on protecting the rights of Protestant, American-born white male citizens.

Level II Articles

1. Armey, Dick. Freedom's Choir. *Policy Review,* Winter 1994. The new Republican party as a "party of freedom."
2. Fiorina, Morris. The Decline of Collective Responsibility in American Politics. *Daedalus,* Summer 1990. Reforming the party system has actually weakened it.
3. Hale, Jon. The Making of the New Democrats. *Political Science Quarterly,* Summer 1995. Turning the liberals into moderates.
4. Lind, Michael. The Southern Coup. *The New Republic,* June 19, 1995. How the South became Republican.
5. Starobin, Paul. Party Hoppers. *National Journal,* February 7, 1998. A surprising trend—rich Republicans disillusioned with their party are switching their votes.
6. Wattenberg, Martin. When You Can't Beat Them, Join Them: Shaping the Presidential Nominating Process in the Television Age. *Polity,* Spring 1989. Why nominating conventions are declining in importance.

VIDEO RESOURCES

1. *Conspiracy—The Trial of the Chicago Eight.* Made for TV, this movie recounts the trial of the activists who disrupted the 1968 Democratic convention held in Chicago. HBO Video, 1987.
2. *Feed.* A documentary that shows the 1992 party nomination process; it includes candid shots of the candidates during the New Hampshire primary. Video Democracy, 1992.
3. *The Best Man.* A classic movie about two presidential candidates who each have skeletons in the closet. United Artists, 1964.
4. *The Last Party.* A documentary about the "political state of the union" during the 1992 presidential campaign. Campaign Films, 1993.
5. *War Room.* PG. A fascinating documentary about the inner workings of the 1992 Clinton campaign. Pennebaker, 1992.

Chapter 10: Campaigns and Elections

BECOMING POLITICAL EXERCISES

1. Collect several examples of campaign literature. What is the appeal? Are they asking for money? Do these samples discuss issues? Promote personalities? How effective do you think these are in influencing voters?
2. Interview someone who has run for public office or who has managed a campaign. How much money did they need? How did they raise the money? How did the candidate decide what issues to press? How successful was the candidate?
3. Research the electoral system of a nation that uses proportional representation, such as Israel, Germany, Belgium, or one of the Scandinavian countries. What are the advantages and disadvantages of their system?
4. Visit the web site of an on-line politician, such as a legislator or state officer. What does the site contain? Is this an effective way of communicating with the public? Does the politician administer the site himself or is it done by others? Can you understand the politician's positions on major issues by consulting the web site?

FOR FURTHER READING

Level I Articles

1. Barone, Michael. Divide and Rule. *National Journal,* July 12, 1997. The return of straight ticket voting.
2. Carney, Eliza Newlin. Opting Out of Politics. *National Journal,* January 17, 1998. Negative campaigns may be turning off voters and reducing voter turnout.
3. Everline, Theresa. Notes of an Opposition Researcher. *Washington Monthly,* July/August 1996. The sleazy life inside a campaign.
4. Ferling, John. 1797: The First Real Election. *American History,* December 1996. After Washington, presidential elections got more interesting.
5. Gans, Curtis. Stop the Madness! *Washington Monthly,* May 1997. Campaign commercials turn off American voters.

6. Hamburg, Dan. In the Money: A Congressman's Story. *Nation,* May 5, 1997. Inside look at the powerful pressures on congressmen to raise money.
7. Judis, John B. Goo-Goos Versus Populists. *American Prospect,* January–February 1997. Campaign finance reform proposals examined.
8. Mann, Thomas E. Deregulating Campaign Finance. *Brookings Review,* Winter 1998. Here's a novel proposal: do away with all limits on contributions to campaigns.
9. Miller, Ellen S. Clean Elections, How To. *American Prospect,* January–February 1997. Campaign reformers should adopt the Clean Money Option.
10. Sabato, Larry and Simpson, Glenn. Vote Fraud! *Campaigns & Elections,* June 1996. You thought vote fraud was history? Voting fraud is back, bigger than ever.
11. Sabato, Larry and Simpson, Glenn. When Push Comes to Poll. *Washington Monthly,* June 1996. Negative campaigning disguises itself as research.
12. Starobin, Paul. Man Trouble. *National Journal,* December 6, 1997. The "Guy Gap" in the Democratic party.
13. Starobin. Paul. The New Mugwumps. *National Journal,* November 1, 1997. How the elites promote good government today.
14. Teixeira, Ruy. Voter Turnout in America: Ten Myths. *Brookings Review,* Fall 1992. Destroys the myths we hold about why people don't vote.

Level II Articles

1. Ansolabehere, Stephen et al. Does Attack Advertising Demobilize the Electorate? *American Political Science Review,* December 1994. Statistical proof that negative campaigns reduce voter turnout.
2. Chavez, Linda. Hispanics, Affirmative Action, and Voting. *Annals of the American Academy of Political and Social Science,* September 1992. Explores Hispanic political activity.
3. Clark, Janet. Getting There: Women in Political Office. *Annals of the American Academy of Political and Social Science,* May 1991. Theories about why so few women hold public office.
4. Dahl, Robert. The Problem of Civic Competence. *Journal of Democracy,* October 1991. How decentralization, citizen assemblies, and technology can increase voter awareness.

5. Ganz, Marshall. Motor Voter or Motivated Voter? *American Prospect,* September–October 1996. Will "motor voter" laws increase political participation?
6. Kaminer, Wendy. Crashing the Locker Room. *The Atlantic Monthly,* July 1992. Problems women face when they run for office.
7. Lind, Michael. Alice Doesn't Vote Here Any More. *Mother Jones,* March–April 1998. Why we should adopt proportional representation.
8. Lind, Michael. A Radical Plan to Change American Politics. *The Atlantic Monthly,* August 1992. Implementing proportional representation in American elections.
9. Ornstein, Norman. Money in Politics. *The Ripon Forum,* July–August 1992. We need more money in campaigns, not less—and how to get it.
10. Schrag, Peter. California, Here We Come. *Atlantic Monthly,* March 1998. How voter initiatives can destroy representative government.
11. Zimmerman, Joseph. Alternative Voting Systems for Representative Democracy. *PS: Political Science & Politics,* December 1994. Outlines different types of election and voting systems, such as alternative vote, cumulative vote, and proportional representation.

VIDEO RESOURCES

1. *Majority Rule.* A TV drama about a woman general who decides to run for president. 1992.
2. *Nashville.* R. A musical satire about a political campaign and a music festival in Nashville in the 1970s. Paramount, 1975.
3. *Power.* R. A heartless political consultant markets political candidates like soap. Lorimar, 1986.
4. *Primary Colors.* R. Join the guessing game: how much of this movie is based on Bill Clinton, and how much is fiction? Mutual Film Company, 1998.
5. *Primary Motive.* R. A candidate lies about his background and is exposed, but still wins the public-opinion polls. Ascension Films, 1992.
6. *Running Mates.* PG-13. A Hillary Clinton look-alike falls in love with a bachelor presidential candidate. HBO Video, 1992. [Note: There are two movies by this name.]
7. *The Candidate.* PG. A great satire of the political process as Robert Redford is packaged for a senatorial campaign. Warner Brothers, 1972.

Chapter 11: Groups and Interests

BECOMING POLITICAL EXERCISES

1. Locate and read an article in the library that discusses the power of an interest group such as the National Rifle Association or the American Association of Retired Persons.

2. Analyze some organization to which you have belonged—a high school club, a fraternity, a church group, a band. How can you describe the internal decision-making process? Were you part of the leadership? If so, how did you become a leader? How did the group recruit new members? Did this group have a free-rider problem? How did they deal with it? Does this analysis help you understand why interest groups have to work so hard to get members?

3. Interview a lobbyist to learn about what he or she does, how influential they believe they are, techniques they use, and where their money comes from.

4. Select a hot topic, such as gun control, environmentalism, reproductive rights, or animal rights, and go on-line to find two organizations representing different sides of the debate (for example, the National Rifle Association and Handgun Control, Inc.). Summarize the information found on their web sites. What do the two sides have to say about the issues, and about each other?

FOR FURTHER READING

Level I Articles

1. Bailey, Charles W. Snakes in the Grass. *Washington Monthly,* September 1996. How grassroots lobbying is manipulated by public relations firms.

2. DiLorenzo, Thomas J. Who Really Speaks for the Elderly? *Consumers' Research Magazine,* September 1996. Challenges the assumption that AARP speaks for all the elderly.

3. Georges, Christopher. Old Money. *Washington Monthly,* June 1992. AARP as a multi-billion dollar business.

4. McWilliams, Rita. The Best and Worst of Public Interest Groups. *Washington Monthly,* March 1988.

5. Pianin, Eric and Babcock, Charles. Working the System. *Washington Post National Weekly Edition,* April 13, 1998. The sordid side of campaign fundraising.

6. Rauch, Jonathan. Blow It Up. *National Journal,* March 29, 1997. Suggests that public financing of campaigns combined with deregulation might clean up the mess.
7. Sanchez, Samantha. How the West Is Won. *The American Prospect,* March–April 1996. How the "wise use" movement (timber and mining interests) uses "astroturf" lobbying.
8. Silverstein, Ken. "Hello. I'm Calling this Evening to Mislead You." *Mother Jones,* November–December 1997. The inside scoop on "astroturf" lobbying.
9. Silverstein, Ken. My Life as an Undercover PAC. *Nation,* May 5, 1997. When you have money to give, your social life improves immeasurably.
10. Trento, Susan. Lord of the Lies. *Washington Monthly,* September 1992. Influence peddling in Washington.
11. Victor, Kirk. Lost Cause? *National Journal,* March 1, 1997. Just how effective is Common Cause anyway?

Level II Articles

1. Berry, Jeffrey. Citizen Groups and the Changing Nature of Interest Group Politics in America. *Annals of the American Academy of Political and Social Science,* July 1993. The rise of public interest groups has made politics more open and participatory, but also more complex.
2. Covington, Sally. How Conservative Philanthropies and Think Tanks Transform U.S. Policy. *Covert Action Quarterly,* Winter 1998. Money, influential people, recruitment.
3. Herrmann, Robert. Participation and Leadership in Consumer Movement Organizations. *Journal of Social Issues,* Volume 47, No. 1, 1991. Organizes consumer groups into four categories with different agendas and tactics.
4. Peterson, Paul. An Immodest Proposal: Let's Give Children the Vote. *Brookings Review,* Winter 1993. Satirical approach to understanding interest groups.
5. Rauch, Jonathan. The Hyperpluralism Trap. *The New Republic,* June 6, 1994. Special interests have taken over the government, but there are some things we can do to regain control.
6. Shaiko, Ronald. Greenpeace U.S.A.: Something Old, New, Borrowed. *Annals of the American Academy of Political and Social Science,* July 1993. Analyzes a radical public interest group.

VIDEO RESOURCES

1. *Born on the Fourth of July.* R. The story of Ron Kovic, a Vietnam veteran who became a key leader in the anti-war movement. Fourth of July, 1989.
2. *Portrait of a Rebel: Margaret Sanger.* A TV movie about the efforts to repeal the Comstock Act in order to allow dissemination of birth-control information. 1982.
3. *Tucker: The Man and His Dream.* PG-13. The true story of Preston Tucker, who fought the Detroit automakers and the Michigan politicians in order to create a safer automobile. Lucasfilm, 1988.
4. *When You Remember Me.* A TV movie about a real-life fourteen-year-old boy who fights to improve conditions for the disabled. 1990.

CHAPTER 12: CONGRESS

BECOMING POLITICAL EXERCISES

1. Visit the local office of a congressperson or a state legislator. Find out what the office does, how much staff it maintains, and how the legislator spends his or her time.
2. Legislators get many of their ideas for new policies from "think tanks," or private organizations that research public problems and develop innovative policy proposals. Locate the web site of one of these organizations and report on its current policy interests:

   Conservative think tanks: American Enterprise Institute, Cato Institute, Heritage Foundation, Hudson Institute

   Liberal think tanks: Twentieth Century Fund, Russell Sage Foundation, Urban Institute, Brookings Institute, Center for Budget and Policy Priorities
3. Draft a letter to a U.S. senator or congressperson, stating your opinion on a current issue. Bring the draft letter to the group for review. E-mail the letter and see if you get a response.
4. Watch Congress or its committees in session for at least one hour on C-SPAN. Then watch the British parliament's "Question Time" on C-SPAN (Sunday nights). Compare the two legislative bodies.
5. Congress's web site (http://thomas.loc.gov) provides information about bills passed in this and past sessions and gives the status of pending legislation. Track a topic that you are interested in to see what legislation has been proposed in this or the last few sessions.

FOR FURTHER READING

Level I Articles

1. Barnes, Fred. The Unbearable Lightness of Being a Congressman. *New Republic,* February 15, 1988. How Congress turns idealists into drudges.
2. Bumpers, Dale. Capitol Hill's Longest-Running Outrage. *Washington Monthly,* January/February 1998. Senator Bumpers gives an inside view of how powerful interests can block legislation.

3. Chiles, James R. The Really Good, Really Old Days on Capitol Hill. *Smithsonian,* November 1995. At least congressmen today don't spit on the floor.
4. Georges, Christopher and Boo, Katherine. Capitol Hill 20510. *Washington Monthly,* October 1992. How Congressmen try to turn themselves into media stars.
5. Lind, Michael. 75 Stars. *Mother Jones,* January/February 1998. Here's an absurd proposal—reapportion the United States Senate.
6. Meacham, Jon. Hill Climbers. *Washington Monthly,* June 1993. The congressional staff as a professional cadre.
7. Nivola, Pietro. The New Pork Barrel. *Brookings Review,* Winter 1998. How government regulations are another form of pork.
8. Stern, Philip. The Tin Cup Congress. *Washington Monthly,* May 1988. How congressmen spend their time—and it's not on legislation.
9. Waldman, Steven. How Washington Tries to Strangle Even the Best Ideas. *Washington Monthly,* January–February 1995. Excellent analysis of the legislative process, using the student loan reform bill as an example.

Level II Articles

1. Fiorina, Morris. An Era of Divided Government. *Political Science Quarterly,* Fall 1992. The President and Congress of different parties may be a long-term trend as ticket-splitting increases.
2. Fowler, Linda L. Who Runs for Congress? *PS: Political Science & Politics,* September 1996. Socioeconomic status and political experience are key variables.
3. King, Anthony. Running Scared. *Atlantic Monthly,* January 1997. Today's legislators are slaves to public opinion.
4. Mason, David. Let Congress Be Congress. *Policy Review,* Fall 1992. Useful and practical list of reforms Congress should make, such as term and session limits, staff cuts, and getting out of the casework business.
5. Stark, Steven. Too Representative Government. *The Atlantic Monthly,* May 1995. Americans dislike Congress but still expect it to solve their problems.

VIDEO RESOURCES

1. *Adam.* A TV movie about how John Walsh and his wife lobbied Congress for help in the search for their kidnapped son. International, 1983.

2. *Advise and Consent.* The story of a Senate battle over confirmation of a Secretary of State. Columbia, 1962.
3. *Bob* Roberts. R. A satire about a folk singer who runs for the Senate. The Bob Roberts Co., 1992.
4. *Mr. Smith Goes to Washington.* This classic Jimmy Stewart movie shows a naive businessman who takes a courageous stand as a senator and is nearly destroyed by it. Columbia, 1939.
5. *Quiz Show.* PG13. A 1950s congressional subcommittee discovers that TV quiz shows are rigged. Hollywood Pictures, 1994.
6. *Tail Gunner Joe.* A TV movie about the rise and fall of Senator Joseph McCarthy. 1977.
7. *The Seduction of Joe Tynan.* R. A senator faces moral dilemmas. Universal, 1979.

Chapter 13: The Presidency

BECOMING POLITICAL EXERCISES

1. Select a newspaper cartoon about the president and write a brief report, analyzing the symbols and images used, the issue depicted, and the cartoonist's point of view. Be sure to include a copy of the cartoon in your report.
2. Draw your own cartoon about the president and some issue in the news.
3. Research a first lady to learn about her family, education, political interests, the problems she encountered when her husband was president, and the effect of public office on her and her children.
4. The vice presidency is an oft-forgotten position, but several vice presidents have been notable. Research the career of one of the following vice presidents: Aaron Burr, George Clinton, Henry Wallace, Spiro Agnew, or Nelson Rockefeller.
5. White House information can be found at the White House web site and the Americans Communicating Electronically Gopher. Check out a web site and look for press releases, and official documents. What did you find?

FOR FURTHER READING

Level I Articles

1. Anthony, Carl. The First Ladies: They've Come a Long Way, Martha. *Smithsonian,* October 1992. Historical development of the unelected post of First Lady.
2. Broder, David. The Story that Still Nags Me. *Washington Monthly,* February 1987. Did Senator Muskie really cry, or was it snowing? Broder's conscience still bothers him.
3. Solomon, Bert. Do We Ask Too Much of Our Presidents? *National Journal,* June 18, 1994. Why aren't these presidents superheroes?
4. Sorensen, Theodore. From the Eye of the Storm. *Washington Monthly,* November 1997. Insider's view of the decision-making process during the Cuban missile crisis.

Level II Articles

1. Cronin, Thomas. The Paradoxes of the Presidency. *Skeptic,* September–October 1976. Conflicting roles of the presidency.
2. Eastland, Terry. Reconsidering Presidential Power. *American Enterprise,* May–June 1992. The paradox of a conservative president who is also a strong president.
3. Kennedy, John F. *Inaugural Address.*
4. O'Sullivan, John. After Reaganism. *National Review,* April 21, 1997. Republicans need to redefine themselves in light of the movement to the center by the Left.
5. Wildavsky, Aaron. The Two Presidencies. *Society,* January–February 1998. Contrasts the president's foreign policy powers with his domestic powers.

VIDEO RESOURCES

1. *All the President's Men.* PG-13. The true story of the investigation of the Watergate break-in that led to President Nixon's resignation. Warner Brothers, 1976.

2. *Eleanor and Franklin.* A TV movie about the relationship between Franklin Roosevelt and his wife, Eleanor. 1976.

3. *In the Line of Fire.* R. A Secret Service agent tries to prevent a presidential assassination. Apple/Rose Productions, 1993.

4. *Kennedys of Massachusetts.* A TV biography of one of America's most important political families. 1990.

5. *Missiles of October.* A TV movie portraying the Cuban missile crisis of 1962. MPI, 1974.

6. *Secret Honor.* Richard Nixon's search for meaning. Sandcastle 5, 1985.

7. *Seven Days in May.* Military leaders plot to overthrow the American government. Seven Arts, 1964.

8. *Sunrise at Campobello.* FDR contracts polio and must decide if he has to give up his career in politics. Warner Brothers, 1960.

Chapter 14: Bureaucracy in a Democracy

BECOMING POLITICAL EXERCISES

1. Interview someone who holds a professional position in federal, state, or local government. Find out how they got their job, be able to describe their duties, their work environment, and their agency's promotion policy. Ask this person to cite some pros and cons of working for the government.
2. Take the sample test found in the application form for the foreign service. Most college career centers have copies. What was your score? Was the test difficult?
3. Select a federal agency that interests you and research it on the Internet. What did you learn about this agency? Is the agency larger and more complex than you had thought?
4. If you are interested in working for the federal government, locate the web site of the Office of Personnel Management (http://www.usajobs.opm.gov) to check out current listings. What occupations are in demand? Are there any summer jobs available in your area? How about entry-level jobs in your career field?

FOR FURTHER READING

Level I Articles

1. Franklin, Daniel. The FEMA Phoenix. *Washington Monthly,* July/August 1995. Federal agencies can reinvent themselves.
2. Helvarg, David. "It Was Like a Wild West Chase on the High Seas." *Smithsonian,* February 1997. The dangerous life of a National Marine Fisheries Service agent.
3. Helvarg, David. Open Hostilities: National Park Personnel Are Increasingly Targeted by the Wise Use Movement's Campaign of Violence. *National Parks,* September–October 1996. Working for the federal government isn't for wimps.
4. Hodges, Glenn. Dead Wood. *Washington Monthly,* October 1996. Time to reform the Forest Service.
5. Levin, Blair. Mama, Don't Let Your Babies Grow Up to Be Regulators. *Washington Monthly,* January/February 1998. Lessons learned from someone who worked for the Federal Communications Commission.

6. Peters, Charles. From Ouagadougou to Cape Canaveral: Why the bad news doesn't travel up. *Washington Monthly,* April 1986. Why bureaucrats are afraid to tell their bosses about the problems in their agencies.
7. Piore, Adam. Mission Creep. *Washington Monthly,* April 1997. A look at the antiquated and wasteful Veterans Administration.
8. Scher, Abby. Tax Attack: The Right Targets the IRS. *Dollars & Sense,* March–April 1997. The most-feared federal agency attacked by the Christian Patriot movement.
9. Waldman, Amy. Government's Nine-to-Fivers. *Washington Monthly,* July–August 1996. Serious problems in the civil service system lead to waste and inefficiency.
10. Watson, Bruce. The New Peace Corps Steppes Out—in Kazakhstan. *Smithsonian,* August 1994. The Peace Corps goes to a new part of the world.

Level II Articles

1. Behn, Robert. The Big Questions of Public Management. *Public Administration Review,* July/August 1995. The Three M's of public management: micromanagement, motivation, and measurement.
2. Frederickson, H. George and Frederickson, David. Public Perception of Ethics in Government. *Annals of the American Academy of Political and Social Science,* January 1995. Discusses accountability and the public trust.
3. Thompson, Dennis. Paradoxes of Government Ethics. *Public Administration Review,* May/June 1992. Government ethics differ from personal ethics because government officials must serve a democratic society.

VIDEO RESOURCES

1. *Afterburn.* A TV movie based on the life of a military widow who disagreed with the Defense Department's conclusion that her husband's death was due to pilot error; she eventually took a contractor to court and proved that the military was covering up for the company. HBO Video, 1992.
2. *Article 99.* R. A veterans' hospital dismisses a doctor who defies the military rules about treating veterans. Article 99 Productions, 1992.
3. *Dead Ahead:* The Exxon Valdez Disaster. PG-13. The bureaucratic impediments to cleaning up the oil spill in Alaska. Imperial, 1992.
4. *Marie.* PG13. The true story of Marie Ragghianti, who fought corruption in government while chairing the Tennessee Parole Board. DEG, 1985.

5. *Nightbreaker.* A TV drama about a doctor who was part of the military's experiments exposing soldiers to atomic radiation in the early 1950s. Turner Entertainment, 1989.

6. *Silkwood.* R. The true story of nuclear-plant worker who was a whistleblower and died under mysterious circumstances while on her way to meet with a reporter. Fox, 1983.

7. *The Children Nobody Wanted.* A TV true story about Tom Butterfield, an unmarried Missouri college student who fought the bureaucracy in order to adopt homeless children. 1981.

8. *True Colors.* R. Two lawyers take different paths—one to fight for right in the Justice Department, the other heading into politics. Paramount, 1991. [Note: There are two movies by this name.]

Chapter 15: The Federal Courts

BECOMING POLITICAL EXERCISES

1. Select one current or former Supreme Court justice and research his or her background and career on the bench. What has been this justice's judicial philosophy?
2. Visit a courtroom and spend at least one and a half hours observing the activities. Take special note of the roles and actions of the jury, the attorneys, and the judge. Describe the procedures followed by the court. What is your overall evaluation of the experience?
3. Interview someone who has served on a jury to learn how the process works. How were they selected? What sort of cases did they hear? What do they think of the jury system—should it be changed in any way? Would they support the idea of professional jurors (people who are trained and hired just to serve on juries)?
4. Get a copy of the LSAT application from your school's career center and take the sample test. What sort of skills are law schools looking for? Does this increase or decrease your interest in law school?

FOR FURTHER READING

Level I Articles

1. Braun, Stephen. Rogue Courts: Their Own Kind of Justice. *National Times,* January 1996. Illegal "common law" courts are "playing Dungeons and Dragons with the legal system."
2. Doherty, Brian. We the 50 Peoples. *Reason,* March 1997. State courts disagree with the federal courts, creating some serious constitutional conflicts.
3. Holland, Barbara. Do You Swear That You Will Well and Truly Try. . . ? *Smithsonian,* March 1995. History of trial by jury.
4. Minow, Newton and Cate, Fred. What the Jury Doesn't Know . . . Could Hurt You. *Washington Monthly,* September 1994. Why juries should be told about a defendant's criminal record.
5. Moore, W. John. Court Is in Recess. *National Journal,* October 30, 1993. The Supreme Court is hearing fewer cases and tackling fewer controversial cases.

6. Neely, Richard. Loser Pays Nothing; Breaking Out of the Courtroom. *Washington Monthly,* June 1983. Attacks trial lawyers' compensation system.
7. Schwartz, Herman. One Man's Activist. . . *Washington Monthly,* November 1997. Surprise! Republican judges are activists, too.
8. Zobel, Hiller. Naming a Justice: It Has Always Been Politics as Usual. *Smithsonian,* October 1991. Historical review of the nomination process.
9. Zobel, Hiller. The Jury on Trial. *American Heritage,* July–August 1995. Should we abolish citizen juries and hire judges to do the job?

Level II Articles

1. Berns, Walter. Judicial Review and the Supreme Court. *The World and I,* September 1987. Judicial review as necessary for constitutional government.
2. Costanzo, Mark and White, Lawrence. An Overview of the Death Penalty and Capital Trials: History, Current Status, Legal Procedures, and Cost. *Journal of Social Issues,* Summer 1994. Explains why the death penalty is so costly.
3. Lemov, Penelope. The Assault on Juvenile Justice. *Governing,* December 1994. How states are trying to deal with violent youth offenders.
4. Luginbuhl, James and Burkhead, Michael. Sources of Bias and Arbitrariness in the Capitol Trial. *Journal of Social Issues,* Summer 1994. Good analysis of the trial process.
5. Quirk, William. Judicial Dictatorship. *Society,* January/February 1994. How the "least dangerous" branch became so powerful.
6. Schulhofer, Stephen. Access to Justice for the American Underclass. *The World and I,* June 1991. Inability of the poor to get equal treatment by the courts.
7. Wilson, James Q. Criminal Justice in England and America. *Public Interest,* Winter 1997. Greater flexibility in the British system allows more than just public opinion to be served.

VIDEO RESOURCES

1. *And Justice For All.* R. Intended as satire, this depiction of the American legal system is more real than parody. Columbia, 1979.

2. *Guilty of Innocence—The Lenell Geter Story.* A TV movie based on the true story of a black engineer wrongly sentenced to prison for armed robbery. His release resulted from a 60 Minutes story. Vidmark, 1987.

3. *Howard Beach: Making the Case for Murder.* A TV drama about a black man killed in an all-white neighborhood of Queens and the state prosecutor who worked to bring the case to trial. 1989.

4. *Incident at Oglala: The Leonard Peltier Story.* PG. The true story of a Native American activist who is accused of murdering two FBI agents but is considered by Amnesty International to be a political prisoner. Seven Arts, 1992.

5. *The Verdict.* R. Paul Newman plays an ambulance-chasing attorney who wins a big case against powerful interests. Fox, 1982. [Note: There are several movies by this name.]

6. *Twelve Angry Men.* One juror holds out against the others who just want to get this over with and go home. Orion, 1957.

Chapter 16: Government and the Economy

BECOMING POLITICAL EXERCISES

1. Construct a crossword puzzle using at least ten terms from this chapter. Make a copy for each person in your group and report their scores. You could make a wordfind instead, but use clues rather than the words themselves in the list.
2. How important is the interest rate to the economy? Call a bank loan officer to find out how much the payments would be for the following: a $15,000 car loan for 3 years and for 5 years; a $95,000 mortgage for 30 years at 6 percent versus 30 years at 8.5 percent. Then compute the difference to determine how much interest you would pay. What does this tell you about the importance of the interest rate?
3. Study the impact of rising and falling interest rates. Interview one of the following persons to find out how the change in interest rates affects them: a realtor, a small business owner, a car dealer, a retired person.
4. If you live near a Federal Reserve Bank, take a tour to learn about its operations.
5. Get out your income tax return for last year and calculate: (1) how much tax you would pay if you paid 17 percent for all earned income above $35,000; (2) how much tax you would pay if we had a national sales tax of 25 percent (estimate your spending); (3) compare both with what you actually paid in federal income tax. Did you pay more in income tax or in Social Security and Medicare taxes? What tax do you support?
6. How does the government work with business to create jobs? Contact your local chamber of commerce or economic development agency to get information about their programs, including tax abatements, job training programs, freeport exemptions, and so on.

FOR FURTHER READING

Level I Articles

1. Aizenman, Nurith C. The Case for More Regulation. *Washington Monthly,* October 1997. Deregulation leads to calls for re-regulation.
2. Chiles, James. Bang! Went the Doors of Every Bank in America. *Smithsonian,* April 1997. The bank holiday of 1933.

3. Cottle, Michelle. The Real Class War. *Washington Monthly,* July/August 1997. Recent tax cuts benefit the rich.

4. Hage, David. A Guide to the Slowing Economy. *U.S. News and World Report,* July 3, 1995. A useful guide to those "leading economic indicators."

5. McIntyre, Robert S. The Flat Taxers' Flat Distortions. *American Prospect,* Summer 1995. Lowering taxes on the rich will bring higher taxes on the middle class.

6. Mitchell, Daniel. A Flat Tax with No Mortgage Deduction Would Probably Help Homeowners. *American Enterprise,* May/June 1996. Good contrast to the McIntyre article above.

7. Reich, Robert. The Missing Options. *American Prospect,* November–December 1997. Trickle down prosperity isn't reaching the people at the bottom, but the two parties don't want to talk about it.

8. Shenk, Joshua. The Perils of Privatization. *Washington Monthly,* May 1995. Privatization has many advantages, but some dangers as well.

Level II Articles

1. Chait, Jonathan. The Flat Tax Scam. *New Republic,* December 15, 1997. Claims that the flat tax serves the elite, not the general public.

2. Galbraith, John Kenneth. The Surrender of Economic Policy. The *American Prospect,* March–April 1996. When the government refuses to challenge the macroeconomic policies of the Fed and balanced budget supporters, it is avoiding dealing with the centers of power.

3. Gordon, John. American Taxation. *American Heritage,* May/June 1996. History of federal taxes in America with special emphasis on the income tax.

4. McCormack, John. The Conspiracy Bugaboo. *Liberty,* March 1996. A right-wing magazine attacks a popular right-wing theory about the power of the Federal Reserve System.

5. Starobin, Paul. Bankers' Dozen. *National Journal,* November 26, 1994. The Federal Reserve's twelve district banks wield extensive power, but operate virtually out of sight.

6. Starobin, Paul. Rethinking Capitalism. *National Journal,* January 18, 1997. Some leading conservatives create the "civil society movement" to battle the excesses of capitalism.

7. Sum, Andrew et al. The Economics of Despair. *American Prospect,* July–August 1996. Analyzes the labor market crisis facing young adults.

8. Zimmerman, Christopher. Flat Tax, Sales Tax, or VAT? *State Legislatures,* October–November 1995. Good discussion of pros and cons of each.

VIDEO RESOURCES

1. *Country.* PG. Farm crises of the 1980s seen through the eyes of a family whose farm is about to be auctioned off. Walt Disney Productions, 1984.
2. *Gung Ho.* PG-13. When a Japanese company takes over an American automobile-manufacturing plant, the two cultures clash. Paramount, 1985.
3. *Matewan.* PG-13. A movie about organizing a union in West Virginia in the 1920s. Red Dog, 1987.
4. *Norma Rae.* PG. The true story of a Southern textile worker who helps organize a labor union at her mill. Fox, 1979.
5. *Riding the Rails.* Documentary describing the poverty of the Great Depression which forced four million Americans (including 250,000 children) into riding the rails. Out of the Blue Productions, 1997.
6. *Roger & Me.* R. How people coped when General Motors closed a plant in Flint, Michigan. Warner Home Video, 1989.
7. *Signs of Life.* PG-13. A boat-building business in Maine shuts down and leaves an emptiness in the community. American Playhouse, 1989.
8. *The Grapes of Wrath.* The dramatization of a John Steinbeck novel about Okies who migrated to California during the Great Depression. Fox, 1940.
9. *The Fight in the Fields.* Documentary of Cesar Chavez and his work organizing migrant workers into the United Farmworkers Union. Paradigm Productions, 1997.
10. *The Molly Maguires.* PG. The true story of a secret society formed in the Pennsylvania coal mines to fight for better working conditions. Tamm, 1970.

Chapter 17: Social Policy

BECOMING POLITICAL EXERCISES

1. Interview someone who can recall the Great Depression of the 1930s. How did he or she feel about the government's policies? About President Roosevelt? About his or her own future at the time?
2. Mr. and Mrs. Adams, who are in their seventies, live in Texas and receive a monthly food stamp allotment of $200, or $50 a week. Plan healthy, nutritious meals for one week, meeting the USDA food guidelines of at least five servings of fruit and vegetables, two to three of meat, poultry, fish or eggs, and two to three of dairy products each day. Be sure to check current prices at the grocery store.[1]
3. Investigate the requirements for participating in a government welfare program, such as food stamps, Medicaid, WIC, a Pell grant, or a farm subsidy.
4. Research the social benefits of a democratic socialist country, such as Sweden, England, or Denmark. Compare the taxes paid and the benefits received with those of the United States.

FOR FURTHER READING

Level I Articles

1. Baker, Dean. The Privateers' Free Lunch. *American Prospect,* May–June 1997. Reasons to oppose privatizing Social Security.
2. Conte, Christopher. Will Workfare Work? *Governing,* April 1996. Working to get off of welfare requires higher paying jobs.
3. Dreyfuss, Robert. The Biggest Deal: Lobbying to Take Social Security Private. *American Prospect,* May–June 1996. A look at the interest groups behind privatization.
4. Longman, Phillip. Entitlement Junkies. *Washington Monthly,* April 1995. The "dirty little secret" of the middle class is that they have their own entitlements.

[1]You might want to call your county welfare office to get current data for your state.

5. Rowe, Jonathan and Cobb, Clifford. The Worst Tax. *Washington Monthly,* July/August 1997. Analyzes the impact of payroll taxes on the working class.
6. Sarasohn, David. Hunger on Main St. *Nation,* December 8, 1997. Food banks are strained and welfare reform has just begun.
7. Serafini, Marilyn Werber. Oh, Yeah, the Uninsured. *National Journal,* Nov. 15, 1997. The number of people without health insurance is growing, but no one wants to deal with it.
8. Skocpol, Theda. Delivering for Young Families. *American Prospect,* September–October 1996. The GI Bill changed a generation; could we do it again?
9. Stanfield, Rochelle. Between the Cracks. *National Journal,* October 11, 1997. The real problems of welfare reform.
10. Tisdale, Sallie. Good Soldiers. *The New Republic,* January 3, 1994. How the Salvation Army performs services for the government.
11. The Family: Home Sweet Home. *The Economist,* September 9, 1995. How government policies in Sweden, Germany, Great Britain, and the United States affect families.
12. Wildavsky, Ben. Social Insecurity. *National Journal,* October 11, 1997. Both sides of the debate on privatizing Social Security.

Level II Articles

1. Burtless, Gary. Paychecks or Welfare Checks: Can AFDC Recipients Support Themselves? *Brookings Review,* Fall 1994. The problem of job creation in workfare plans.
2. Christensen, Kimberly. As If That Wasn't Bad Enough. *American Prospect, May*–June 1997. Response to the Jencks' article below.
3. Cutler, David and Katz, Lawrence. Untouched by the Rising Tide: Why the 1980s Economic Expansion Left the Poor Behind. *Brookings Review,* Winter 1992. "Trickle down" economics and the poor during the Reagan era.
4. Ellwood, David. Welfare Reform as I Knew It: When Bad Things Happen to Good Policies. *American Prospect,* May–June 1996. Excellent analysis of the first round of welfare reform.
5. Galston, William. Divorce American Style. *The Public Interest,* Summer 1996. The failure of no-fault divorce.
6. Horn, Wade and Bush, Andrew. Fathers and Welfare Reform. *Public Interest,* Fall 1997. How to make fathers responsible.

7. Jencks, Christopher. The Hidden Paradox of Welfare Reform. *American Prospect,* May–June 1997. Problems single mothers face under welfare reform.

8. Kotlikoft, Laurence J. and Sachs, Jeffrey. Privatizing Social Security: It's High Time to Privatize. *Brookings Review,* Summer 1997. Arguments in favor of privatization.

9. Quinn, Joseph F. and Mitchell, Olivia S. Social Security on the Table. *American Prospect,* May–June 1996. Looks at the problems facing Social Security and some of the proposed solutions.

VIDEO RESOURCES

1. *Boyz N the Hood.* R. Young black men struggle to overcome their depressing poverty-ridden environment by going to college. Both, Inc., 1991.

2. *Conrack.* PG. The true story by Patrick Conroy of his experience as a teacher to black children on a remote South Carolina island. Fox, 1974.

3. *Hoop Dreams.* PG-13. An excellent depiction of obstacles facing young black men who hope to rise above their meager circumstances. 1994.

4. *Powwow Highway.* R. Two Native Americans observe the conditions under which many of their people live. Cannon, 1989.

5. *Stand and Deliver.* PG-13. The true story of a high school math teacher whose poor Hispanic students take the AP calculus test and astonish the College Board people. American Playhouse, 1988.

6. *Taken Away.* A TV movie about a single working mother whose child is taken away by authorities because she cannot afford daycare. MCA, 1989.

Chapter 18: Foreign Policy and Democracy

BECOMING POLITICAL EXERCISES

1. Interview someone who served in the military in the Vietnam war to learn what it was like, why the person served, and what his or her thoughts are on the war twenty-five years later.
2. Research the breakup of the Soviet empire. Select one country, such as the former East Germany or the Ukraine and analyze the political and economic effects of the loss of communist control.
3. Research the effects of the atomic bombs dropped on Hiroshima and Nagasaki in World War II.
4. Interview a foreign student at your school to learn about his or her country and its foreign policy toward the United States.
5. Research and write a 500-word report on a biological or chemical weapon, such as anthrax. How would such a weapon be delivered? How serious a threat is this weapon? If Iraq is producing such weapons, what should be the response of the United States?

FOR FURTHER READING

Level I Articles

1. Diamond, Edwin and Bates, Stephen. The Ancient History of the Internet. *American Heritage,* October 1995. The Department of Defense created the Internet to fight the cold war.
2. Kirschten, Dick. The New Peace Corps. *National Journal,* April 18, 1998. The Peace Corps' slogan is right—"The hardest job you'll ever love."
3. Kitfield, James. Front and Center. *National Journal,* October 25, 1997. How women are reshaping the American military.
4. Maddox, Robert. The Biggest Decision: Why We Had to Drop the Atomic Bomb. *American Heritage,* May/June 1995. Rebuts the revisionists' argument that the bombs were unnecessary.
5. Noah, Timothy. We Need You: National Service, An Idea Whose Time Has Come. *Washington Monthly,* November 1986.

6. Oberdorfer, Don. The Peacemaker. *Washington Monthly,* December 1997. Jimmy Carter's peacemaking efforts with North Korea.

7. Schuck, Michael. When the Shooting Stops: Missing Elements in the Just War Theory. *Christian Century,* October 26, 1994. Just war theory needs to include repentance and honorable surrender.

8. Thomas, Evan. Bobby Kennedy's War on Castro. *Washington Monthly,* December 1995. The truth about the CIA's attempts to assassinate Fidel Castro.

9. Weissman, Stephen. Addicted to Mobutu: Why America Can't Learn from Its Foreign Policy Mistakes. *Washington Monthly,* September 1997. Why do we persist in supporting friendly dictators?

10. Wilson, William. I Had Prayed to God that This Thing Was Fiction. *American Heritage,* February 1990. The government's chief investigator of the My Lai massacre describes the horror he uncovered.

11. Wolkomit, Richard and Wolkomit, Joyce. After the Breakup, Who's Minding the Bomb? *Smithsonian,* February 1997. The Center for Nonproliferation Studies tracks the spread of nuclear fuels.

Level II Articles

1. Bennahum, David. The Internet Revolution. *Wired,* April 1997. How Serbian students used the Internet to promote revolution.

2. Kirkpatrick, Jeane. The Lesser Evil Over the Greater Evil. From "Human Rights and American Foreign Policy: A Symposium" in *Commentary,* November 1981. The problems of combining human rights policies with foreign policies.

3. Mann, Charles. How Many Is Too Many? *Atlantic Monthly,* February 1993. Population pressures are creating a world-wide problem.

4. Preston, Richard. The Bioweaponeers. *New Yorker,* March 9, 1998. Scary article all about biological weapons.

5. Ricks, Thomas. The Great Society in Camouflage. *Atlantic Monthly,* December 1996. Costs and benefits of the culture of the U.S. Army.

6. Ricks, Thomas. The Widening Gap Between the Military and Society. *Atlantic Monthly,* July 1997. Argues that the military culture is both conservative and politically active.

7. Schaefer, Peter. Foreign Policy: Repairing the Damage, Rethinking the Mandate, Rewriting the Law. *American Enterprise,* November/December 1992. Reorganizing our foreign policy programs.

8. Smith, Robert Barr. Justice Under the Sun: Japanese War Crimes Trials. *World War II,* September 1996. Postwar justice.

9. Tonelson, Alan. America First—Past and Present. *Society,* September/October 1992. America needs to seek its self-interest first.

10. Tonelson, Alan. Human Rights: The Bias We Need. *Foreign Policy,* Winter 1982–83. A human rights policy is necessary for national security.

VIDEO RESOURCES

1. *Andersonville Trial.* A TV movie about the war-crimes trial of Confederate captain Henry Wirz; raises important moral questions. International, 1970.
2. *Apocalypse Now.* R. The classic movie about the insanity of war. United Artists, 1979.
3. *Casualties of War.* R. This movie is based on true story of an army private who spoke out against war crimes he witnessed. Columbia, 1989.
4. *China Beach.* A TV movie about the Vietnam War through the eyes of several women who served. Warner Home Video, 1988.
5. *Dear America: Letters Home From Vietnam.* PG-13. A documentary of actors reading from letters sent home from Vietnam. HBO, 1988.
6. *Friendly Fire.* A TV movie about how the parents of a soldier killed by "friendly fire" try to learn the truth about his death. Foxvideo, 1979.
7. *In Love and War.* R. The story of James Stockdale, Ross Perot's running mate in 1992, and his years of torture in a Vietnam POW camp. Vidmark, 1988.
8. *The Killing Fields.* R. The true story of American reporter who tries to help his Cambodian interpreter when his life is in danger. Enigma, Goldcrest, 1984.
9. *My Father, My Son.* A TV movie about Admiral Elmo Zumwalt, who ordered the Agent Orange spraying in Vietnam, and his son who later died of cancer caused by the spraying. 1988.
10. *Platoon.* R. Everything about Vietnam you ever wanted to know. Hemdale, 1986.
11. *Trial of the Catonsville Nine.* PG. The true story of the trial of nine anti-war protestors led by Catholic priest Daniel Berrigan. 1972.